Frederic William Farrar

In the days of the youth

sermons on practical subjects, preached at Marlborough College, from 1871 to 1876

Frederic William Farrar

In the days of the youth
sermons on practical subjects, preached at Marlborough College, from 1871 to 1876

ISBN/EAN: 9783742860248

Manufactured in Europe, USA, Canada, Australia, Japa

Cover: Foto ©Lupo / pixelio.de

Manufactured and distributed by brebook publishing software (www.brebook.com)

Frederic William Farrar

In the days of the youth

"IN THE DAYS OF THY YOUTH."

*SERMONS ON PRACTICAL SUBJECTS,
PREACHED AT MARLBOROUGH COLLEGE,*
From 1871 to 1876.

BY

F. W. FARRAR, D.D., F.R.S.,

CANON OF WESTMINSTER; RECTOR OF ST. MARGARET'S, WESTMINSTER;
CHAPLAIN IN ORDINARY TO THE QUEEN; FORMERLY FELLOW OF TRINITY COLLEGE,
CAMBRIDGE; AND LATE MASTER OF MARLBOROUGH COLLEGE.

London:
MACMILLAN AND CO.
1876.

DEDICATION.

To the Council of Marlborough College;—to the beloved memory of Bishop Cotton;—to my honoured friend and predecessor, the Master of University College, Oxford;—to my Colleagues, whose high aims and self-denying labours have secured the progress and prosperity of the College during the past six years;—to the Prefects, who have been my immediate pupils, and of whom I trust that many will henceforth be lifelong friends;—to the hundreds of Marlborough Boys, whose diligence, goodness, and loyalty have caused me such deep and enduring happiness—

I Dedicate

These few of the many Sermons delivered in the College Chapel between January 29, 1871, and July 23, 1876.

PREFACE.

THE following Sermons are, almost exclusively, occupied with practical subjects bearing upon school life. The publication of them is the last proof I can give of the undying affection which I shall always retain for Marlborough College, and of the deep and sacred interest which I shall always feel in those among whom, for six years, it was my privilege to live.

This volume must not be regarded as representative of my entire teaching. Asked to publish some of my school sermons, I have selected those only which were more or less special in character or treatment. Hence I have excluded from this volume the many sermons which I preached on the great doctrinal truths of Christianity; those which were suggested by the Fasts and Festivals of our Church; those on different Scripture characters; those which pleaded the cause of various charities; those that dwelt exclusively on the Life, the Parables, the Miracles, the Cross and Passion, the Resurrection and Ascension, of our Saviour Christ. Many of these might doubtless, in a literary sense, have been regarded as better and more valuable than some here published. But this volume is not published on literary grounds at all. All my sermons were necessarily composed as they were required, in brief intervals from much labour and incessant interruption; they were never intended for publication; and have neither been altered nor elaborated since.

Any value they may possess depends on their being left as they were written—with all their intentional repetitions, with the absence of references and authorities, which I could not always give, and in the style intended solely for oral delivery. I know that those who heard them, and for whose sake they are mainly published, will receive them kindly, and will read them with no other desire than that of reviving those good impressions which I trust that, by God's grace, they sometimes produced in faithful hearts.

ST. MARGARET'S RECTORY, WESTMINSTER,
October 9, 1876.

CONTENTS.

SERMON I.
STANDING BEFORE GOD 1   PAGE

SERMON II.
LITTLE FAITHFULNESSES 11

SERMON III.
HUNGERING AND THIRSTING AFTER RIGHTEOUSNESS . . . 21

SERMON IV.
THE RIGHT USE OF SPEECH 39

SERMON V.
SMOULDERING LAMPS 41

SERMON VI.
ASPICE, PROSPICE, RESPICE 51

CONTENTS.

SERMON VII.
LITTLE GIVEN, LITTLE ASKED 61

SERMON VIII.
QUIETNESS AND CONFIDENCE 72

SERMON IX.
THE GRAIN OF MUSTARD SEED 80

SERMON X.
INNOCENT HAPPINESS 89

SERMON XI.
SCHOOL AND HOME 99

SERMON XII.
SELF-CONQUEST 110

SERMON XIII.
THE PERIL OF WASTE 119

SERMON XIV.
CALLING THINGS BY THEIR WRONG NAMES 129

SERMON XV.
COUNTERBALANCE EVIL WITH GOOD 139

CONTENTS.

SERMON XVI.
THINKING OF GOD 148

SERMON XVII.
THE OMNIPOTENCE OF PRAYER 159

SERMON XVIII.
SOWING AMONG THORNS 169

SERMON XIX.
HOW TO KEEP GOOD RESOLUTIONS 179

SERMON XX.
THE OBJECTS OF SCHOOL LIFE 189

SERMON XXI.
EXCUSES TO MAN AND TO GOD 199

SERMON XXII.
THE TEMPLE OF THE GOD OF TRUTH 209

SERMON XXIII.
DRIFTING AWAY 219

SERMON XXIV.
THE HISTORY AND HOPES OF A PUBLIC SCHOOL 230

CONTENTS.

SERMON XXV.
THE NEED OF CONSTANT CLEANSING FROM CONSTANT ASSOILMENT 243

SERMON XXVI.
SOBERMINDEDNESS 254

SERMON XXVII.
NOT FAR FROM THE KINGDOM OF HEAVEN 265

SERMON XXVIII.
RUNNERS FOR A PRIZE 275

SERMON XXIX.
THE CONTINUITY OF GODLINESS 285

SERMON XXX.
HOW TO RESIST THE DEVIL 297

SERMON XXXI.
HOLIDAY ADVICE 307

SERMON XXXII.
BLAMELESS AND HARMLESS 316

SERMON XXXIII.
HANDWRITINGS ON THE WALL 325

SERMON XXXIV.
THE COURAGE OF THE SAINTS POSSIBLE IN BOYHOOD . . 337

SERMON XXXV.
THE TRIPLE SANCTIFICATION 349

SERMON XXXVI.
TRUTHFULNESS AND HONESTY 358

SERMON XXXVII.
SCHOOL GAMES 367

SERMON XXXVIII.
FROM SORROW TO REPENTANCE 376

SERMON XXXIX.
LAST WORDS 389

IN THE DAYS OF THY YOUTH.

Sermons Preached in Marlborough College.

I.—STANDING BEFORE GOD.

DEUT. xxix. 10.

"Ye stand this day all of you before the Lord your God."

So spake Moses, the strong and patient servant of God, in one of those powerful addresses with which the Book of Deuteronomy is filled. They were uttered at the close of the wanderings in the wilderness, when the prophet was already old; but as the one hundred and twenty years of his marvellous life had not dimmed his eye or abated his natural force, so neither had the cares and sorrows of a dread responsibility quenched the fire of his words or the force of his convictions. Disappointed of the high reward for which his soul had longed, suffered only to see the Holy Land which he had once hoped that his feet should tread, he still remained faithful and tender, and wavered neither in his allegiance to God nor in his love to man. Unselfish to the last, the old chieftain summoned around him the children of his heart; and as the captains of the tribes, and elders, and officers, and all the men of Israel, nay, even their little ones, and the hewers of wood and drawers of water, sat listening at his feet, he reiterated again and again, in language which must have smitten their hearts like the thunders of Sinai, the blessings and curses, the sanctions and prohibitions of the fiery law! And then, inviting them to bind their souls with a sacred covenant, he prefaces it with these words of solemn import: "Ye stand this day all of you before the Lord your God."

Intense in their significance—fresh in their solemnity—as when Moses uttered them to the listening multitudes on the farther shores of Jordan, the echo of those warning words rolls to us across the centuries. They express the formative principle, the regulating conception, the inspiring impulse of every greatly Christian life. The very differentia of such a life,—that is, its distinguishing feature,—is this, that it is spent always and consciously in the presence of God.

> "It shall be still in strictest measure even
> To that same lot, however mean or high,
> Towards which Time leads us, and the will of heaven.
> All is if I have grace to use it so,
> As ever in my great Taskmaster's eye."

And in proportion to our faith is the vividness and reality wherewith, like Moses, we see God—like Enoch walk, like Abraham converse, like Jacob wrestle with Him, like Elijah thrill to the inward whisper of His still small voice. There are, indeed, some eyes so dim that they catch no gleam of His Presence; some ears so dull that they never hear the music or the thunder of His voice; and there are moments when even to the best of men He seems silent or far off. But when the eyes are opened by prayer and penitence, when the ear is purged by listening humbly for the revelation of His will, then all life, all nature, all history, are full of Him.

Then, Conscience, speak she never so faintly, becomes His articulate utterance. Then Experience, seem it never so perplexing, is but the unknown pattern which He is weaving into the web of our little lives. Then even amid the crash of falling dynasties, and the struggles of furious nations, we see His guiding hand. Then the great open book of the universe reveals Him on every page, while, legibly as on the tables of Moses, He engraves His name upon the rock tablets of the world; and clearly as on the palace wall of Belshazzar, He letters it in fire amid the stars of heaven, in flowers among the fields of spring. But whether we see or see not, whether we hear or hear not, whether conscience and life be voiceful to us or silent, assuredly He is and He speaks to us; assuredly not this day only, but every day, we stand each and all of us before the Lord our God.

I. Let us first strive, my brethren, to recognise the fact, and then to consider its consequences. By recognising the fact I mean that we should endeavour to impress it on our thoughts; to make it not only theoretical, but intensely practical; to realize it as the principle of action, to build upon it as the basis of life. Oh, on this first Sunday of a new half-year let every one of us, from the oldest to the youngest, strive to feel and know that God is; that He is the rewarder of all them that diligently seek Him; that every sin we commit is committed in His presence; that His eye is always upon us, never slumbering nor sleeping: in the busy scenes of day about our path; in the silent watches of the night about our bed. Who, my brethren, whether in defiance or in terror, whether in prosperity or in despair, ever succeeded in concealing himself from God? Adam in his shame and nakedness strove to hide himself among the garden trees, and that Voice called him forth. Cain would have fled from Him into the land of exile, but even there he felt the branding finger upon his brow. Hagar despaired of Him, and lo, His angel of mercy shone before her at the Beerlahairoi. Jonah rose to flee from Him in ships of Tarshish, and met Him in the shattered vessel, on the tempestuous sea. He flashed upon the dreams of Jacob, in a vision of forgiveness, as he slept on the rocky stairs of the steep hill-side. "Whither," sang David the guilty adulterer, David the weeping penitent, "whither shall I go then from Thy Spirit, or whither shall I go then from Thy presence? If I climb up to heaven, Thou art there; if I go down to hell, Thou art there also; if I take the wings of the morning and abide in the uttermost parts of the sea, even there shall Thy hand lead me, and Thy right hand shall guide me."

Yes, "Thou, God, seest me!" And when we have felt this truth, how does the thought affect us? what is its meaning for us? Does it inspire us with love, or with hatred? with comfort, or with despair?

II. (1.) Our first lesson from it, my brethren, is a sense of *warning*. Surely there is a warning—for the forgetful a startling, for the guilty a terrible, even for the good man a very solemn warning, in the thought that not only our life in its every incident, but even our heart in its inmost secrets, lies naked and open before Him with whom we have to do. When we remember that He, who chargeth even His angels with folly, and in whose sight the very heavens are not clean, is always with us; that the very loneliest solitudes are peopled with His presence; that walls do not hide, nor inner-chambers conceal us from Him; that the deepest curtains of secrecy and midnight are to Him transparent as the blaze of noon,—are we indeed so pure and innocent, is the white robe of our baptism so utterly unstained, that there is no warning for us in that thought? If the Gadarenes, anxious for their swine, could flock to Christ to entreat that He would depart out of their coasts; if even St. Peter, troubled by the sudden apocalypse of His tenderness and power, could fall at His feet, saying, "Depart from me, for I am a sinful man, O Lord;" must there not be a similar repugnance and alarm in every willingly sinful soul? Oh if there be such alarm in your soul, be warned in time. If you hate, if you are terrified by the thought of God's perpetual presence, then be sure that there must be some deep disharmony in your being, and be sure that, while this continues, you cannot be fulfilling the law of your creation, you cannot be at peace with God.

(2.) But we, my brethren, are Christians; it ought not to be so, I trust that it is not so, with us, for to all who have learnt to love and to trust in God, the thought that we stand before Him involves not only a sense of warning, but, secondly, a sense of *elevation*, of ennoblement. It is a sweet and a lofty doctrine, the highest source of all the dignity and grandeur of life. It is the very thing which distinguishes us from the beasts that perish. They, so far as we know, feel no responsibility, rise to no worship, attain no knowledge, cherish no hope for the future, and but a dull, blind memory of the past; until, their unimmortal but sinless destiny being accomplished,

> "Something in the darkness draws
> Their foreheads downwards, and they die."

But man, how different a life is his! "How noble in reason! how infinite in faculty! in form and moving how express and admirable! in action how like an angel! in apprehension how like a god!"[1] And why? Because He is a son of God, made in His image, an inheritor of His kingdom, conscious of His presence. In childhood how is he clothed with the charm of innocence; in youth, if he be true to himself, how does the grace of Heaven take early hold of him as he grows in wisdom, and stature, and favour with God and man; in manhood how does he ever become sweeter and purer, nobler and loftier; and in old age, at last, how does the fire of his life as it wanes in lustre increase in loveliness—as the sun before his setting is gazed upon with more of admiration, if with less of awe, while he makes even the clouds around him and the waters underneath his feet flush into a softer purple and a purer gold!

(3) And besides a sense of warning and of elevation, a third consequence of life spent consciously in God's presence is a firm, unflinching, unwavering sense of *duty*. And surely this sense of duty, so marked a feature in every good man's character, is a thing of extraordinary dignity. Certainly without it life is singularly contemptible, inevitably miserable. Compare a river which has burst its banks, and whose waters, shallow, polluted, dangerous, first flood the fields with devastation, then poison them with malaria—compare it, I say, with the same river flowing in its ordered courses, majestic with its rejoicing depth, enriching the plains with fertility and health, filling (as an Arab poet expresses it) its bosom with gold, and robing its path in emeralds:—such, my brethren, is a human life without, and a human life with, the sense of duty. Or compare, again, a vessel, rolling, waterlogged and helpless, at the mercy of the storm,—a wind-tossed, melancholy hulk on the waste of waters, or a desolate wreck upon

---

[1] Shakspeare, *Hamlet*.

the lonely shore,—compare it, I say, with the same vessel obeying a very small helm, and therefore cutting through the frustrate billows in victorious career, and making the very hurricane speed it onwards toward the destined shore;—such again, my brethren, is a human life without, and a human life with, the sense of duty. A life regardful of duty is crowned with an object, directed by a purpose, inspired by an enthusiasm, till the very humblest routine, carried out conscientiously for the sake of God, is elevated into moral grandeur; and the very obscurest office, filled conscientiously at the bidding of God, becomes an imperial stage on which all the virtues play. To one who lives thus the insignificant becomes important, the unpleasant delightful, the evanescent eternal.

> "A servant with this clause
> Makes drudgery divine;
> Who sweeps a room as for Thy laws
> Makes that and the action fine."

And do not for a moment, my brethren, suffer this idea of Duty to wear a harsh or repulsive aspect to your thoughts. Oh give your hearts to her, serve her with a manly devotion, and so far from being severe or unlovely, this "stern daughter of the voice of God," hand in hand with her sister Wisdom, shall guide you along the path of a godly and honourable life, till at the touching of their sacred feet the very wilderness, aye, the very thorns of the wilderness, shall blossom as the rose.

(4.) But, as a fourth consequence, there is something loftier and lovelier than even a sense of duty, which results from a consciousness of standing in the presence of God—it is the sense of *holiness*. It is a solemn thought that a man may perform his duties, and yet not be a holy man; he may be apparently upright, not really innocent; outwardly conscientious, not inwardly sincere. It is one thing to be "not far from the kingdom of God," another to be a member thereof; one thing to be near the gate of heaven, another thing to be therein. I do not mean that men are open and conscious hypocrites. These, I believe, are very rare. But it is mostly some cherished idol, some wilful reservation, some favourite temptation, in a word, some besetting sin, that makes men fall short of that truth in the inward parts which God requires, and which, to those who seek for it and love it, He will give. For God says—tenderly indeed, yet absolutely—"My son, give Me thine heart." He says, "Be ye holy, for I am holy." He forbids us, not only to seek our own pleasure, or do our own ways, but even to think our own thoughts; He requires not only duty, but holiness; He searcheth the spirits; He discerneth the very reins and hearts.

(5.) Who, my brethren, is sufficient for these things? If we have fallen far short of duty, how then shall we attain to holiness? And yet without holiness no man shall see the Lord. Oh, who shall arm us for the dread struggle of the future? Who shall forgive us all the sad failures, all the foolish errors, all the wilful wanderings, of the past? My brethren, this text will give us the answer. We stand, all of us, before the Lord our God. The knowledge of this not only warns us, not only ennobles us, not only inspires us with a sense of duty, not only convinces us of the necessity for holiness, but lastly, it encourages us with a *certainty of help* and strength. That God before whom we stand is not only our Judge and our Creator, but also our Father and our Friend. Behold Him revealed to us in Christ, our elder Brother in the great family of God! He feels for all our infirmities. He can sympathise in all our sorrows.

He has conquered all our temptations. He has borne the dread burden of all our sins. The pulse of every beating heart is known to Him. He sees every tear we shed. He considers every wish we cherish. He answers every true prayer we breathe. In the depth of humiliation He is with us. In the rough places His angels catch us by the hand. In the valley of the shadow of death—where none can accompany us—His brightness illumines every dreadful downward step. My brethren, doubtless we shall all find difficulties, troubles, temptations here, and the very worst of them will come from our own wayward, wandering hearts; well, let us face them bravely, humbly, cheerfully; let us remember that it was He who placed us in the midst of them, because He meant us to resist, because He will help us to conquer them. Fear not; even the youngest and weakest here He loves; let us be true to the higher law of our nature; let us remember that God sees us; and then let us doubt not, but earnestly believe that He will accept us in the Beloved as His redeemed, forgiven sons. Only believe in Him, and He will lead you by the hand through a happy and uncorrupted youth to the firm threshold of a godly manhood; will, in the hour of death, fling open before you the gates of everlasting life; will, in the day of judgment, pronounce those blessed words, for which a life of the worst agony would cheaply pay,—" Servant of God, well done !"

Lessons, then, of warning, of elevation, of duty, of holiness, of help,—these are what we should set before us. Oh, my brethren, that we may learn these lessons, keeping them before us consciously; knowing ourselves to be bound by them inflexibly; feeling ourselves encouraged by them daily and hourly! For in a sense yet more solemn than ordinary do we stand, all of us, on this day, on this first Sunday of a new half-year, before the Lord our God. On this day He gives you the inestimable blessing of a fresh start in serving Him, a new opportunity to devote yourselves to Him. Oh may you who are new boys among us determine on this day to commit yourselves and your ways unto the Lord, sure that if you do He will be your shield and buckler. And you who are already familiar with this place, if you have by His blessing humbly striven to serve Him hitherto, oh seek by His grace to serve Him also henceforth with yet deeper devotion, with yet sincerer earnestness; and if you have been faithless, unholy, guilty before Him, oh let the time past suffice, and turn to Him now in this accepted time, now on this day of salvation. So may His best blessing, without which nothing is strong, nothing is holy, rest upon us all: on us who teach, inspiring us with wisdom, and self-denial, and unwearied energy, and holy purpose; on you who learn, clothing you with the heavenly grace of reverent and earnest spirits; kindling your ardour with the certain victory of the strong in faith; crowning your efforts with the priceless beatitude of the pure in heart. And that this blessing may rest upon us, let us seek it now, out of a pure heart fervently. Brethren, pray for us. Let us, as we kneel in earnest prayer, each ask God's blessing for himself, as each also for one another, and all for this place which we all love, that it may be always a place of sound learning and religious education, and that each son of this school may rise hereafter to call it blessed, having been trained therein to be a profitable member of the Church and commonwealth, that he may be hereafter, by God's grace, a partaker of the immortal glory of the resurrection through Jesus Christ our Lord.

February 12, 1871.

SERMON II.

LITTLE FAITHFULNESSES.

LUKE xvi. 10.

"He that is faithful in that which is least is faithful also in much: and he that is unjust in the least is unjust also in much."

You have just been listening, my brethren, to the parable of the Unjust Steward, of which these words form the sequel. Into the difficulties of that parable it is not now my purpose to enter; but surely they have been greatly exaggerated. The master of the steward approved of his dexterity, not of his fraudulence; he praised him, not because he had done wisely, $\sigma o \phi \hat{\omega} \varsigma$, but prudently, $\phi \rho o \nu i \mu \omega \varsigma$. The parable is but another illustration of the warning, "Be ye prudent, $\phi \rho o \nu \iota \mu o \grave{\iota}$, as serpents, yet harmless as doves." If, in the thirst for power—if, in the greed of gain—the children of this generation can show tact and zeal, imitate those qualities in a better cause, win the treasures of heaven with that toil wherewith they heap up for themselves the wealth of earth, And, in doing this, neglect nothing;—underrate no virtue because you esteem it trivial—commit no wrong because you hold it small. There is a duty and a glory in little faithfulnesses. There is a peril and a shame in little sins.

You will see that there are two parts of the text, and we might dwell with profit upon either. "He that is unjust in the least is unjust also in much." What a world of warning lies in those words! The little foxes that spoil the vines—the little canker that slays the oak—the little leak which ever gains upon the vessel till it sinks—the little fissure in the mountainside, out of which the lava pours—the little rift within the lute that, slowly widening, makes the music mute—what are all these, in their ruinous influence, but a fit emblem of the sinfulness of little sins? how do they illustrate that old proverb that the mother of mischief is no bigger than a midge's wing! Yes, my brethren, small injustices are but the wet and slippery stepping-stones down into deeper waters. He who is unjust in a penny now may be so in thousands of pounds hereafter. He who is not perfectly honest in trifles now, may, if unchecked, develop, in later life, a character radically untrustworthy — fundamentally unsound. Therefore, my brethren, let us be in all our dealings transparent as the day; let us all proudly and kindly encourage each other to shun and to scorn, in all our doings, the faintest spot of suspicion and dishonour; let us, if it occurs, put our foot firmly upon it as we would upon a spark where a magazine was near, knowing with what a monotonous and fatal echo the records of men's lives sigh back their confirmation to that solemn warning, "He that is unjust in the least is unjust also in much."

But, my brethren, though it may often be our duty to dwell on topics such as these—though, as we were wisely warned last Sunday, it is a dangerous and timid optimism which is afraid to call sin sin, or to ignore the shame and the sorrow wherewith God has burnt a mark upon its brow, yet it is always a happier and more hopeful thing to dwell upon the other side—on obedience rather than on transgression—on the high happiness which ministers to virtue rather than on the retribution which dogs the heels of vice. Let us, then, this morning, passing by the sombre conclusion of the text, touch lightly—for more than this is impossible—upon its happy prophecy: let us take for our brief meditation the glory and the blessing of little faithfulnesses.

1. Little faithfulnesses: it is all the more necessary for us to contemplate them, because it is not these in general which men venerate or admire. We praise the high—the splendid—the heroic: we dwell on the great deeds—on the glorious sacrifices. When you read how the lady of the house of Douglas thrust her own arm through the bolt grooves of the door and let the murderers break it while her king had time to hide; or how the pilot of Lake Erie stood undaunted upon the burning deck, and, reckless of the intense agony, steered the crew safe to the jetty, and then fell dead among the crackling flames; or how the Russian serf, to save his master and his master's children, sprang out from the sledge among the wolves that howled after them through the winter snow; or, once more, how, amid the raging storm, the young girl sat with her father at the oar to save the shipwrecked sailors from the shrouds of the shattered wreck—whose soul is so leaden that it does not thrill with admiration at deeds like these? But think you, my brethren, that these brave men and women sprang, as it were, full-sized into their heroic stature? Nay; but, like the gorgeous blossom of the aloe, elaborated through long years of silent and unnoticed growth, so these deeds were but the bright consummate flower borne by lives of quiet, faithful, unrecorded service; and no one, be sure, has ever greatly done or gloriously dared who has not been

familiar with the grand unselfishness of little duties; who has not offered to God—more precious than the temple altars smoking with hecatombs of spotless lambs —the daily sacrifice of a contrite heart—the daily discipline of a chastened life. You would be like these ? Well, it is a great ambition. But if you would not be false to it, show now, in little things, of what stuff your hearts are made, and you will not then be unprepared if God should ever require of you the hero's courage or the martyr's faith. Fourteen years ago, when England had been agonised by the horrors and massacres of the great Indian mutiny, then the daring genius and inflexible will of one great soldier carried a handful of troops across flooded rivers and burning plains. He was an old man, for the fire of life may die away in the white ashes of a mean career, but it glows to the last in the generous and the true, and he died in the effort before he knew of the honours heaped upon him by grateful England, though not before he had saved the brightest jewel in England's crown. To Sir Henry Havelock the opportunity for showing to all the world the moral greatness which was in him did not come till he was sixty-two; but do you think that, in God's sight, that pure and unselfish life would have been one whit less beautiful if the opportunity had never come ? Had Henry Havelock died a poor struggling officer, unknown beyond the limits of his own regiment, think you that in the angel-registers the record would have been less bright ? Or may it not rather be that,—in those biographies which are written only in God's Book of Life—the quiet patience of one who had been but a neglected lieutenant till the age of forty-three—the unmurmuring simplicity with which, on the very morning of victory, he resigned the chief command into another's hands,—the moral courage, which, amid a godless society, made him invite his men to join with him in prayer, and not wince under the sneering title of Havelock's saints,—may it not be, I say, that these little faithfulnesses are written in brighter letters than the victory at Alumbagh, or than the salvation of India by that great march, through scorching heat and drenching rain, from Cawnpore to Lucknow? If then you would do great deeds hereafter, prepare for them, rehearse them, show yourselves fit for them now. "He that is faithful in that which is least is faithful also in much."

2. But, secondly, remember that if the opportunity for *great* deeds should never come, the opportunity for *good* deeds is renewed for you day by day. The thing for us to long for is the goodness, not the glory, and in the words of the poet—

> "One small touch of charity
> Would raise us nearer godlike state,
> Than if the crowded orb should cry
> As those who cried Diana great."

Do you desire that, hereafter, the world should ring with your name coupled to some heroic action, or that, in the annals of earthly goodness, it should be emblazoned in lines of gold? Well, as you grow older and wiser, as your eyes are enlightened to distinguish the substance from the shadow, you will learn to value and covet the spirit, not the sign of it; the high motive, not the tangible result; the simple faithfulness, not the echoing recognition; the quiet lightning-deed,

> "Not that applauding thunder at its heels
> Which men call fame."

You will repeat the prayer which an unhappy queen of our own royal house inscribed with a diamond upon her castle window, "Oh keep me innocent, make others great." Most of us, my brethren, perhaps every one of us will but die in the round of common duties, in the fulfilment of an ordinary routine; happy if that routine be accepted loyally; happy if those duties be faithfully performed. For if life be a battle-field, then, like other battle-fields, it is won by the nameless multitudes, by the unrecorded hosts. The great leaders fight and fall conscious that theirs shall be the glory of the victory; but as the thin red lines advance to battle amid the storm of shells, each peasant-soldier knows well that where he falls the poppy and the violet shall but blossom over a nameless grave, and yet they advance unflinching to the batteries whose cross-fire vomits death upon them, and so—as a generous leader once exclaimed—and so "they die by thousands those unnamed demi-gods."[1] They give their lives; and what can a king do more? And we too—however common-place, however humble—we too can keep the ranks unbroken; we too can be of "the faithful who were not famous;" we too can make sure that where we stand, there at least, in the great Armageddon, by the grace of God, there shall be no swerving in the line; and thereby shall our little service be, as has well been said, "precious as the continuity of sunbeams is precious, though some of them fall unseen and on barrenness;"[2] precious as the drops of rain are precious, though some of them seem to be wasted in idle dimples upon the shipless main!

3. Little faithfulnesses then are not only the *preparation* for great ones, but little faithfulnesses are in themselves the great ones. Observe the striking fact that our Lord does not say, "He that is faithful in that which is least will be faithful also in much," but "He

[1] Kossuth. [2] George Eliot.

that is faithful in that which is least *is* faithful also in much." The essential fidelity of the heart is the same whether it be exercised in two mites or in a regal treasury; the genuine faithfulness of the life is equally beautiful whether it be displayed in governing an empire or in writing an exercise. It has been quaintly said that if God were to send two angels to earth, the one to occupy a throne, and the other to clean a road, they would each regard their employments as equally distinguished and equally happy. In the poem of *Theocrite*, the Archangel Gabriel takes the poor boy's place:—

> "Then to his poor trade he turned,
> By which the daily bread was earned;
> And ever o'er the trade he bent,
> And ever lived on earth content;
> He did God's will: to him all one
> If on the earth, or in the sun."[1]

Yes, the insignificance of our worldly rank affects in nowise our membership of the spiritual aristocracy. The thing really important is, not the trust committed to us, but the loyalty wherewith we fulfil it. All of us may be, in St. Paul's high language, fellow-labourers with God; and he who is that, be he slave or angel, can be nothing better or greater. The mountains cease to be colossal, the ocean tides lose their majesty, if you see what an atom our earth is in the starry space. Even so turn the telescope of faith to heaven, and see how at once earth's grandeurs dwindle into nothingness, and Heaven's least interests dilate into eternal breadth. Yes, to be a faithful Christian is greater in God's sight than to be a triumphant statesman or a victorious emperor. "God's heroes may be the world's helots." "God's prophets, best or worst, are we—there is no last or first."

[1] R. Browning.

4. Let a very few remaining words endeavour, yet more practically, to apply to our present needs and circumstances these mighty and consoling truths.

I. And first I would ask, Do any of you regard your boyhood, with its subjection to parents and masters, and its general state of discipline and tutelage, as "that which is least?" Do you yearn for the greater day, as perhaps you think it, when you shall be free to choose in life your own path and your own pursuits, none hindering you? Well, to you I say solemnly, "He that is faithful in that which is least is faithful also in much; and he that is unjust in the least is unjust also in much." What you are now the chances are that, in the main, you will be hereafter. The boy is father to the man. Be false and treacherous, be unjust or impure, be indolent and disobedient now, and you will either be saved so as by fire, or you will grow up into a useless, dangerous, degraded man. And, on the other hand, be good and faithful, be pure and honest, be brave and generous now, and then be very sure that God will make you a worthy son of the school that trained, a worthy citizen of the nation that nurtured you; nay more, a true child of God, a certain inheritor of the kingdom of heaven. The servant that used rightly his two talents was made ruler over many things. No servant of God ever yet missed of his infinite reward. "Heaven," as was said by the great teacher of China,[1] "heaven means principle."

II. And lastly, I would say to you, not only be faithful in this the least part of your life, but try to be faithful in the least things which concern it. Count nothing slight, says the wise son of Sirach, whether it be great or small. Life is made up of little things, just as time at the longest is but an aggregate of seconds.

[1] Confucius.

Be an act ever so unimportant, the *principle* involved in our acts is not unimportant. You say that there is very little harm in this or that; if there is even a little harm in it then there is great harm in it. A feather will show you the direction of the wind; a straw will prove the set of a current. And this is why Christ says, "Be ye perfect." It is a precept intensely practical. No day passes but what we can put it into action. Here, for instance, in this your school life, not to speak of the weightier matters of the law, little punctualities, little self-denials, little honesties, little passing words of sympathy, little nameless acts of kindness, little silent victories over favourite temptations—these are the little threads of gold, which, when woven together, gleam out so brightly in the pattern of a life that God approves. Let me illustrate the last only, and it shall be from a source which you will all reverence, for it is from the life of that good Bishop to whom Marlborough looks as her father and second founder. Bishop Cotton was blessed, says his biography, with a remarkably sweet and even temper, but in India a land of many irritations and small worries, it was often tried. A cloud would gather for a few moments on his countenance; but ordinarily by entire silence he checked the hasty word. Very rarely, however, an expression of annoyance escaped him; and here comes what I would ask you to consider. Surely, you will say, a passing irritation, a momentary haste, were very small faults, hardly faults at all. Not so, thought that noble heart. He was faithful, you see, in little things. "His self-condemnation afterwards," continues his biographer, "was truly that godly sorrow that worketh repentance, and could spring only from the heart and conscience of one who

[1] *Life of Bishop Cotton.*

feels that he has, for the moment, failed in allegiance to Him in whom alone lies the strength for a sinner's victory." "In the most trivial temptations he sought to maintain that warfare against sin which made his whole life, as it ripened towards its close, a religion, a devotion, an act of faith."

That example, my brethren, belongs especially to us; we claim it, and we feel it to be ours; like a sweet savour, like a precious heritage, it lingers here; and that life was pre-eminently moulded on the principle which I have roughly striven to illustrate: "He that is faithful in the least is faithful also in much; and he that is unjust in the least is unjust also in much."

March 5, 1871.

SERMON III.

HUNGERING AND THIRSTING AFTER RIGHTEOUSNESS.

MATT. v. 6.

"Blessed are they which do hunger and thirst after righteousness: for they shall be filled."

IT was indeed a new revelation that Sermon on the Mount, to part of which you have just been listening;—new in its method, new in its substance, new in its results. It was new in its *method*;—for at Sinai out of the thick darkness, amid the rolling thunder, God had spoken of old to a wandering nation as they trembled at the base of the burning hill; but now on the green grass, among the mountain lilies, beside the limpid lake, with the infinite tenderness of sympathy and sorrow, the lips of the Son of Man spake softly the utterance of God. It was new in its *substance*;—for there were no narrow prohibitions here, no Levitical ceremonies, no transitory concessions, no statutes that were not good, and judgments whereby they should not live, but the eternal, transcendent, unshaken law of mercy and self-denial, of tenderness and love. It was new in its *results*;—for that fiery law did but curb and crush one obstinate and rebellious people with a burden which neither they nor their fathers were able to bear; but this was to be a delight for all and for ever, it was to come like a fresh youth to a diseased and decrepit world, revivifying as the summer sunlight, beneficent as the universal air.

Whichever one we selected of those divine beatitudes, with which, as with a song sweeter than ever angel sang, our Lord began His Sermon on the Mount, we should find it full of instruction, and we should find it opposed diametrically to the vulgar teaching of the world. And let us admit at once that there are aspects in which these beatitudes seem too high for your youthful age. "Blessed are the poor in spirit;" but how impetuous and resentful, how swift and self-reliant is the heart of youth! "Blessed are they that mourn;" but can we dwell on this to you at an age which, as the poet-preacher expresses it, "danceth like a bubble, empty and gay, and shineth like a dove's neck, or the image of a rainbow which hath no substance, and whose very imagery and colours are fantastical." "Blessed are the merciful;" "Blessed are the peace-makers;" "Blessed are the pure in heart." Yes, these, doubtless, you might learn even now to practise and to understand, but can we hope that you will see any force in this also, "Blessed are they that hunger and thirst after righteousness: for they shall be filled?" It was natural for David, the old worn king, for David, who, after all the buffetings of a stormy life, had learnt, even if it were by evil, that good was best—it was natural, I say, for him to exclaim, "As the hart panteth after the waterbrooks, so panteth my soul after thee, O God!" But such would be in general but exotic and artificial language for most of you. Look at the corn-fields now, and you will see only the green blade, barely struggling into the sunlight out of the frosty soil: we do not look yet for the ear, much less for the ripe corn in the ear; nor in the inexperienced neophyte and the timid catechumen do we expect the vision of the mystic and the rapture of the saint. Some, indeed, there may be of you, of whom, in silence and in secret, the grace of God has taken such early hold that to them even such words as these may come of right; but for most of you, as yet, it is enough if the hunger and thirst after righteousness has taken *this* form :—that you abhor that which is evil, and cleave to that which is good; that, recognizing the blazonry of your high birth, you scorn and loathe all meanness and malice, all cruelty and lies; that, feeling, as it were, the symbol of certain victory which was marked upon your forehead in your baptism, you turn with a certain honest haughtiness of nature from the baser and more degrading forms of vice; that in the determination to live by God's grace lives pure, and brave, and serviceable, you have, as it were, already set your feet upon the mountain and turned your eyes towards the sun. Would to God that every one of you had gone as far as this! It is true that righteousness, in the language of Scripture, means more than this,—more than moral culture, more than gradual improvement, more than the natural integrity of a rightly-constituted soul. It means the devoted service of God; it means the constraining love of Christ; it means the unutterable yearning of the Spirit for all that is divine. But, nevertheless, virtue, if it be not as yet righteousness, is yet the sweetest flower which blooms beside that narrow path. It has been truly said by a moralist of the eighteenth century— may you all remember that admirable definition !—that virtue is the conquest of self for the benefit of others ; and in this aspect, at least, to disparage virtue because as yet it is not holiness, is to disparage the blossom because it is not yet the fruit. And if you are aiming at this, if you have realised already the sanctity of such service, if your one main desire is that you should be yourself good and happy, in order that others may be the better and the happier for you—in one word, if you recognize that you are not your own, but are God's child, and must therefore by living for others do His work—then fear not; this is at least the dawn which shall broaden and brighten into the boundless day. It shall never be yours to cry in disappointment with the dying Brutus: "Oh virtue, thou art but a name!" Nay, more, you may fearlessly claim the gradual fulfilment of the divine beatitude, "Blessed are they that hunger and thirst after righteousness: for they shall be filled." For observe, my brethren, there are some—alas! there are many—in the world who seem to hunger and thirst after *nothing*. It is a type which in this age is getting more and more common, the type of those who live as though they had no souls, as though no God had made them, no Saviour died for them, no Spirit shone in the temple of their hearts. They live but little better than the beasts that perish, the life of dead, stolid, spiritless comfort, the life without purpose, without effort, without nobility, without enthusiasm, "the dull, grey life, and apathetic end." The great sea of human misery welters around them; but what is that to them, while the bread is given and the water sure? Over them, vast as the blue dome of Heaven, brood the eternal realities; before them, deeper than ever plummet sank, flows the river of death; beyond it, in gloom unutterable or in beauty that cannot be described, is either the outer darkness or the City of our God; but it seems as though they had neither mind to imagine, nor faith to realize, nor heart to understand. These are they whom in his awful vision the great poet of the Middle Ages saw whirled like the autumn leaves, round and round the outer circle of the prison-house, aimlessly following the flutter of a giddy flag, hateful alike to God and to His enemies, whom, in his energetic language, Heaven despises and Hell itself rejects. These are they of whom, in language no less energetic and intense, the divine poet of the Apocalypse exclaims: "I know thy works, that thou art neither cold nor hot: I would thou wert cold or hot. So then because thou art lukewarm, and neither cold nor hot, I will spue thee out of my mouth." It is sad, but it is true, that they are nothing, they do nothing, they learn nothing, they add nothing to the sum of human happiness—*numerus et fruges consumere nati*; their lives, one had well nigh said, worth less to humanity than the very flower that grows upon their graves. Oh! be not you like these. Be something in life, do something, aim at something; not something great, but something good; not something famous, but something serviceable; not leaves, but fruit. You are planted in the vineyard of God, you are watered by the dews of Heaven; let the great Husbandman not look in vain, when He looketh that ye bring forth grapes; for if not, then lo! even now, in the hands of the watchers and the holy ones, the lifted axe may be swinging through the parted air, even now the dread fiat be issuing forth: "Cut it down; why cumbereth it the ground?"

2. But there are others who hunger and thirst indeed, but it is not for righteousness; hunger and thirst, oh, how fiercely, oh, with what futile pain, spending their money for that which is not bread, and their labour for that which satisfieth not. Some — hundreds — like Balaam, are greedy of gain, and if they succeed, then all that they touch seems to turn to gold, and, like

the foolish king of the legend, they starve in the midst of it. Or they are greedy of sensual pleasure, they rush madly to the "scoriac river of passion," and consume their very beings with draughts of its liquid fire. Or they are greedy of power and fame, and chase those dancing bubbles till at a touch they burst, while, with the echoes of mocking laughter, they themselves fall through some sudden gap of death into the rolling waters of the prodigious tide below. Over and over again, in book after book, in age after age, does Scripture warn us of the emptiness, the unsatisfactoriness of human wishes; it compares them to the vanishing brooks dried up in the summer heat, when they are needed most; it compares them to broken cisterns which will hold no water. A modern army was once crossing a desert, scorched with heat, agonized with thirst; suddenly before them gleamed lakes and rivers, green with their grassy margins, bright with the soft inversion of reflected trees. They pressed forward in their weary hunger, in their raging thirst; warned in vain that it was but a mocking phantom, they pressed forward only to be undeceived with double anguish; they pressed forward to find nothing but the circle of sun-encrimsoned wilderness, nothing but the glare of illuminated sand. They had seen that mirage which is the truest type of the devil's promise and the worldling's hope, the false spectre of waters which are not, and of fruits that fail,— that mirage of the desert, which is but too apt to deceive us all, till death disenchants the dreaming eyes.

3. But "blessed are they that hunger and thirst after righteousness: for they shall be filled;" filled with the heavenly manna of which he that gathered least had yet no lack, sated with the water which he who drinketh shall thirst no more. There is no false glamour.

no raging hunger, no scorching thirst in those green pastures, beside those still waters, whither God leadeth His children's feet. The voice of Scripture, which warns us so often of the perils of being deceived by dangerous desires, tells us also again and again that the kingdom of heaven is righteousness, and joy, and peace. "Great is the peace," sang David, "which they have who love Thy law." "Her ways," said Solomon, "are ways of pleasantness, and all her paths are peace." But if any doubt, I will not ask them to believe on the testimony of Scripture only. Scripture is but one of God's revelations, and none of His revelations can contradict each other. But take in hand the unsuspected page of history; read the rich volumes of biography; decipher the tablets of conscience as the light of God's law falls full upon them: will they contradict the warning? will they alter the advice? Nay, let the best-read here find me in all the history of the dead, point to me among all the myriads of the living, but one single man, be he the most gifted, the most successful, the most superior, who has been *satisfied* and *supported* by what earth can give, or who, having eaten the fruits of sin, has not found them venomous and bitter; or, on the other hand, one single man, be he the very poorest and most despised, who, having with his whole soul sought righteousness, has not thereby been *fully* satisfied, infinitely content—find me, I say, but one permanently happy worldling, but one permanently miserable Christian, and I will admit that Scripture errs. But, my brethren, you cannot, even with all the records of the ages and all the literature of the godless to aid your search. Wickedness, even exalted on the throne, even robed in the purple, even lolling at the feast, is gnawed by the secret viper at the heart; righteousness, even lurking in the catacomb, even tortured in the dungeon, even quivering in the flame, rejoiceth in its deepest sorrow, and is assurance, and life, and peace.

Observe, we do not pretend to offer you a life of unbroken prosperity or of undisturbed repose. Righteousness will give you love, joy, peace; but it will not give you an invincible amulet against misfortune, or a continuous immunity from pain. Pain, bereavement, failure may be the needful fire to purge away the dross of your nature from the seven-times refined gold. Let Satan tempt you with the transient spasms of enjoyment or the mean baits of ease: the service of God disdains such lower allurements. Yes, the path of evil is broad, and smooth, and downwards, and near at hand; but toil stands in the path of righteousness, and that path is narrow, and steep, and rough; but who would exchange its saddest sigh for the laughter of fools, which is as the crackling of thorns under a pot? Who would exchange the tears which God's hand shall wipe away for "the troubles of the envious or the fears of the cowardly, the heaviness of the slothful, or the shame of the unclean?" Nay, who would exchange the banquet of the prodigal at its maddest and most luxurious moment for the sternest duty and the heaviest affliction of his Father's home? Whatever happens to you, if you hunger and thirst after righteousness, you shall be satisfied; for then your hunger is not for the stones of the wilderness, but for the tree of life; your thirst not for poisoned fountains, but for the river pure as crystal proceeding out of the throne of God and of the Lamb. For you that tree was planted; for you that river flows: Christ is the river of living water; Christ is that tree of life. "All things are yours, and ye are Christ's, and Christ is God's." Young as you are, have you never thirsted for something to calm, and satisfy, and give peace to your souls? Well, he that cometh to Christ shall never hunger, and he that believeth on Christ shall never thirst. And if you have failed to win that blessing, may there not be a special meaning for you in that appeal, "Oh that thou hadst hearkened to my commandments; then had thy peace been as a river, and thy righteousness as the waves of the sea"? But if you have hearkened to God's commandments—if you have at least striven to hearken to God's commandments—then you see that what God gives He gives richly, He gives abundantly. It is no dribbling rivulet of peace which He pours into the thirsty soul, but a rejoicing river; no transitory torrent, but an abounding tide; rising in His children as water rises in a fountain, dwelling in them as water dwelleth in a mighty sea. This is His promise, and, if we fulfil its conditions, it can never fail; for the mouth of God hath spoken it, and God is true.

May 7, 1871.

SERMON IV.

THE RIGHT USE OF SPEECH.

MATT. xii. 36.

"I say unto you that every idle word that men shall speak, they shall give account thereof in the day of judgment."

GUIDED by the lessons of each Sunday, we have striven to think together over the great truths of our belief; to cleanse, to strengthen, to uplift our souls by the awful verities of death, judgment, and eternity. But such thoughts are worse than useless if they produce no effect upon our lives. The test of their reality is not the idle leafage of profession, but the rich certainty of fruit. The tree of life beside the pure river bare twelve manner of fruits, and yielded her fruit every month. What are those fruits? They are the golden apples of each fair virtue. To the consideration of one such virtue our Lord's words to-day invite us; a single virtue, but manifold in its operation—that high virtue which consists in the right use of speech.

Our life, like the fancies of our sleep, is blended of the intermingling realities of the unseen and the seen. All of us live two lives in one : the outward, temporal, accidental life of routine and circumstance; and that inward, invisible life, which is unlimited by time or space, which can either soar into the heaven of heavens, gaze undazzled upon the very throne of God, and move untrembling, the Arm that moves the world; or which, sinking downwards into the very deepest and deadliest abysses, can dwell familiarly in the evil darkness, with all monstrous and prodigious things. And this inner and outer life are often wholly disparate; in some men they brighten and fade into alternate prominence and oblivion; in some the outer life is all, the inner nothing; in some the inner is the awful reality, the outer but a passing and inconsiderable dream. And again, the relations between these two lives often wholly differ. In some the outer life is false—a mere hypocrisy; a whitened sepulchre covering the deep uncleanness; a fair face hiding the inward leprosy; the network of sunbeams over a treacherous and turbid sea. In some this outer life is not false but inadequate; it fails somehow to express and reflect the inward goodness; it creates an unjust prejudice, like the rough robe that conceals a king, or the stained fringe of the shallow waves that are so poor an outcome of the mighty sea. And there are some again—oh happy they!—whose two lives, the outer and the inner, are mutually expressive, exquisitely harmonious.

"How sour sweet music is,"

sings our great poet,

"When time is broke, and no proportion kept;
So is it with the music of men's lives."

And the outer lives of these of whom I speak are, as it were, a sacrament: the outward and visible sign of an inward and spiritual grace given unto them. In them, by God's blessing, there is no painful dislocation between the thing that they weakly approve and the thing they basely do; their outward life is calm and holy, because their inward life is inviolate and pure.

The soul of a bad man, or a worldly man, may, I suppose, in course of time die down to the ground; may, as it were, be eaten out of him by lusts and cares, and then he can scarcely be said to have an inner life at all; but for all save these, the inner life is the real being, as the soul is the truest self; and this is the object of what I have been saying—our genuine words are the shadows of our souls. None can read our thoughts; none can see our souls; but when the lips speak, then that which is within us is revealed, revealed for ever. The pulses of articulated air may pass away from the cognisance of the senses, but as no motion can ever wholly cease, they quiver in that sensitive medium until the end; and even were it not so, yet for every idle word we speak, we shall, for Christ's own lips have said it, be called to account upon the judgment day. "Then," says the prophet Malachi, "they that feared the Lord spake often to one another, and the Lord hearkened and heard it, and a book of remembrance was written before Him for them that feared the Lord and thought upon His name." And is there no other book of remembrance, a book of remembrance which must also be a book of condemnation? Do you think that those who have willingly defied God's laws, even if they die splendid and prosperous in the scarlet fruitage of their sins, do you think that they have escaped the Divine justice? Ah no; there is many a word of thine written on those awful pages, and by thy words thou shalt be justified, and by thy words thou shalt be condemned. Evil thoughts are deadly and dangerous, but they are less guilty than evil words, less guilty than evil deeds; they are the sparks which may indeed, at any moment burst into flame; and the spark may be trodden out while it is yet a spark; but who shall stay the raging conflagration? Yet evil thoughts are full of peril, and if all our sins of thought were but written upon our foreheads, there would be dire need for us to stand with bowed heads and downcast eyes as we await the verdict before the solemn bar; yet if we have conquered them as thoughts, then far less will be the wrong that we have done, far less damning will be the witness of our accusing consciences against ourselves. But every word we speak falls on the ears of others; and who shall brave the witness of others against him? "Words, words, words," it has been exclaimed, "good and bad, loud and soft, millions in the hour, innumerable in the day, unimaginable in the year:— what then in the life? What in the history of a nation? What in that of the world? And not one of them is ever forgotten. There is a book where they are all set down."[1] Oh let the thought add dignity, add solemnity, add truthfulness, add absolute and perfect purity, add sacred and illimitable charity to all we say!

Let us then consider briefly and imperfectly, for more is not possible in the time before us—some of our duties and some of our dangers—for the two are correlate—in the use of speech. What classes of idle words must we avoid? You will, I think, find that they fall mainly under four heads: words that sin against truth, against reverence, against purity, against Christian love; our duty is to see that all our words be holy words, true words, clean words, charitable words; our effort, if herein we would live nobly, should be to avoid all impurity, all impiety, all malice, and all lies.

[1] Dean Alford.

1. Let us take words of falsehood first. In all ages, pagan no less than heathen, from the old poet who sang

> "Who dares think one thing, and another tell,
> My soul detests him as the gates of hell,"[1]

down to the living one who exclaims

> "This is a shameful thing for men to lie,"[2]

the best and loftiest of mankind have ever been the most incisive in branding the sin of lies. There is something specially contemptible in the cowardice, the treachery, the meanness of this sin; the trail of the serpent is peculiarly upon it; even men of the world are sickened by it. A man of honour could not tell a lie even if he would: in uttering it he would be unable to repress the rising gorge of self-disgust; the blush of his indignant honesty would burn through the smooth, false visage of deceit. But though I trust that there are but very few of us who need to be warned against positive open lies, may we not all aim at more absolute and perfect accuracy? aim never to colour any statement, however slight, by our interests or our wishes? aim not only to speak the truth always, but always also the whole truth and nothing else? And although I know that there are scarcely any of you who would *tell* a deliberate lie, let me warn you, my young brethren, against *acting* one; against little concealments, against little dissimulations, against little dishonesties, against little deceits. In form, for instance, the surreptitious leaf, the dishonest aid, the copied exercise, the note written in school: these are the fruitful sources of temptation; and therefore, if you would be perfectly honest, never pretend to be doing what you are not

---

[1] Homer.   [2] Tennyson, *Morte d'Arthur*.

doing; never pretend to have done what you have not done; never be surprised into a concealment or startled into a falsehood; such "manslaughter on truth" always ends in murder. Excuse develops into subterfuge; subterfuge degenerates into equivocation; equivocation ends in lies. If you set a stone rolling on a mountain it acquires at every moment a more and more hideous velocity and force; and so many a boy, suddenly charged with some trivial wrong, suddenly detected in some venial fault, suddenly afraid of some insignificant punishment (oh, whenever such a thing occurs to you, pause, and think, and keep your lips as it were with a bridle, before you speak!)—yes, even a boy of natural honour has often ere now found himself landed in the shame, found himself branded with the stigma, of distinct and undeniable falsehood. We may hate lies and abhor them; but depend upon it, only by God's grace and our own careful watchfulness are any of us safe from anything. And oh, knowing that we may, in violation of our own real and truest nature, become false by carelessness, by timidity, even by a mere social assentiveness and wretched complaisance, let us draw for ourselves a deep and severe boundary line herein.

"My sin, Ismenius, hath wrought all this ill,"

says an old dramatist;

"And I beseech thee to be warned by me,
And do not lie if any man do ask thee
But how thou dost, or what it is o'clock :
Be sure thou do not lie—make no excuse ;
For they above (that are entirely truth)
Will make the seed that thou hast sown of lies
Yield miseries a hundred-thousand-fold
Upon thy head, as they have done on mine."

2. About the idle words of irreverence I shall say but little. Common as is the senseless vice of profanity—

a profanity caused in the uneducated by mere brutal ignorance, and in others by an imitative weakness or petty irascibility—I venture to hope and to believe that by God's blessing it is not in its worst forms common among you. How can it be common among Christian boys? But if any one of you is in the habit of using oaths, I rede his sleeping conscience to beware of their guilt and folly. This futile gratuitous insult against sacred names and solemn truths is nothing more or less than the mere vulgarity of guilt. It is a sign of mental imbecility and social ill-breeding, no less than of moral death. Other sins offer at least some ghastly simulacrum of a pleasure, or some poor excuse of a temptation; this sin of swearing offers none. What? to use the name of God, and of God's most dread judgments, in the mere riotous intemperance of brainless speech; to fling about thoughts so dread that they should be immured "like the garden of Eden with the swords of the cherubim," and to prostitute them into petulant curses or idle expletives —one hardly knows whether most to admire the stupidity of such a degradation or to detest its guilt. But remember that there are other, and alas! far commoner ways of taking God's word in vain. You may take it in vain by the irreverent utterance of a petition, by the empty repetition of a creed, by the undevotional singing of a hymn: you may take it in vain as you read a lesson in chapel, or say a grace in hall—ay, take it in vain, though the lips move not, as you join in acts of adoration and listen to words of prayer. Oh, let there be reverence among us for sacred things; and here in this chapel, by deep silence, by the thoughtful attention, by the reverend attitude, by the hearty and devout response, may you learn that humble and holy fear which shall make all carelessness about the name or the thought of God impossible to you henceforth for ever.

3. But commoner by far than the idle words of falsehood, and the idle words of irreverence, are the idle words of uncharity: and though it would be impossible to dwell upon them now, whose conscience does not accuse him here? Ill-nature, gossip, spite, malice, slander, whispering, backbiting, detraction, calumny, alas! the multitude of the names,—and I have not half exhausted them,—proves the prolific danger of the thing. Yes, there are "the unknown voices that bellow in the shade and swell the language of falsehood and of hate;" there is "the diseased noise and scandalous murmur" of petty criticism; there is the thick scum of city loquacity, and the acrid jealousies of provincial sloth. Among you, I doubt not, there is all the petty, ignoble, seething tittle-tattle of constant and promiscuous talk. These things do not all spring from wicked bitterness, they are not all the symptoms of the empty head and the corrupted heart; sometimes they are simply the offspring of intellectual feebleness trying to seem clever by the attempt at satire; sometimes a mere effort of those who are weary of themselves and envious of others, to break what has been called "the pattering monotony of life;" sometimes a sort of disappointed egotism, and morbid self-conceit, because

"It's always ringing in their ears,
'They call this man as good as me.'"

But whatever it be, it becomes a disease. It makes the mind like those looking-glasses in the temple of Smyrna which gave a false and distorted reflection even of every innocent and happy face that looked upon them. It is a great curse to the possessor—this mocking, carping, detracting, grumbling spirit; men please it not, nor women neither; it makes us, like that ancient satirist, the natural product of a corrupt and decadent civilisation, who lets his tongue "rage like a fire among the noblest names, defaming and defacing,"

> "Finding low motives unto noble deeds,
> Fixing all doubt upon the darker side,"

until to him not even Helen was beautiful or Achilles brave.[1] Kind words, and liberal estimates, and generous acknowledgment, and ready appreciation, and unselfish delight in the excellences of others—these are the truest signs of a large intellect and a noble spirit: while proneness to discover imperfection, and love of finding fault, and exultation in dwelling upon failure, and fondness for inflicting pain, are the certain marks of an unchristian temper and an ignoble heart.

4. On the fourth and last class of idle words—words of impurity—I shall scarcely even touch. More criminal even than irreverence, more degrading even than falsehood, more pestilent even than slander—oh, if there be a sin which needs "the fiery whip of an exterminating angel," it is the sin of those who degrade one of the highest gifts of God to do the vilest office of His enemies. What should we think of one who smeared the walls of a city with the elements of plague? what of him who on the most dangerous headlands kindled, of purpose, the wrecker's fire? Yet even he would be doing the devil's work less obviously and less perilously than he who, into the ear of another, pours the leperous distilment of his own most evil thoughts. The influence of such words is truly baleful; their effects often terribly permanent. They paint the soul's inmost chambers with unhallowed imagery; they break on its

[1] Lucian.

holiest memories with satanic songs. The troubled sea, when it cannot rest, whose waters cast up mire and dirt—raging waves, foaming out their own shame—such are the Scripture metaphors for these. And from all such—from all such, more and rather than from every other class of the sinful—from their words that eat as doth a canker, from the contagion of their presence, from the infection of their touch, from the contamination of their very look—from all such may God mercifully preserve the school we love!

Oh, then, my brethren—and above all you who are now about so soon to renew with your own lips your baptismal vow—make for yourselves, in conclusion, at least this one resolution—that you will set a watch before the door of your mouth. Let no oath, no privy slandering, no corrupt communication, no word that is not true, ever again cross or sully those lips that, more surely than with a living coal from the altar, have been hallowed by the utterance of a Christian vow. Against meanness, profanity, pollution, let there henceforth be an impassable barrier there. And let all of us strive, more earnestly and more continuously, after the dignity of severer speech. If we cannot otherwise trust ourselves, then,—from all morbid egotism, from all ungenerous depreciation—let us take refuge in that silence which, under such circumstances, is a better thing than speech, being innocent as childhood, and "harmless as a breath of woodbine to the passer-by." Better to be silent, and silent for ever, than to speak words false, or uncharitable, or impure. And some there are—some still among the living—who, because their spirits are always walking like white-robed angels among the white-robed companies on high—because their eyes and their thoughts are among the stars and not upon the dust, who, because they gaze upon the golden brow of humanity and not upon its feet of clay —who, because they look upon their fellows with the larger, other eyes of sunny, genial, loving natures, speak no words now that are not pure, and sweet, and noble, and charitable, and kind. Oh, may we learn to be like them, for the Saints of God are these, though no visible aureola gleam as yet around their brow! Nay rather, may we be like Him, who, though He loved us so much that for our sakes He emptied Himself of His glory, and became obedient unto death, even the death of the Cross, yet gave His solemn warning that for every idle word that men shall speak, shall they give account at the judgment day.

May, 17, 1871.

SERMON V.

SMOULDERING LAMPS.

MATT. xxv. 8.

"*Our lamps are gone out.*"

THERE is much to say, and but little time to say it in. We must feel that often; we must feel it especially on an occasion such as this, when, besides the ordinary Sabbath quietude and Sabbath prayer, there is triple reason why to-day we should call this Sabbath a delight, holy of the Lord, honourable.

1. In the first place it is Whit-Sunday, the White Sunday, the birthday of the Christian Church. And remember that what we commemorate to-day is not only the sound as of a rushing mighty wind, and the shaken house where the Apostles were assembled, and the saintly foreheads, each mitred with its cloven flame—not only the Gift of Tongues, and the Word of God shining like the lightning from East to West—not only the burning words of Peter and the first great harvest of regenerated souls: historic reminiscences like these may become dim with time and overshadowed with unreality —but we commemorate the deepest and greatest of Christian truths, the presence in our hearts of an in- dwelling Spirit, to be the eternal aid to an increasing

holiness, to be the eternal witness of an unshaken faith. On other days we thank God for the gift of some special blessing, to-day we thank Him for the imparting of Himself, not only into our nature, as on Christmas Day, not only into our death as on Good Friday, but the gift of Himself into our hearts. This is the very noontide of the Christian day—a noontide without an evening—a day on which no night need ever more descend.

2. But further, this is not only Whit-Sunday, but to many of you also the first Sunday after your confirmation. In infancy, even at the tenderest dawn of life, you were brought to the arms of Christ, and there with "a few calm words of faith and prayer," and "a few bright drops of holy dew," you were signed with the sign of the cross, in token that hereafter you should not be ashamed to fight manfully under Christ's banner, and to be His faithful soldier and servant unto your life's end. In the ancient Church, and even down to the Reformation, another significant ceremony was added; the child was clothed by the minister in a white robe, called the chrisom robe, as a sign that he was washed from sinful defilements and had put on Christ, while the words were used, "Take this white vesture as a token of the innocency which by this Holy Sacrament of Baptism is given unto thee, and as a sign whereby thou art admonished, so long as thou livest, to innocency of living, that after this transitory life thou mayest be a partaker of life everlasting." And though in no earthly vestry, yet amid the eternal treasuries, that chrisom robe of innocence is laid up as a mute witness against you. For then as a river rises, pure as crystal, among the moss of some green mountain side, even so your life began; then were those bright and happy years in the dear old home when you were taken in the arms of God's

holy ones, and knelt in prayer beside His saints; the days of every redeeming grace, of every softening virtue, of every refining and purifying influence, of every sacred and tender memory; the days when your innocent heart was a bright temple, wholly God's, when the child folds his little white hands as he lisps out of stainless lips his holy prayers, and when as night by night he lies down in his little cot, the angels of God close to the doors of his happy heart, and weave under his curtained eye the radiant fantasies of untroubled sleep. Yes that was

> "Before we knew to fancy aught
> But a white celestial thought,
> Before we taught our tongues to wound
> Our conscience with a guilty sound;
> But felt through all this earthly dress
> Bright shoots of everlastingness."[1]

And if indeed the river of your life have been stained since then by any of the bitter soils through which its course has run, yet now once more have you been affectionately urged, gently aided, to calm and cleanse the turbid waves. Surely on the first Sunday after your confirmation you feel, all of you, the richer, the holier, the happier. You have experienced, I trust, already that God's Holy Spirit can indeed, if you rightly seek Him, draw His sevenfold veil between you and the fires of youth; and with the shadow upon your heads of the hand that blessed, you have been strengthened to take your stand boldy and nobly on the side of all that is great and true. Oh, that on this day He would indeed outpour upon each youthful head the crysmal fires of His sevenfold gifts; and if, indeed, any of you have sinned and fallen and desecrated His temple; if in any of your hearts have been the spirit of folly and

[1] H. Vaughan.

blindness, the spirit of ignorance and effeminacy, the spirit of forgetfulness and self-indulgence, and the spirit of evil defiance against His law, oh, may He henceforth grant you instead, and grant you richly, according to the prayer we prayed, the spirit of wisdom and understanding, the spirit of counsel and ghostly strength, the spirit of knowledge and true godliness, and the spirit of His holy fear.

3. And once again, this, not only a Whit-Sunday, not only the first Sunday after your confirmation, is to many of you ever-memorable as the day of your first Communion, the day on which you are first admitted to the highest privilege of the Christian's life. Coming immediately after your confirmation, and henceforth continually, until it be, as it were, the very *viaticum* at your journey's close, what a blessing, my brethren, may this be to you: at the most solemn crisis of youth a gracious reminder of all that Christ your Saviour has done for you, and all that you have vowed for Him—at the most dangerous period of life a living Sacrament, the outward and visible sign of an inward and spiritual grace—when the passions are strongest and pleasure wears its most falsely-destructive smile—a fresh call to repentance and self-devotion, a fresh grace of strength and purity, a fresh stimulus to charity and faith and prayer.

And I doubt not that, all this being so, there is some gleam of brightness in the saddest heart among you all. How shall I aid you to feel it permanently, to feel it increasingly, to feel it even until the end? For alas! warm feelings, though happy, are not religion; and high hopes, though inspiring, are not holiness; and religious excitement, though awakening, is not strength. My brethren, I cannot, for human opportunities are scanty, and human words are weak; but to the Holy Ghost the Comforter, who loveth before all temples the upright heart and pure, to Him who can send forth His seraphim with the fire of His altar to touch and hallow the lips of whom He will,—I pray to Him that in this His house, on this His day, He would take of the things of Christ and show them unto you; that He would Himself make intercession for you with groanings that cannot be uttered.

Let me then take but a single point: let me take the imagery of my text, and strive to fix it upon your hearts. Into your hands has been put a lighted lamp; into the hand of every one of you the lighted lamp of conscience, of the Word of God, of the Spirit of Christ; into the hands of many of you to-day the same lamp, indeed, but fed with an oil more fragrant, and burnished into a purer gold.

And when I describe this guiding principle of life as a lamp put into your hands, you will recognise at once the imagery of Christ's parable, which you heard in the evening lesson two days ago; you will recall that lovely and pathetic picture of the bridegroom setting forth to his bride's house to bring her home; of the virgins, her companions, awaiting them far on into the starry coolness of the oriental night; of their slumber in the midnight silence; of the cry, "Behold, the bridegroom cometh;" of the hurry, the alarm, the shame, the anguish, when the foolish virgins found that their oil was exhausted and their lamps had burned too low. And then you will remember how the bridal procession passed into the glorious and happy banquet, and the door was shut. In vain, with their miserable smouldering lamps, they stand, terrified, remorseful, agitated, at the closed door and knock. To that wild, eager, importunate knocking, in his festal robes, the garlands of rose and myrtle on his brow, the bridegroom came, and over his fair presence, through the opening door, streamed the echoes of lordly music and the glow of odorous lights. But for these foolish virgins there were no words of welcome now, and upon their terror-stricken hearts sank like heavy snow-flakes the chilly words, "I know you not." It was too late. The door was shut. It was dark and cold, and the birds of night were flitting, and the thick dews fell, and in that chilly darkness their lamps were going out.

Our lamps are being quenched. And, using the same metaphor, "Quench not," says the great Apostle of the Gentiles, "quench not, put not out the Spirit." Can, then, the light of God's holy Spirit be quenched within us? If so, how can that light be quenched? Whereby can it be kept alive?

i. Let me answer both questions as briefly and simply as I may. And first, the lamp, the light within us, can be quenched in two ways: the one active, the other passive; the one by forgetfulness of God, the other by familiarity with vice. The bright lamp is in your hands, but it can die out if you yield to sloth; it will be extinguished if you give yourself to sin.

By sloth, for instance. Oh, my brethren, set it down as a certain fact in the revelation of God's will that the life which is content without one effort after holiness must be content also without one hope of heaven. You know it is so in the physical domain: there you cannot attain to excellence without care and practice; you know that it is so in the intellectual domain—there you cannot win either knowledge or distinction without study and self-denial; and think you that it shall not be so also in the spiritual domain?

Think you that there the great victory will be given to yawning satiety and drowsy ease? Should the young Greek athlete be content to submit to rough training and eat hard fare before he could even hope for his withering garland of Isthmian pine? And shall you dream that the crown of life, the wreath of amaranth that cannot fade, will be dropped, even unasked for, upon the glutton's banquet or the sluggard's bed? Nay, but believe me, "the kingdom of Heaven suffereth violence, and the violent take it by force." Even the heathen saw that toil is the janitor at the gate of virtue, and that he who would win must strive.

You have heard that your bodies are temples of the Holy Ghost; but a temple that is not desecrated must be tended and adorned. The great city of Ephesus was proud to call herself upon her coins the Νεωκόρος, "the temple-sweeper" of her heathen fane; and will you make no effort to cleanse and tend that heart which is the living temple of the one true God? Oh, if not, beware lest the temple of a living God become the tomb of a dead soul, and the lamp which now shines peacefully within it first wane, then glimmer, then expire.

ii. But more swiftly and more violently than by sloth, in yet a deadlier and yet a surer way, may the light of God's Holy Spirit be quenched by sin. Oh, thus it is that from the temple of the heart the Spirit is driven, even as the Prophet saw the rushing splendour of the Divine presence as it departed from the polluted shrine, first rise high into the air, then retire till it stood over the gate of the city, then remove to the hills beyond it, then vanish away for ever into the unutterable gloom. Oh, thus it is that, as in the doomed cities of old on the eve of their destruction, voices are heard as of offended

deities, saying to each other in awful accents, Μετα-
βαίνωμεν ἐντεῦθεν, "Let us depart hence." Oh, my
brethren, you who will go forth on the path of life to
meet the bridegroom, beware but of one conscious, one
admitted, one unresisted sin. Nothing quenches more
surely the holy lamp. You may try to think of the sin
as venial; you may try to hold each fresh commission
thereof light; but it is even thus that, star by star, the
whole heavens fade away from the human soul; even
thus that one by one its excellences vanish, its virtues
faint, its graces cease to shine. As when a man descends
slowly into some dark mine and carries a taper in his
hand, and knows that so long as the flame of that taper
burns bright and clear, so long the atmosphere he
breathes is safe; but as he gets lower the flame begins
to contract and to grow pale, and then to waver, and
at last, as the foul fog-damps surround and imprison
it, it becomes but a faint and dwindling flicker, and
finally, amid the blue and poisonous vapours, expires
with a foul breath of sickening fume; even so it is,
alas! with him who, from the sunlight of God's countenance, descends deeper and deeper—with conscious
self-surrender, with willing guilt, with impotent, because
with unresisting will—into the deep, dark underground
of a besetting sin.

iii. But, my brethren, we are persuaded better things
of you, and things that accompany salvation though we
thus speak. Your lamps, I trust, some of your lamps I
know, are burning brightly now: brighter from recent
thoughts, and recent blessings, and recent prayers,
brightly with holy purposes, brightly with hopeful
efforts, brightly with strong resolves; not yours, by the
grace of God, not yours shall be the sad confession and
the shameful history of the downward course, the

growing degeneracy, the smouldering lamp; not yours the increasing degradation, the gathering midnight, the deepening sleep; oh, may it not be for any one of you to watch in anguish the fungous growths that clog the untrimmed wick, or its silvery lustre sinking into noxious dimness as the gloom threatens to swallow for ever the dying flame. Oh, surely you will be of the wise who took with them oil in their vessels with their lamps. Prayer, effort, watchfulness, penitence for past sin, effort to aid the souls of others: these are the means of grace which are like fresh oil and fragrant in the lighted lamp of a Christian's soul. Each time you kneel beside your beds, each time you meet in this chapel, each hour of quiet thought in which you go forth to meet your Lord, each Sunday spent in a calm and holy faith, above all, each Holy Sacrament at which you kneel with peace in your penitent cleansed hearts towards God and man, these shall widen around you the circle of heavenly light, these (and God grant they may!) shall so make the lamp beam in the temple of your souls that even into its darkest recesses soon no evil thing shall dare intrude. Thus shall your care be

> " Fixt and zealously attent
> To fill your odorous lamps with deeds of light
> And hope, that reaps not shame."

iv. And if any of you need a word of special comfort, oh, bear with me while I speak one word of comfort more. The lamp, my brethren, in this life never goes quite out. The text is mistranslated: it is not " are gone out," but " are going out;" it is not " are quenched," but " are being quenched." Not while life lasts does God's Spirit desert utterly, finally, irrevocably, the human soul. Even the steely-hearted murderess in the splendid tragedy has yet this touch of grace, that she loves her aged father; even the adulterous usurper has yet this hope, that he can kneel upon his knees. And therefore I bid you take courage. Even if in your slothfulness the lamp has burned too low, even if in your sinfulness it has been all but smothered, yet, oh believe that even now there is One who will not quench the smoking flax, there is a breath of God which even now, like a stream of fire, can rekindle the smouldering flame. To the very saddest and most unhopeful of you all to-day, to him who has wandered farthest from innocence, to him who has fallen deepest into sin, even to him I say— yet not I, but the voice of God's own promises— My young brother, God's grace is sufficient for thee. His Spirit is striving with thee now. Oh despise not His gracious influence; oh reject not His offered love. Lo, for thy lost innocence, God offers thee repentance. Lo, for the cleansing of thine hidden leprosy, He stretches from heaven the finger of a healing hand. Lo, for the recovery of thy lost health He holds to thee a green leaf from the tree of life. Lo, at this great Pentecost He rekindles the dying spirit with His descending flame. Courage, my brother; that lamp may have burnt low, but it has not yet burnt out. " Hast thou not known, hast thou not heard, that the everlasting God, the Lord, the Creator of the ends of the earth, fainteth not neither is weary? there is no searching of His understanding. He giveth power to the faint; and to them that have no might He increaseth strength. Even the youths shall faint and be weary, and the young men shall utterly fail. But they that wait upon the Lord shall renew their strength; they shall mount up with wings as eagles; they shall run and not be weary; they shall walk and not faint."

Whitsunday, May 30, 1871.

SERMON VI.

ASPICE, PROSPICE, RESPICE.

Phil. iii. 13.

"Forgetting those things which are behind, and reaching forth unto those things which are before."

Next Sunday, my brethren, will find this chapel empty and silent. Now it contains the beating hearts of many worshippers,—the mysterious thoughts, the wandering fancies, the solemn hopes, the evanescent gladnesses, the sorrowful regrets of some 500 boys; but next Sunday it will be untenanted, unless the fancy can give life to the sunbeams that play upon its floor; empty unless some of that host of God whom Jacob met at Mahanaim still find cause to linger and meditate in a place which has been, we trust, to many a house of God and a gate of heaven. The court, too, and the College buildings will be almost melancholy in their desertion and silence; the school-rooms closed, the playground noiseless, the whole life of the place arrested for a time. And we, who, day after day, for more than eighteen weeks, have been worshipping here, who have strolled about these fields, who in that sunny playground have felt it almost "a luxury to breathe the breath of life,"—we too shall be scattered; worshipping some of us in quiet country churches, lingering some of us for health and change by the margin of the summer sea, wandering some of us over wood and hill in the purple heather and the tall green ferns; but all of us I trust retaining a sense of our duties here, and all of us rich in the enjoyment of a rest sweetened by innocence and earned by toil. For a time severe tasks will be laid aside, examinations over and settled; you will be among the scenes which you have known and loved from childhood; among the bright and happy faces of brothers, sisters, friends; encircled by that holy and tender love of father and mother which distance cannot abate or time abolish. Oh the sunny memories of those long holidays! Oh the unalloyed happiness of the day which welcomes back our boyhood to the threshold of its home! I do not envy the boy who is not even now counting up the hoarded treasury of those home thoughts, enjoying, by anticipation, hours which are among the simplest and sunniest which earth shall yield.

But there is a little pause to-day. To-day for the last time shall this congregation meet in this chapel; a few weeks will pass and we shall re-assemble, but the congregation which shall then meet here will be the same yet not the same; the river is the same, but the wave is different; different in its constituent elements though identical in its continuity of life. This very fact preaches to us to-day; it bids us forget those things which are behind and reach forth to those that are before; and all that I desire is to articulate its unspoken utterance. For to-day is at once a close and a beginning. Forecast, meditation, retrospect—these are what it demands. *Aspice,* it seems to say, *Prospice, Respice;* look thoughtfully at the present, look forward to the future, look backward at the past; at the present with firm and holy resolution, at the past with humble and penitent gratitude, to the future with calm and earnest hope.

Have you ever, my brethren, on some sea-voyage left your companions and strolled to the stern, and there leant over the taffrail to watch the blue waves gliding under you, and the white cliffs fading into the distance, and the wastes of untrodden water lengthening in the rear? It is a position eminently provocative of thought. Let us in imagination take it to-day. We too are voyagers on a broad sea; some of you as yet have had but little experience save of cloudless skies above you, and the rippling of white foam about the bows; the wind plays with the streamer and swells the sail, and under the sunlight the waves before you are flashing into gold. But others of us are farther on our way; the *placidi pellacia ponti* deceives us not; we know that on that great sea there are sunken reefs and iron shores; we know that of the ships which traverse it, some, alas, founder in the billows, and others split upon the rocks:—

> "And where a home hath he
> Whose ship is driving on the driving sea?
> To the frail bark now plunging on its way,
> To the wild waters shall he turn, and say
> To the plunging bark or to the salt sea foam,
> *You* are my home?"

Ah no! my brethren, the true home for us lies beyond these waters; and oh, the rudder needs a firm hand, and the voyage a stout heart, for though short it is often perilous and always onward. So then, whatever our voyage may hitherto have been when we have gazed from the stern together on the shores that fade behind us,—and afterwards as we turn away again to look on the misty uncertainties of all that may await us in our future course, let us pray that touching prayer of the Breton mariners. "Save us, oh God! thine ocean is so large, and our little boat so small!"

I. *Respice*, look backward—thankfully, if God have been sensibly drawing you nearer and nearer to Himself; with penitence, and resolve, if you have been wandering farther and farther from him; but in any case, not in the vain hope, not in the futile fancy that we can regain what once is past. On this mysterious sea of time there is no rest, no retrogression. As wave after wave ripples past us, as mile after mile of water rushes by, they are gone, gone for ever, beyond the power of even Omnipotence to recall. The memory of those past days may be as a halcyon calming them under its brooding plumes, or like the petrel hurrying over them with the prophecy of storm; they may have been traversed in a direction straight for heaven, or they may be separating us more and more widely from the haven where we would be,—but they are ours no longer; they belong to eternity; they belong to God; they have glided into the dark backward, they have been swallowed up in the unknown abysm. These years that are past, where are they? This half-year that we are just ending, where is it? Dawn after dawn has broadened into noonday; noonday after noonday has faded into evening; evening after evening has deepened into night; have they left us without a blessing? Is their memory for any one of us a sigh? It is not so I trust for many of us; but is it so for any? Is it so for one? If so, be it so; it cannot now be altered. You may call to them, but you will call in vain; there will be neither voice, nor any to answer; the wealth of empires, the intercession of angels could not recover one wasted hour, or recall one vanished day.

And therefore, because the past is wholly irrevocable, therefore at the best there is a sadness in retrospect. That must be a very dull heart, or a very sleepy conscience, or a very shallow experience, that finds no cause for sorrow in "thinking of the days that are no more." None of us, not even the very best, are as holy or as noble as we might have been; many of us are not even what we were; some of us, we must fear, are but the miserable changelings of ourselves. Yet, if even the best man must feel sorrow and shame in remembering how little worthy his life has been, how far he has fallen short of his own ideal, how often he has swerved from the high laws of duty to God and charity to man,— if, I say, even the best man may feel sorrow, let not even the lowest feel despair. Is any one of you, my brethren, troubled by the sense of a hitherto ignoble life, by sinful thoughts and sinful habits, and the reproaches of a self-condemning heart?—how shall you allay the misery? St. John tells you, "if our hearts condemn us, God is greater than our hearts." St. Paul tells you, "Forgetting the things that are behind." You may have been very sinful, you may have been deplorably foolish, you may have been sadly tried: and the world can do nothing for you—it has neither a heart to pity, nor an arm to save; but your God has, and in His book, and in His works, and in your consciences, you may all hear a Voice saying cheerfully, encouragingly, very tenderly, to the sinful, "Go and sin no more;" to the foolish, "Seek the wisdom which is from above;" to the sad, "Come unto me all ye that are weary and heavy-laden, and I will give you rest;" and, as the sweet Voice speaks, a gracious hand holds forth to you a cup of cold water, which is the water of Lethe, the river of oblivion of sin repented of, the true mandragora for every guilty and sleepless soul. Yes, the retrospect of a sinful man or of a sinful boy if it be long-continued, if it be morbid, if it be absorbing, becomes an evil. Let it not be an evil: let the dead past bury its dead. It is Christ's own Voice which says to us, "Let the dead bury their dead, follow thou me." Let the time past of our lives suffice for folly and for sin. "Forgetting that which is behind," not indeed forgetting its mercies, for they may be remembered with eternal thankfulness, but forgetting its sinful allurements, because they have been displaced by nobler thoughts—forgetting its failures, because they may be still repaired, —forgetting its guilt, because in Christ's blood it can be washed away,—forgetting even its successes, because the goal of yesterday should be but our starting-point to-day. Whether they speak the language of reproachful menace, or the language of old temptation, there is nothing but peril in listening too long to the voices of the past. "Come back," they cry to us, "come back," when our course should be onwards: but

> "Back flies the foam, the hoisted flag streams back,
> The long smoke wavers on the homeward track;
> Back fly, with winds, things which the winds obey:
> The strong ship follows its appointed way."

II. And therefore *Aspice*,—having looked at the past turn your eyes to the present. Yesterday is yours no longer; to-morrow may be never yours; but to-day is yours, the passing hour yours, the living present yours, and in the living present you may stretch forward to the things that are before. The metaphor of St. Paul is the metaphor of a charioteer in some great race. It may be that from his prison in the Palatine he heard the shouts that rang from the Circus Maximus beneath him; it may be that looking through the grated lattice he saw the wild-eyed charioteers leaning over their steeds with twisted lash. The chariots bounded on amid dust and danger, but the racer recked neither of past accident nor present toil, while his eye was fixed on the goal that seemed to fly before him, and the prize that awaited his efforts there. And the quick imagination of the brave old prisoner found in these scenes fresh comfort for an undaunted heart. His gallant spirit could transmute even its trials into gold, as the sunbeams fire the sullen pines. Is he chained to a Roman soldier?—the sword and the breastplate and the helm inspire him with the immortal imagery of the armour of righteousness; does he hear the rattle of chariots in the shouting course? chained there by the arm in his wretched prison, a weary and decrepit prisoner, awaiting his doom of death, he yet remembers that he too is running a mighty race, at which the angels are spectators, and the Agonothetes is God, and in that glorious contest for a crown of amaranth he hangs over his winged and immortal steeds. Be it so with us! Life is but one passing "now," until with one last "*now!*" like a clap of thunder, the hour of judgment comes. And, therefore, oh give the present moment wholly, heartily to your Father in Heaven, now, and at yonder holy table, offering yourselves, your souls, and bodies, a reasonable lively sacrifice,—now, in silent prayer consecrating your hearts to God. Oh, buy your eternity with this little hour. *Ex hoc momento*, says the famous sundial, and there is deep truth in its eloquence of warning, *pendet æternitas!*

III. *Aspice, Respice, Prospice.* Besides the present, and

the past, there is a future. It is indeed a page as yet
unwritten, but you may determine, every one of you,
with unerring certainty, what shall be written therein.
Even now you can make that fair white page for you a
page of the Book of Life, and, secure in the love of God,
forgiven by the redemption of Christ, strong in the
strength of the Spirit, you can, as it were, bid the Angel
of Record there to inscribe your names. What external
events shall happen to you in life? how shall the
divinity shape the ends that you rough-hew? You may
indeed lead happy and comfortable lives, liable only to
the great danger of settling upon the lees, and so, amid
the world's gross self-complacencies, suffering your dead
hearts, in the scornful language of Scripture, to become
fat as brawn; or, on the other hand, calamity may burst
upon you like a deluge, and in His very love to you, and
in order that He may turn your thoughts to Him, God,
in the shipwreck of your every earthly fortune, may vex
you with all His storms. And whether it shall be so
or not you cannot tell: but one thing you may certify,
and that is that they shall not change you. You may,
with God as your guardian, pledge yourself, with unshaken certainty, that never of *you* shall it be said, in
the pathetic language of the poet, *Dissimiles, hic vir et
ille puer.* You may suffer, but they whom the love of
God supports in suffering, suffer no longer; you may
fail, but for them that strive even defeat is victory.
There is something sublime in this conviction. Not
know the future? Nay, we know it; if we be Christians
we know it; not, indeed, this little future of joys that
break as the bubble breaks, or of brief afflictions which
are but for a moment; not that little future of diseased
egotisms and contracted selfishness which is not life;
but that great future of the single in purpose and the

pure in heart, that great future which blooms to infinitude beyond the marge of death,—*that*, if we be children of God, we know. For we are pressing forward to the mark of the prize of our high calling, and that mark we cannot miss, and there it shines for ever before us—a crown of life, a crown of glory, a crown that fadeth not away. The true Christian need know no fear. Be true to yourselves, be true to God, be true to the kindred points of heaven and home, and then even the gay Epicurean lyrist will tell you, and tell you truly :—

> "Si fractus illabatur orbis
> Impavidum ferient ruinæ."

On the steep hill of Difficulty, in the Valley of the Shadow, amid the crash of a universe smitten into indistinguishable ruin, "Thou shalt keep him in perfect peace whose mind is stayed on Thee!"

One last word. You are all going home; may the coming weeks of holiday be very happy weeks to us all, and may those of us who return, return more faithful, full of vigour, full of purpose, full of self-denial, full of the spirit which recognizes only that life is not selfishness but service; full of the determination to do our duty here, and to adorn this our Sparta with loyal, energetic, devoted toil. Let your loved ones see that the months of absence have been months of progress; gladden their hearts by your gentleness, your honour, your modesty, your worth. And what last word shall we say to you, dear brethren, who will not return to us? to whom this is the last Sunday; for whom one leaf is about to be turned, one volume of their lives to be closed for ever? Here have many of you been led— been led by wise and kind hands almost from childhood to the threshold of a strong and upright manhood.

Here have you been taught and encouraged to act nobly and to think purely. You love your school, you are grateful to it, you have profited in it, you will endeavour to serve it loyally hereafter, you will not leave it without an affectionate memory and a quiet tear. Fain would you keep with us, but that may not be, and though you leave us now, yet our kneeling together at yonder Holy Table shall be our pledge that we shall continue united in the common noblenesses of life, and the common hopes of heaven. Go forth then, my brethren, pass forth into the world, and may God's best blessing go with you. By the loftiness of your purpose, by the manliness of your conduct, by the sincerity of your love to God, by the devotion of your service to men, be an honour to us in the days to come; leave to all Marlborough boys who shall follow you hereafter your good names as a legacy, your unstained character as an example. We have spoken of life as a voyage, sail forth then with the favouring gale of our affections; we too, are sailing with you, and, swept by the same current, guided by the same compass, through light, through darkness, shall meet in the same haven at the last.

> " But oh, blithe breeze! and oh, great seas!
> Though ne'er—the present parting o'er—
> On yon wide plain we meet again,
> Oh lead us to yon heavenly shore.

> " One port, methinks, alike we seek,
> One purpose hold, where'er we fare;
> Oh, bounding breeze! oh, rushing seas!
> At last, at last, unite us there."

June 25, 1871.

SERMON VII.

LITTLE GIVEN, LITTLE ASKED.

Matt. xxv. 23.

"His lord said unto him, Well done, good and faithful servant; thou hast been faithful over a few things, I will make thee ruler over many things: enter thou into the joy of thy lord."

Of all the glorious aspects of that holy faith which we profess—of all those points of spiritual elevation and moral beauty which, to the world's end, shall give it such infinite charm for every generous and unselfish soul—there is none more noticeable than the fact that it allied itself with the world's feebleness, not its strength. It was with "the irresistible might of weakness"[1] that it shook the nations. Herod sat in his golden palace at Tiberias in dissolute splendour and cruel luxury, but for him Christ had no other notice than "Go ye and tell that fox;" the Pharisees swept through the Temple courts in their fringed robes in all the haughtiness of a sacerdotal clique; and for them Christ had no words but to hurl on their hypocrisy the scathing flame of his indignation and rebuke. The dreaded Emperor was all-powerful at Rome; the mighty legionaries were encamped on the Danube and the

[1] Milton.

Ebro; but neither to Emperor nor legionary did Christ appeal. For pride—for cruelty—for scornful laughter—for insolent lust—He had nothing but the thunder: but for all that suffers—for all that is humble—for all that is faithful—for all that is oppressed—He had an infinite, unfathomable, all-embracing love. To the one He was wrathful as the whirlwind: to the other gentle as the summer breeze. He loved those whom none had loved before; He loved them as none had loved before. He loved the poor: He loved the sick: He loved the ignorant: He loved children: He loved sinners;[1] and among sinners, He, the friend of sinners, loved most those who had suffered most—those who were most worthy of His divine compassion—the feebler sex and the feebler age—little ones who were tempted—women who had sinned.

It is in the great Roman poet a topic of praise that his philosophic husbandman had neither pitied the poor nor envied the rich—

"Nec illa
Aut doluit miserans inopem aut invidit habenti."

But Christ did pity the poor, for He had been poor Himself. Born in the manger of Bethlehem, his youth and manhood had found their homes in the shop of the carpenter at Nazareth, and the hut of the fisher at Bethsaida. Let the world's insolent philosophers go learn of Him. They kindled their poor faded torches at His light, and they boast that *they* can illuminate the world. It was not they, but Christ, who emancipated our race from the dull fascination of wealth, and the abject flattery of power. It was not they but He who taught the inherent dignity of man—who showed that

---

[1] See Dupanloup, *Vie de Notre Seigneur.*

man was to be honoured for being simply man, and that his nature, if undebased by sin, may, in the humblest child who was ever born, be great with all the greatness of virtue, and awful with all the awfulness of immortality. The "*Tu, homo, tantum nomen, si te scias,*" of St. Augustine,—the "We are greater than we know," of Wordsworth—are not the exultant utterance of philosophic heathens, but of humble Christians; they were learnt not in the schools of Confucius or of Zoroaster—not in the groves of Academe, or in the monasteries of Sakya Mouni,—but at the feet of Him who did not blush to sit at the banquet of the publican —who shrank not from the white touch of the leper, and felt no pollution from the harlot's tear.

The life, the teaching, the very incarnation of Christ were all meant to impress upon us this awful and elevating truth : that "each man is as great as he is in God's sight and no greater;" that God distributes His earthly gifts differently, yet loves His children all alike. Surely this is a thought full of consolation for you and for all the vast, obscure, nameless, insignificant multitude. We are not kings, or great men, or mighty men, not rich, or powerful, or renowned; no: but Ὀὐ προσωπολήπτης ὁ Θεός. God is no respecter of persons. How can He be ? before Him all mankind is but as the small dust of the balance. Is it anything to the ocean whether one foam-speck be larger or smaller, of those that float on its illimitable breast ? can there be any gradations or eminences in the infinitely little ? No. A king dies, and the great bells toll, and the long processions stream, and the gaiety of nations is eclipsed, but to the great God before whom his soul passes in all its nakedness he is of no more import than the little nameless outcast who dies in the city street without a friend. O let us thank God that He has taught us to reverence ourselves: let us thank God that in His sight all are equally great, all equally little. Be it true that we are but of the smallest consequence to the world in which we live; that when we die few will hear of it; and there shall be but a few tears in a few faithful eyes, but not in many, and not for long, and then the unbroken ripple of human life shall flicker onward in the sunshine, and in a few years our very names be illegible, as the lichen eats out their crumbling letters on the churchyard stone. Ay so!—but our souls shall be as safe, shall be as immortal, in God's holy keeping as though our ashes had been entombed in pyramids or inurned in gold. To God nothing is common, nothing is obscure; to God everything is sacred, everything precious, if it fulfil its appointed functions in His great design.

> " Each drop uncounted in a storm of rain
> Hath its own mission.
> The very shadow of an insect's wing,
> For which the violet cared not while it stayed,
> Yet felt the lighter for it vanishing,
> Proves that the sun was shining by its shade."

And can we—drops from the eternal fountain—shadows of the living light—can we have been made for nought? No; the only real, the only permanent, the only essential greatness open to man is that of duty and of goodness; and that is as open, is as free, is as possible to every man as the sunlight that shines on us, or as the sweet air we breathe.

These lessons, my brethren, spring immediately from this parable of the talents, from which our text is taken, which you have just heard read to you in the second lesson of to-day. That parable contains of course far more than we can exhaust; is rich in many other great and important lessons on which we cannot touch; it shows that all that we have is received from God—is not a thing to be haughtily valued but humbly cherished, seeing that it is not our own but given; it shows to us that the object, the sole object, of all the talents we receive is not self-glorification, but use and service; but it shows also the lesson on which I have hitherto dwelt, that God values us not for the splendour or amount of the gifts which He has given, but for the manner in which we use them;—and that however mean our gifts, however small our opportunities, we may know for our consolation and encouragement that our reward will be, not great, but infinite, if we use them right. To some of His servants their Lord gave five talents, to others less gifted He gave but two; yet mark, for surely it is worth our notice, that though they who had five talents, being faithful, had gained five more, and those who had but two, though faithful, could but add to them two more—though therefore the one had produced in their Lord's service less than half produced by the other, yet these latter, no less than the other, hear the same words of approval, Εὖ δοῦλε, ἀγαθὲ καὶ πιστέ, "Well done, good and faithful servant;"—these, no less than the other, receive the same reward, the reward of new and larger opportunities in place of the smaller faithfully employed; these, no less than the other, experience the same beatitude, and are bidden to 'enter into the joy of their Lord.' Nay, even he to whom but one talent had been given would, had he used it rightly, have been no less tenderly received. All have had something entrusted to their care; all, in that something, possess means whereby they may happily serve their God, and their brother here, and enter into his joy hereafter. Is not the lesson a lesson of hopefulness and comfort? Look up to the sky this evening, and you will see some stars preeminent in magnitude, while others, set in the galaxy, are lost in one white undistinguishable haze. Yet though, as the great apostle says, one star differeth from another star in glory, all are of the same pure essence, all of the same divine origin:

> "All are the undying offspring of one sire."

And, therefore, if—as is indeed the case—

> "If thou indeed derive thy light from heaven,"

then, whether it be the most immeasurable radiance or the tiniest and feeblest gleam, still

> "To the measure of that heaven-born light,
> Shine, Christian, in thy place and be content."

i. Let me take two instances, wherein men differ very widely in the gifts they have received: and first the instance of poverty and riches. "Money," says the book of Ecclesiastes, "is a defence," and therefore one who is poor in this world's goods has, so far, a talent—that is an opportunity, and means of service—the less. Others obtain with ease the advantages which he cannot even win by effort. Well, my brethren, remember that in God's sight poverty, so far from being a disgrace, is a beautiful and hallowed lot. You have but little of this world's goods; oh be faithful with that little, and you shall find it more than much. There are, I admit, two kinds of poverty—the one murmuring and envious, and mean, and greedy, and idle; the other manly and noble and helpful,—possessing indeed but little save daily bread, but possessing also the lovely virtue of contentment to make it sweet. Now it may be that some of you come from poor homes—it may be that many of you in this crowded nation and competing age may grow up yourselves to feel the cares and struggles which poverty entails; and it is perfectly true that the world which is not only often coarse and cruel in its conduct, but also intensely and essentially vulgar in its estimates, is ashamed of poverty,—scorns the necessity of self-denial, blushes at the scant table and threadbare garb. My brethren, may your education here save you from that utter vulgarity of mind and heart. Say with the poet:—

> "Lives there for honest poverty
> Who hangs his head and a' that;
> The coward slave, we pass him by,
> And dare be poor for a' that."

Yes, since there is such a thing as a poverty which is rich in every element of a noble life—since many a foul, false heart has beaten under the velvet and the ermine, and many a true and royal heart been covered by the poor man's serge—nay, since Himself and all His apostles, and well nigh all His martyrs and well nigh all His saints were poor—then of poverty no man need ever be ashamed. If you come from poor homes now, hail it as a voice of God speaking to you in kindly accents, and bidding you by cheerful activity, by honest labour, to lighten the burden of those you love. If you are poor hereafter, learn that a poverty which scorns luxury—which can dispense with superfluities—which can find life purest and strongest and sweetest when it is disciplined under the beneficent laws of "high thinking and plain living," is wealthier in every element of happiness than

> "Twenty seas, though all their shores were pearl,
> Their waters crystal, and their rocks pure gold."

Do not imagine even that it will enable you to do less for God. The lips of the contemptuous Pharisee might curl when the poor widow dropped her two mites into the gorgeous treasury, but in the eyes of Him on whom they were bestowed, that poor widow had given more than they all. Many a struggling curate does more for God in the way of charity than many a vulgar millionaire. The kind word spoken in His service—the cup of cold water given in His name—these are possible to the poorest, and kings can give no more. "My most dear God," wrote Luther, "I thank Thee that Thou hast made me poor and a beggar upon earth. Therefore I can leave neither house nor fields, nor money to my wife and children after me. As Thou hast given them unto me I restore them to Thee again. Thou rich, faithful God, feed them, teach them, preserve them, as Thou hast fed, taught, and preserved me, O Father of the fatherless and Judge of the widow."

ii. Secondly and lastly, take the instance of stupidity —of deficiency in gifts of the intellect. Here again there are two kinds of stupidity. There is the wilful stupidity of blank, unimpressible, contented ignorance—the stupidity of the horse or the mule that have no understanding—of natures impenetrably sluggish and sensually base. There is nothing beautiful in that, for it has its root not in the appointment of God, but in the obliquity of man. But there is another kind of stupidity, if we can apply to it that name at all, which is neither ignoble nor offensive, nay, more, which has a certain calm and gentleness, a certain worth and beauty of its own. Intellectual gifts, if precious, are also perilous, and not seldom in this world's history have they been shining instruments in the hand of ambition,

"To render faults
Illustrious, and give infamy renown."

But when God has created one, who being endowed with but small capacities, yet firmly, honesty, humbly does his best, then to the dignity and sweetness of such a character my whole heart opens, and such as these, both in boyhood and manhood I have observed to be among the noblest I have known. "If there be one thing on earth," said a great teacher, "which is truly admirable, it is to see God's wisdom blessing an inferiority of natural powers when they have been honestly and zealously cultivated. To so and so," he used to say, mentioning a good but dull boy, "I would stand hat in hand."

Oh, if I am speaking to any here who are sometimes vexed by the thought that they can only plod on in the paths of humble usefulness, and never compete with their more brilliant schoolfellows; to any who sorrowfully think that the world's great successes are not for them; to any who feel that God has given to them but the one talent, not the two or the five; I would remind them how infinitely the great are transcended by the good, I would say to them, work on without one shadow of discouragement, without one pang of self-depreciation. Do your best, assured that God loves you as though the soul of Plato or of Shakspeare were your own; work with as manly a self-respect as though Empires would be moulded by your counsels, and Senates listen to your words; work with as calm a certainty that he will accept and will bless and will reward that work, as though the sunbeam that falls upon you were streaming down direct from His hand of fatherly blessing, held in invisible consecration over your stooping head. Yes, my young brother, be thou faithful unto death, and whether rich or poor, whether dull or intelligent, whether unknown or renowned, He will give thee, for He has promised, the crown of life. Thou, too, with angels and archangels, and all the company of heaven, shalt enter into the joy of thy Lord; to thee too, no less loudly, with no less soul-thrilling emphasis and sweetness, than to the lordliest and most glorious souls, shall peal forth from the highest empyrean, the blissful utterance of final approbation,

"Servant of God, well done!"

I have not said the half of what I meant or wished to say, and I have said it poorly and feebly, but I must conclude. Yet let me conclude with one allusion. The grave, my brethren, has scarcely closed over one who not long since was one of your number; whom many of you remember as a school-fellow, whom still more of you saw here as a visitor during last half-year. I knew enough of him to know how simply and honourably in his short life he had used the talents which God had given him, and striven to carry out some of the lessons which I have striven to indicate to-day, and I can testify to his simplicity and modesty, to that quiet humility of the Christian, united in him with the courteous culture of the gentleman. Those who had the pleasure of knowing him better could add much more; and one of his friends and school-fellows pronounced upon him this high eulogy, that whether as a boy, or a youth, or as a man, no one knew harm or evil of Thomas Ragland Dumergne. Faithful over a few things, we know well that all such shall be rulers over many things. For they fulfil in their lives that one rule, which though not in so many words recorded in the gospels, is recorded by the earliest Church-tradition as having been uttered by the lips of Christ Himself, Γίνεσθε δοκιμοὶ τραπέζιται, 'Be good exchangers;'—use, that is, to the very utmost the gifts which God has entrusted to you; use them cheerfully, use them vigorously, use them humbly, use them happily, use them with the certainty of God's approval, whether those gifts be great or small.

Sept. 24, 1871.

SERMON VIII.

QUIETNESS AND CONFIDENCE.

Is. xxx. 15.

"In quietness and in confidence shall be your strength."

THE connection of this text, my brethren, with the name and life of the apostle St. Andrew is not quite meaningless or artificial. The very little that is known of him exhibits forcibly that quietness and confidence to which our text exhorts. It was to his calm and strong conviction—it was to that untroubled vision enjoyed by the pure in heart and hand—that he owed by God's blessing the proud pre-eminence of being among the very earliest of our Lord's disciples; and this is the reason why his name stands first, stands in immediate connection with Advent Sunday, in the bright calendar of the Apostles and Saints of God. More than one of the few and slight notices recorded of him might furnish us with profitable thoughts; as, for instance, the ready faith with which he called the Saviour's attention to the little lad with five barley loaves and seven small fishes; or the brotherly love which made him first and at once find his own brother Simon and bring him to his Master's side. Let us rather, however, dwell on the quiet faith, the patient strength, the holy self-possession of soul which can alone account for all that is recorded of him. There is a singular contrast between him and his more illustrious brother Simon Peter. St. Andrew seems to have been all peace and restfulness; St. Peter all fervency and flame. St. Peter's character has been well touched in a little book called *Life in Earnest*, which many of you may have read. " Is Jesus encompassed," it says, "by fierce ruffians? Peter's ardour flashes in his ready sword, and converts the Galilean boatmen into the soldier instantaneous. Is there a rumour of the resurrection? John's nimbler foot distances his older friend, but Peter's eagerness outruns the serener love of John, and past the gazing disciple he hurries breathless into the sepulchre. Is the risen Saviour on the strand? His comrades turn the vessel's head for shore, but Peter plunges over the vessel's side, and struggling through the waves falls in his dripping coat at his Master's feet. Does Jesus say 'bring of the fish that ye have caught?' Before anyone could anticipate the words, Peter's brawny arm is tugging the weltering net with its glittering spoil ashore, and every eager movement unwittingly is answering beforehand the question of his Lord, 'Simon, son of Jonas, lovest thou me?'" A noble character, my brethren, a character intensely lovable with all its faults: and yet perhaps not nobler, and certainly less rare than the unresting duty, the unhasting calm, the unclouded conscience, the unwavering faith of that gentler and less famous brother, who first uttered to his astonished ear, that great eureka, Εὑρήκαμεν τὸν Μέσσιαν, "We have found the Messiah, which is, being interpreted, the Christ."

1. There are two kinds of character, my brethren,—the fervent and the contemplative—the enthusiastic and the peaceful—and each of them is admirable and each

necessary for the progress and well-being of the world. But, as the ancients said, *Corruptio optimi pessima*, and each of these is liable to a certain degeneracy which is very common, so that instead of fervour we find restlessness, and instead of quietude lethargy. Of the one—which as it is the least amiable and the least hopeful, is also happily the rarer—I will not speak. It is the cold, dead, lethargic, unemotional character: always contented in its self-satisfaction, always imperturbable in its conceit. Of these I will only quote the words of Scripture to the Angel of the Laodiceans: "Thou sayest I am rich, and increased with goods, and have need of nothing; and knowest not that thou art wretched, and miserable, and poor, and blind, and naked: I counsel thee to buy of me gold tried in the fire, that thou mayest be rich; and white raiment, that thou mayest be clothed, and that the shame of thy nakedness do not appear; and anoint thine eyes with eye-salve, that thou mayest see. As many as I love, I rebuke and chasten: be zealous therefore, and repent."

2. But the other character is fussy, and flurried, and restless—totally without repose, totally without dignity, always in extremes. There is no perspective about it, no silence, no sobriety, no self-control; it values no blessing which it has, because it is always yearning for some blessing which it has not; it enjoys no source of happiness in the present, because it is always fretting, and if I may use the phrase fidgeting for some source of happiness in the future. At School it is restless and dissatisfied because it is not at the University; and at the University because it is not yet in the active work of life; and in the active work of life, because the harvest of its poor

endeavours is not reaped well-nigh as soon as it is sown; and so the inevitable days slip on and the man dies or ever he has lived. Often this restless discontented misery is the Nemesis of a sinful life, for St. Jude speaks of those who are like "raging waves of the sea foaming out their own shame," and the prophet Isaiah tells us, "The wicked is like the troubled sea, when it cannot rest, whose waters cast up mire and dirt. There is no peace, saith my God, to the wicked." But often it is not so bad as this; it is the mere restlessness, and excitement, and discontent bred by a soul which has no sweet retirements of its own, and no rest in God, no anchor sure and steadfast on the rushing waves of life. It is bred by a harassed age in which we find no leisure; in which

> "The world is too much with us; late and soon
> Getting and spending, we lay waste our powers.
> Little we see in Nature that is ours;
> We have given our souls away, a sordid boon;"

or, in which, as another expresses it, we

> "See all sights from pole to pole,
> And glance, and nod, and bustle by;
> And never once possess our soul
> Before we die."

3. Now to both these common characters this text offers an antidote; to the self-satisfied, a confidence which is not conceit, a quietude which is that of a glassy sea, not that of a stagnant and corrupting pool; to the restless and anxious, a quietude and a confidence which are nothing else than a calm faith and happy trust in God. And therefore the text, beautiful in itself, has had for many a singular charm. It is, as you know, the motto of that quiet and holy book which has soothed so many

restless souls—*The Christian Year.* And to us in this place it ought to have a deeper and yet more real interest, because it was the favourite motto of that good and eminent man—to whom to the latest day of its existence Marlborough will owe so much, and who to some of us here present was once a beloved and living friend, and not merely a hallowed memory. When at a time of deep anxiety he came to the place it was the one thought which he carried with him. Many would have shrunk with dread from the responsibility before him, but he did not, because to him responsibility was but the quiet, earnest, faithful fulfilment of the duty to which God had called him; many would have been painfully anxious about the success of their work, but he was not, because he knew that duties are always in our own hands, results always and alone in the hand of God. In the very first words which he uttered in this chapel he said to the Marlborough boys at that day, "The very youngest boy in this chapel has hardly so much need to pray for God's grace in the work set before him as I who have urged you to it." And when, though the burden and heat of the day was already over, he was called to another new and arduous work in that toilsome Indian bishopric, it was again these words which consoled and encouraged him. I, my brethren, who stand where he stood, who speak from the very spot where, on these saint's day evenings, he so often spoke—I, who by a slight effort of memory, can recall the very expression of his face and very accent of his voice, and who have wandered with him so often on the terrace, and in the forest, and over the downs—know well, how earnestly, were he now here, he would attribute any particle of success wherewith God blessed his labours to the grace which enabled him to keep this spirit alive in his heart, like a silver lamp shedding its quiet radiance over the darkness—know well that, if his happy spirit still linger here in a place which was so dear to him, and among the successors of those who were once his beloved children in the Lord, there is no lesson which he would urge upon you with a more fatherly gentleness than this—"Thus saith the Lord God, In returning and rest shall ye be saved; in quietness and in confidence shall be your strength."

4. The text opens many a wide vista, and it is impossible at all adequately to illustrate and enforce it. I will, therefore, leave it with you for your own meditation, only praying that God's Holy Spirit may impress it deeply upon all our hearts. But I will merely mention the cause why it suggested itself to me to-day as likely to be profitable to some of you. It was because to many of you—I hope to the large majority of you, certainly to all the noblest and best of you, to all, in fact, except the idle and the frivolous—the two weeks of school-time which yet remain to us, must be weeks of effort and anxiety. You know how very much depends for most of you in the future upon the exertions of the present; you know that in an age of struggle and competition and over-population it will require on your parts a distinct and vigorous effort to secure those conditions which are the ordinary elements of a reasonably happy life; you know that in this age, even as regards mere earthly success and position, the axe is at the root of the barren trees; you know, in fact, that what is called your chance in life depends in great measure on what you do and on what you learn here now. I suppose that for the two-thirds of you the complexion of your future, its earthly prosperity, or its comparative earthly failure, turn on your ability to pass well or ill, or even to pass at all, in

certain competitions which will test how far you have used the opportunities which it is the earnest and faithful endeavour of us, your teachers, to further to the uttermost. And all these are, and ought to be, powerful motives, though even these are, and ought to be, less powerful than the nobler considerations that all who love you will take a keen interest in the success or non-success of your school endeavours, and above all, far above all, that those endeavours being incumbent on you from your very position here, are in reality a part of your duty to your neighbour and your God. And all these considerations ought to produce in your minds a steady, conscious purpose, deliberately to do your best; to waste no time; to cultivate to the utmost, wisely, carefully, and thoughtfully the power both bodily and intellectual, as well as spiritual, which God has given you. But I cannot feel surprised, nor can I blame, a tendency to restlessness and anxiety at a time of examination, any more than I can be surprised if you even look forward with some care and misgiving to the necessary uncertainties of your future life. And, therefore, as the best remedy which I can offer, I would say in sincere sympathy, " In quietness and in confidence shall be your rest." Do not yield to over anxiety. Fevered work, flurried work, anxious work, restless work, is always bad work. Work all of you as if you felt and realised " the dignity of work, the innocence of work, the happiness of work, the holiness of work." Do your best loyally and cheerfully, and suffer yourself to feel no anxiety or fear. Your times are in God's hands. He has assigned you your place. He will direct your paths. He will accept your efforts if they be faithful. He will bless your aims if they be for your soul's good. Regard your present life—the present conditions of your life—

as His assignment and His boon; regard the present hours—yea, the very moments of your life—as no less real, as no less substantial, as no less important, as no less certain to enjoy God's blessing of innocent happiness and cheerful hope—perhaps far more so—than any of the moments which are yet to come. Do your best then in quietness, not in feverish impulse; do your best with confidence,—not confidence in your poor, ignorant, feeble self, but in a merciful and tender God, and be quite sure that whatever else may happen to you, or not happen, this at least will happen—which is greater than all earthly blessing—that His loving Spirit will lead you into the land of righteousness. Neither in these examinations which are immediately before you, nor in any of the competitions on which the future profession of many of you will depend, nor in the increasing labour, and struggles of your future lives—nay, not even in the hour of death or in the day of judgment will *he* have any cause to be unhappy or to fear who has quietly, humbly, faithfully done his best

St. Andrew's Day, *Nov.* 30, 1871.

SERMON IX.

THE GRAIN OF MUSTARD SEED.

MATT. xiii. 21.

"The kingdom of heaven is like to a grain of mustard seed."

THE parable of the grain of mustard seed must be taken in close connection with that of the leaven, and both are meant to illustrate the small beginnings, the silent growth, and the final victory of the grace of God in the human soul. But they belong to different points of view. The one is extensive the other intensive. The parable of the grain of mustard seed shows us the origin and the development of the kingdom of God, in communities and in the world; the parable of the leaven shadows forth its unimpeded influence in the soul of each separate man.

It is not, however, my object to explain either parable, but rather to touch on one or two natural thoughts which their central conception seems to suggest. May God,—who only can,—make even so insignificant a thing as a weekly sermon, one more barrier against evil, one more impulse to good in every heart among us. What so trivial and worthless as an atom of sand? yet God binds even the atoms of sand together into an invincible barrier against the fury of the sea. What so insignificant as a grain of mustard seed? Yet even a grain of mustard seed can grow into an overshadowing tree, and the fowls of the air—the restless haughtinesses, and hopes, and cares, and fears of men—take refuge in its branches.

There are two classes of men in the world, distinctly marked indeed, but of which one contains infinitely few, the other the vast majority of mankind. To the first of these classes belong those who from the earliest dawn of their intelligence, from the first possibility of independent will, in a word, from the earliest day that they can remember, have striven to be, and *have* been the children and servants of God. Innocent-hearted to the last, as when they lifted their little hands to lisp to their Heavenly Father an infant's prayer, they have carried the sweetness and simplicity of childhood into the powers of manhood; they have retained "the young lamb's heart amid the full-grown flocks." To them duty has always been the natural and happy law of life; to them purity of soul and dignity of temper have come like spontaneous growths. The temple of their hearts has not been desecrated; the fountain of their being has not been troubled; the white robes of their baptism have not been stained. The crown is still upon their foreheads, for they have not sinned. To them, as one of our holiest poets has said,

> "Love is an unerring light,
> And joy its own security."

Such a man, upon a throne, was St. Louis of France; such, in a cloister, was Fra Angelico di Fiesole; such, as a reformer, was St. Benedict of Nursia; such, in literature, were John Milton and William Wordsworth.

Nay, what need of meaner examples? Such in his sweet, noble, diligent, submissive boyhood, in the shop of the carpenter at Nazareth, was the Son of God Himself. Lambs of God are these, by the still waters of His comfort, in the green pastures of His love. "It is," says one, "the most complete picture of happiness that ever was, or can be, drawn. It represents the state of mind for which all alike sigh, and the want of which makes life a failure to most. It represents that Heaven which is everywhere if we could but enter it, yet almost nowhere because so few of us can."

Some I trust are here who may humbly claim this happiness,—

> "Glad souls without reproach or blot,
> Who do God's work and know it not;"

yet (thanks to our own wilful and wayward hearts) never and nowhere are there many.

"How," asks one in the Book of Job, "how can man be justified with God? or how can he be clean who is born of a woman? Behold even to the moon, and it shineth not; yea, the stars are not pure in his sight. How much less man that is a worm, and the son of man that is a worm?"

Peace, alas! comes not to most men but by struggle: and only through bitter experience of evil is learnt the ennobling, absorbing lesson, that good is best.

II. Not perfect innocence then, but humble and sincere repentance, forms the main distinction between man and man; and if happy is he who has kept innocency, and done the thing that is right, happy also is he whose iniquity is forgiven and whose sin is covered. These have not always been God's children, but they are so now: they were afar off, they have now been made nigh by the blood of Christ. But how? whence sprang that desire, which became first a prayer, then an effort, until the sinner, in his pride and blindness, learnt finally that it was an evil and a bitter thing that he had forsaken the Lord his God, and that the fear of God was not in him?

My brethren, that change is conversion, beyond all comparison the most entire and awful change that can happen to any man in life. It is in fact a new life; it brings the soul into new relationships with God. The rebel becomes the child, the haughty humble. He who hid himself from God in shame and anger now goes forth to meet Him in boundless joy. Once mean, he now is noble; once passionate, he is now self-controlled; once frivolous, now soberminded; once unclean in every imagination, now sweet and pure; once full of an evil spirit, he is now clothed, and in his right mind; once a leper, his flesh has now come again like the flesh of a little child.

(1.) Now this great change of conversion appears to occur in two ways—sometimes it seems to be the work of an instant, sometimes to be diffused imperceptibly over many years.

Though the world scoff at them, there *are* such things as instantaneous conversions, supreme crises and movements in the history of life, which, like the shock of an earthquake, cleave a sudden rift deep down between all that a man has been and all he is. Such was the vision of Paul on the road to Damascus; such was the sudden arrest which happened to the soul of Bunyan; such the revulsion of horror which changed De Rancé from the dissolute courtier into the devoted saint. And oh, what a change! A man, in his petty conceit, in his small intellectualism, in his insolent self-will, even in his sensual ignorance, has lived in habitual antagonism to some majestic, eternal law, and suddenly, with overwhelming force, there is flashed in upon his conscience an insight that this law which he, poor worm, has been violating and trying to ignore, is eternal, absolute, independent, not made by him, not to be altered by him, but inexorably infinite, and to be disobeyed only at his everlasting peril. And when that sublime ray of light, that lightning flash out of God's eternity, has penetrated his soul, there is an immense untold interval between that moment and the one which preceded it. "The man indeed is left untouched, but there is added to him the God who created him." All vain, idle, furious passions disappear. All the mere emptiness of life becomes repulsive. Things temporal vanish, things eternal dawn on him. An awful sense of reality comes over him, and joy accompanies it. It is as when the weary traveller struggles over the Alps, and a moment comes when the first soft breeze announces his approach to the Italian soil. Before him there may still be barren wastes and icy tempests, but from that moment, as though there were a new heart in him, he fears no danger before him, he forgets every peril and misery behind.

(2.) And yet, even in these sudden conversions as they are called, it remains no less true that the kingdom of God is like a grain of mustard seed: for just as in the workings of the mystery of iniquity no crime is, in reality, what it sometimes seems to be, the fatal inspiration of one miserable moment, because each action is in reality influenced by all past actions—so no man ever really sprang at one bound from a sinner to a saint. The seeds of good must have long been secretly and silently at work. Those who are familiar with tropic forests tell us that for months they look sombre and monotonous, till suddenly on some one day they will rush into crimson blossom, and blaze in masses of floral splendour under the noonday sun; but the glory, so seemingly instantaneous, is in reality a lengthened work, and the sun, and wind, and rain, and the rich air, and glowing sky, nay, even the lost promise and deciduous leaves of many a previous season, must have lent their influence for years together, before the issue of them can stand thus manifest in the eyes of wondering men.

(3.) And more often the conversion of the heart is not even in appearance sudden, but in a long silent growth in grace and holiness, preceded by the day of small things. In the unseen world as in the seen, every man is moulded by myriads of influences, each small as a grain of mustard seed, each rich with a principle of life; and as in nature, so in the spiritual life, but one seed, alas! of many millions may be brought to bear. None can tell which seed shall bring forth. In one man all are hopelessly wasted, on the barren soil, in the rocky obstinacy, in the choked and thorny life; yet, in another, a look, a word, a flower, a breath of spring, a touch of sunset, a sudden memory, the kind warning of a companion, the verse of a hymn, a prayer once uttered at the mother's knee, may make the difference between life and death. A spiritual lustre falls over forgotten or familiar words, like that which gleamed over the graven gems of Aaron's breast, and makes them awful with oracular import, a Urim and a Thummim, a revelation and a light.

The beginnings then are small, and secondly the growth is silent—first the blade, and then the ear, last of all the full corn in the ear. He, in whom it is working, may not at first sight seem different from others, different from what he was before; but he is in reality an altered man. Within him all is different; thoughts which he once harboured with complacency, he now rejects with horror; hopes which once absorbed his energies, now shrink into nothingness; little serpentine envies which once embittered his spirit, now perish or creep away. All dark things, all shameful things fly from the soul that lies open to the sunlight. A hush comes over the turbulence and the sadness of his spirit, and in that hush he hears distinctly, hears, while his heart thrills within him, the still small Voice of God.

III. But thirdly and lastly, though the beginning be never so small, the development never so silent, the victory is final. It was so with the little seed of Christianity in the world. Paganism fled vanquished before it. One abomination after another vanished; one cruelty after another was repulsed; one high quality after another was recognised in principle; one sweet virtue after another realised in practice. So was it in the world; so, my brethren, will it be in you. If conversion have indeed begun in you (and, oh, be sure that if it have not begun, your life is at this moment a sad, a sinful, and a wasted life), but if conversion have begun in you, you will be also growing in grace, you will be growing day by day purer, humbler, more loving, more temperate, more contented, more certain day by day that your life is in God's hands. The process will begin by the gradual but certain victory over your besetting sin. If you would examine yourself before God, if you would test whether, even but like a grain of mustard seed, the kingdom of God is within you, you may do so simply and decisively by telling whether you feel a deepening dislike, whether you are engaged in an ever deadlier struggle, against the sin which most easily besetteth you. If you hate sin less than you did when you first were tempted, if familiarity with sin have made it seem less sinful, then look to it, for evil is before you. He who says I will struggle against sin hereafter, instead of saying I will struggle with it now; he who is content to fight with it in *fancy* "in the green avenues of the future," not in *fact* in the hot plains of to-day—will proceed to make excuses for it, will come at last not even to feel its horror. To put off repentance is to court ruin; to postpone the season is to perpetuate the sin. Even to hesitate is to yield; even to deliberate is to be lost. Take any instance of sin. Take evil thoughts, which are the *fons et origo* of every sin. You are tormented, say, by evil thoughts, by evil thoughts of envy, of hatred, of impurity. Do you really long that God would cleanse the thoughts of your heart by the inspiration of His Holy Spirit? Well, number to yourself the days in which you have not yielded to this temptation. "I did not yield to evil thoughts yesterday, or the day before, or for the last week:" and if indeed a whole month have passed since you succumbed to this temptation, then thank God very humbly on your knees. "For the habit is first loosened, then eradicated."[1] If you can say then on your knees before God, honestly, in the light of your own conscience, —if you can say, I am struggling, I have, even in part, even for a time, succeeded,—then be sure that if you continue to be in earnest, it will soon be all right with you; be sure that then God is leading you by the hand, leading you by His loving Spirit into the land of

[1] Epictetus.

righteousness. Yes, be sure in that case that you are not far from the kingdom of heaven now, nay, more, be sure that the kingdom of heaven is with you, and shall be in you. "For the kingdom of heaven is like unto a grain of mustard seed which a man took and sowed in his field; which is indeed the least of all seeds, but when it is grown it is the greatest among herbs, and becometh a tree, so that the birds of the air come and lodge in the branches of it."

April 14, 1872.

SERMON X.

INNOCENT HAPPINESS.

Eccl. xi. 9.

"Rejoice, O young man, in thy youth; and let thy heart cheer thee in the days of thy youth, and walk in the ways of thine heart, and in the sight of thine eyes: but know thou, that for all these things God will bring thee into judgment."

THERE are two ways, my brethren, in which this text may be read and understood. It may be read as the mocking accent of a pitiless irony; it may be read as the sincere counsel of a noble and loving heart.

According to the first view, the text would mean—Go, poor fool, and snatch such transitory enjoyment as thy youth and gaiety allow; the sea of things seen and temporal sparkles around thee, launch upon it thy little gilded bark, and spread every sail to the prosperous winds; but there, in the deep shadow of the future, hushed in grim repose, the whirlwind waits thee, and the painted shallop which now dances so gaily over the sunlit ripple shall soon be "a dismantled hull upon the troubled waters or a desolate wreck upon the lonely shore." Go then,—rejoice; that mirth is but the fantastic prelude to disappointment and despair.

No doubt, my brethren, there was a time when, sated and cloyed with luxuries, and finding his mouth filled with the ashes of such Dead Sea fruit, Solomon might have been tempted to speak like that. Many a weary worldling, many a worn voluptuary—sick to the very heart at the sight of pleasures which he can no longer enjoy—has said the same. For selfishness always makes the heart callous and cruel, and it is the characteristic of impenitent evil to find self-solace in watching the ruin of others. But though the whole book of Ecclesiastes is the deep sigh of one who was conscious of a wasted life, it is the sigh of a godly and noble penitence. The sadness of the book is a personal sadness, but it is free from all taint of envy, and it is with a sincerity which every good man will echo, that Solomon says " Rejoice, O young man, in thy youth." But because he well knew the danger of unchequered prosperity and joy, therefore he adds, Rejoice, yet accept the warning,—not as though some dark hand wrote in threatening fire upon the walls of thy banquet-house,— but as though an angel voice whispered it gently in thy ears. In the midst of thy mirth remember,—lest it become guilty, lest it become foolish, lest it become excessive—remember in order that it may be sweet, that it may be innocent, that it may be permanent, that this, like every other portion of thy life, will come before a Divine All-seeing Judge.

You see, my brethren, that two different theories of life, and as a natural consequence two different schemes of education, may depend upon the lessons drawn from words like these. Those who find in them a mockery and reprobation of all pleasure have framed their methods of training in accordance with such a belief. They have repressed harshly, they have condemned unhesitatingly, the natural elasticity and mirthfulness of early life ; by formal discipline, by ascetic practices, by incessant surveillance, by close routine they have succeeded in imposing upon boyhood itself the staid looks and frigid formality of soberer years. Those who are familiar with foreign cities will recall the natural results of a system so unnatural; they will remember with pity the boyish faces that had in them no boyhood; the dull depression, the listless bearing, the furtive glance of those who from childhood upward have been taught to regard all play as folly and all gaiety as sin. But this repressive education is the very reverse of that which for centuries has been carried on at our public schools. The instinct and wisdom of England have led her to feel that no warm, glowing, large-hearted manhood can follow on a soured and gloomy youth; have led her to desire for her children an education more hearty, more manly, more liberal. There was indeed one age in which the belief seemed to waver. The Puritanism of one fiery generation achieved in England a great and glorious work, but it partly neutralised that work when it laid upon the nation that iron cramp from which the baser sort broke loose in the foul license and bacchanalian frenzy of the succeeding reigns, and by which some even of the nobler and the better have thenceforth been bound by a needless yoke. Yet surely in all nature, even if we look no further, God has shown us that He desires our happiness. The God who flings the yellow rainbow across His storms, and bids the sunset rim his very thunderclouds with golden light,— that God who gives its splendour to the flower and its pearly lustre to the shell upon the shore,—that God who makes the summer air ring with the hum of insects and the careless melody of happy birds,—surely He did not wrap round this world with sweet air and bathe it in happy sunshine that we should regard gloom as the normal aspect of our lives. Nay, He has shot many a golden thread through the woof of life, and to darken those threads by needless sadness is an offence against His love. There is indeed a sorrow born of deep afflictions, the scathing of the flame which is meant to purge away the dross;—there is a sorrow which springs from that divine and perfect sympathy which can know no perfect happiness while it witnesses the misery of other children in the one great family of God; —there is a sorrow which has its source in that deep penitence which the Peace of God has not yet healed, and these are forms of sorrow which are noble and not sinful: but there is also a sorrow born of sin and egotism, and the fretting of bad passions, and the weight of chance desires, and that sorrow is wholly ignoble, and when it is seen in boyhood, as it is sometimes seen, it is the saddest of all omens for a wasted and miserable life. In the great Poem of the Middle Ages to which I have more than once alluded—it is a storehouse of moral wisdom—the two poets, as they traverse the gloomy circles of the Inferno, come upon a stagnant and putrid fen, and there, buried in the black mud, they see the souls of the gloomy-sluggish, who in expiation of their sinful gloom in life, are ever forced to mutter—

> "We were sad
> In the sweet air made gladsome by the sun,
> Now in this miry darkness are we sad."

You see to be sad in the sunshine was a crime in the great poet's eyes, and the poets and prophets of Scripture were herein at one with him; for David says, "Rejoice in the Lord, oh ye righteous;" and Isaiah, "Thou meetest him who rejoiceth, and worketh righteousness;" and St. Paul, "Rejoice in the Lord always, and again I say rejoice."

And you know, my brethren, nor should any know better than Marlborough boys, that such are the views of those who are placed in authority over you. We are anything but out of sympathy with the mirth, the games, the victories which not unnaturally occupy a large share of your attention. We rejoice at your triumphs, we grieve at your failures; we feel a personal and friendly interest in your individual successes. If we ever moderate any tendency to excess or extravagance in your amusements, it is only because we would not have them incompatible with those deeper, more important, more permanent, more eternal gains which we would still see yours, long after the strong arm has lost its vigour and the keen eye its light. Never forget that you are God's children, that your fear, your gratitude, your worship, your service are due to Him night and day; and then be sure that, so far from having one happy hour the fewer, or one smile the less, the long summer days will catch a gleam of fresh brightness from the spontaneous mirth of an unsullied conscience and a fearless heart; nay, even wet and cheerless days like these will catch the diffusive glow of an inward sunshine. Your lot is a very happy one. You have many an hour of healthy exercise and pleasurable amusement; many a happy afternoon of relaxation and indulgence; many a valuable opportunity for intellectual progress, and for work which makes no too severe demand upon your powers. And now your holidays are rapidly approaching, and many sunlit months are opening before you, Some of you will be among the bracken and the heather on the hills and moors; some of you will be spending the golden days with the laughter of the summer waves to gladden your eyesight, and their murmur to soothe your ears; others, and perhaps not the least enviable these, will be enjoying the peace of their own innocent and quiet homes. Oh, what wealth more golden than gold is here; what a crowd of blessings; what a welling fountain of sweet waters, of which some memory at least should gladden even the thirstiest desert of after years!

Rejoice then as our Heavenly Father wills that you should rejoice. Rejoice,—but evermore remember. Remember that God's eye is upon you, remember that the laws of God, like the laws of the physical world, are entirely independent of you, your likes or dislikes, your knowledge or ignorance, your belief or unbelief, and yet that you are environed by them from the cradle to the grave, and it is at your own peril that you disobey them; yes, remember, without fear indeed yet with deep solemnity and reverence, that "for all these things God shall bring thee into judgment." Such remembrance will not make you *less* happy but *more*.

> "Why should we think youth's draught of joy,
> If pure would sparkle less?
> Why should the cup the sooner cloy,
> Which God hath deigned to bless?"

Innocent happiness, oh what a world of beatific vision is wrapped up in those two words; what a heaven on earth they picture and signify! But if any of you seek for happiness in *sin*, which is the forgetfulness of God and defiance of His will; in *crime*, which is some wicked offence against the welfare, the peace, the purity of man; in *vice*, which is some degraded tendency in your own personal life, then, my brethren, the sin, the crime, the vice leave upon the soul and conscience that dark stain of guilt which is an abiding and horrifying sense of God's wrath, and causes irretrievable shipwreck of all present happiness and all future peace. "Guilty happiness!" there is no such thing on earth. Guilty *pleasure* there is ; a pleasure short, envenomed, ruinous in proportion to its guilt—the sting of the fondled serpent, the poison in the wine-cup's bitter dregs. But guilty *happiness !* if any of you in the secret thoughts of his heart have ever fancied that there is such a thing, oh let him dismiss that false fancy now. For guilt and misery indeed walk this world hand in hand, but guilt and happiness cannot co-exist. Happy while the soul within him is full of leprosy; happy, while his whole life is in disharmony with the will of Heaven; happy, while the fire of remorse will ever and anon leap up within him from its unquenched embers, and the worm of conscience awake from its undying sleep?—no, my brethren, no man can be happy thus. To wander from the safe, the narrow, the holy path of duty and virtue,—to seek in forbidden atmospheres a delusive and corroding pleasure,—is alas ! to destroy within us not only all true happiness, but even the capacity therefor. For happiness is like that manna, the angel food of Israel in the wilderness, which if gathered duly and in moderation, was sweet as honey and pure as the morning dew; but if sought in excess and against God's commandments ceased to be human food at all, and stank, and bred worms, and was corrupt. Oh then learn as the most assured and the most invaluable lesson of your youth that golden rule of David's, "Keep innocency, and do the thing that is right, for that shall bring a man peace at the last." That is my lesson, that my message to you this morning. The bad boy—and you can draw the picture of the bad boy for yourselves—can you conceive of such a boy as happy? If it has ever been your misfortune to know such a boy, have you not also known that he was miserable? What is his guide in life? Is the traveller safe when he turns his eye from the northern star to follow the delusive meteor which flickers over the fields of death? Is the ship safe whose course is steered not by the steady lustre of the beacon, but by the wrecker's deadly fire? My brethren, the traveller may sink in the morass and the ship be torn and shattered upon the sunken reef, yet they are safer than he who has deliberately forsaken the guide of his youth and forgotten the covenant of his God. To lose the blessing of an innocent heart is to lose all that is virtuous and honourable—all that is lovely and of good report—all that sweetens, all that ennobles, all that illuminates the life. For innocence and peace and happiness are three pearls strung together in the same jewel, and if one be lost they are lost together and can never again—never in this world even for the penitent, even for the forgiven—be recovered in their pristine lustre.

I wanted, my brethren, to speak only of innocent happiness to-day, but I have been forced to digress into these harder paths, and

"To support uneasy steps
Over the burning marle, not like those steps
On heaven's azure."

And perhaps it is best that it should so have been, since, as of old, it remains the duty of every teacher to call not the righteous but sinners to repentance. And is all that I have said needless? I know indeed—and heartily do I thank God for it—how much there is in your lives to praise. I know that many a manly and innocent, and high-minded boy is listening to me now; but is there *no* danger? is every heart here indeed pure, every lip reverent and holy? every conscience sweet and untroubled? has no one need of that warning with which my text concludes? There is a book, my brethren, lying ever open before God's throne, and in that book is written every evil thought we have ever thought, every idle word we have ever spoken, every wicked deed that we have ever done. Would you turn the awful pages of that book? would you read its records? You may, nothing hinders: that book though it lie ever open before God's throne, is near you, is with you, is within you. It is the book of your memory. The memory of man is the book of God. And its records, though they appear to be in many places obliterated, are in reality indestructible. Oh, when in after years you are called upon to turn over those folded pages of memory, may you rejoice to know that by God's grace they are clear and clean, and that there is not on them one of those damned spots which wrung even from the lips of David that bitter cry, "Oh, remember not the sins of my youth, nor my offences, but according to thy mercy think thou upon me, O Lord, of thy goodness." For, in one last word, happy, my brethren, is he whose unrighteousness is *forgiven*, whose sin is *covered;*—but happier, far happier is he to whom the Lord imputeth *no* sin, and in whose spirit there is no guile. For though there can be no such thing on earth as a perfectly happy life—though what should be the June of life will often be chilly as its autumn and rainy as its spring—there is a joy which is given only to the pure in their purest hour, and there is a heaven and an earth " undreamt of by the sensual and the proud;" and he has attained most nearly thereto of whose heart the grace of God has taken early hold, and whose spirit, amid all the stormy passions of life, has remained true to his God and Saviour—

"True to the kindred points of heaven and home."

Never out of sympathy with innocence, he is never out of sympathy with joy. As his youth has been unstained, his manhood will be noble, his old age a crown of glory; and death will be to him but a shining messenger sent to fling wide open before him the palace gates of immortality and heaven.

This is innocent happiness; and not now only but through all your lives, out of a full heart, fervently I daily pray that God,—God the Loving, God the Merciful, God your God and Father,—may grant it, my brethren, to every one of you.

June 9, 1872.

SERMON XI.

SCHOOL AND HOME.

1 Sam. ii. 12, 26.

" Now the sons of Eli were sons of Belial; they knew not the Lord. . . . And the child Samuel grew on, and was in favour both with the Lord, and also with men."

On his road from the ancient Bethel to Samaria the traveller will pass a rounded hill separated by narrow valleys from the amphitheatre of hills which surround it. At no great distance is one of those fountains which are so exquisitely dear to the imagination in the burning and thirsty East. Silence and desolation reign around. Those grey heaps of ruin seem as though they were determined to keep their secret.

On this spot three thousand years ago stood the Tabernacle, which was indeed to Israel a Tabernacle of witness. Those boards of acacia wood had been hewn under the granite crags of Sinai. That gold had been molten from ancient ornaments of Egypt. That brazen altar was covered with plates beaten from the censers of Korah and his company. In that Holy of Holies was the Ark of God, overshadowed with the golden wings of the Cherubim, wherein was the golden pot of manna, and Aaron's rod that budded, and the two tables of the covenant. Every colour on those woven hangings, every number in those symmetrical proportions, had its mystic significance.—It was Shiloh, God's bright sanctuary.

And it was naturally a spot most solemn. Up that terraced slope wound the procession of white-robed Levites. By that clear fountain, under the glowing sunlits that fell through the shadowy leaves of the vineyards, the maidens of Israel led their sacred dances. In those courts, day by day, smoked the fumes of the morning and evening sacrifice; and in the holy place the incense breathed its fragrant supplication, and the lamp shed its sevenfold lustre; and into the holiest, in his robes of purple and fine linen—his breast "ardent with gems oracular," and holiness to the Lord upon his brow—entered the high priest, once a year, with the blood of atonement. That high priest was the gentle and venerable Eli;—and in such a home—which seemed to breathe the very atmosphere of holiness and prayer—he trained his sons to take part in that hallowed service.

In the picture of a youth so circumstanced there is an almost idyllic charm. It has furnished to Greek tragedy one of its sweetest conceptions—the young and innocent Ion ministering in the great temple of Apollo at Delphi. And here, too, the sacred historian dwells with evident pleasure on the beautiful, noble, holy boyhood of the child who served before the Lord, wearing a linen ephod, and who, in the visitations of the night, thrilling to the Divine voice which called him by his name, answered fearlessly, "Speak, Lord, for Thy servant heareth." Yet from that same tabernacle, from that same tutelage, from those same influences, came forth also the sons of Eli; and the sons of Eli were sons of Belial; they knew not the Lord.

The training the same, the product how different; the school the same, the boys whom it educated how fearfully contrasted! Such contrasts seem strange, but they are in reality matters of daily experience. Four millenniums ago two boys so unlike as Esau and Jacob played together from infancy in the same pastoral tent. Daily from the same home we see boys go forth, some to live noble self-denying lives, others to live lives that come to nothing, and do deeds as well undone. So too, often, from happy conditions come base characters; from degraded environments strong, sweet natures struggle into the light.

Are there not analogies to this in nature? "It is a marvel," says an American writer, "whence the white pond lily derives its loveliness and perfume, sprouting as it does from the black mud over which the river sleeps, and from which the yellow lily also draws its unclean life and noisome odour." So it is with many in this world; the same soil and circumstances may produce the good and beautiful and the wicked and ugly. Some have the faculty of assimilating to themselves only what is evil, and they become noisome as the poisonous water-plant; some assimilate none but good influences, and their characters become fragrant and spotless. What then is our inference from this? It is, that only the personal devotion of the heart, the personal surrender of the individual will, can save a man or make him holy. The sons of Eli, we read in the next chapter, made themselves vile. A man's life may be *influenced*, but it is not *determined*, by his circumstances. No aid, save that which comes from above to every man, can help him to climb the mountain path of life, or enter the wicket-gate of righteousness; nor, on the other hand, can any will or power except his own retard his ascent or forbid his ingress. On ourselves—on the conscious exercise of our own free will—depends our eternal salvation or ruin. On the one hand, neither man nor devil can control that will if we dedicate it to God; on the other—

> "From David's lips this word did roll,
> 'Tis true and living yet—
> No man can save his brother's soul,
> Or pay his brother's debt."

And is not this thought thus forced upon us by the first lesson of to-day, an important and profitable one at a time when, for a long interval of rest, you are about to exchange the influences of school for the influences of home? May they not help you to understand better the meaning and purpose of your present life, and the reason why parents—even the most loving, the most tender, the most scrupulous—yet send you away from the shelter and innocence of home to the dangers and temptations of a public school?

Let us pause for a few moments on this question of school and home.

Those of you who know anything of our own literature will remember how, in the bad days of the last century, the poet Cowper was sent from a home of the most exquisite delicacy and refinement to a school in which reigned, unrepressed, those traditions of cruelty, traditions of idleness, traditions of disobedience, traditions of every form of vice, which, thank God, have as traditions been well-nigh swept away by the reviving earnestness and decency of a better age. And you will remember the consequences. Depressed, unhinged, spirit-broken, by all he had been forced to undergo as a young and sensitive boy, a cloud of melancholy, verging at times on actual insanity, settled upon his mind, and all the happiness of his life suffered an awful shipwreck. He has described that home, in all its tender sweetness, in the immortal *Lines on the receipt of his mother's picture*; he has described that school in all its repulsive vileness in the *Tirocinium*. He must have indeed a dull and cold heart who can read to himself that sweet picture of a mother's love to her little boy without tears in his eyes, or can wonder that long years after, in his old age, the poet could write—

> "O that those lips had language! Life has passed
> With me but roughly since I saw thee last;
> Those lips are thine: thy own sweet smile I see,
> The same that oft in childhood solaced me;
> Voice only fails, else how distinct they say,
> Grieve not, my child, chase all thy fears away."

And when we turn from them to the *Tirocinium*, and know that the stern, sad picture was yet a true one, can we wonder that he describes a good father laying his hand on his son's head and saying—

> "My boy, the unwelcome hour is come,
> And thou, transplanted from thy genial home,
> Must find a colder soil, a bleaker air,
> And trust for safety to a stranger's care."

And then the poet, expostulating with the father for trusting his child to such risks, continues—

> "Thou could'st not, deaf to Nature's tenderest plea,
> Turn him adrift upon a rolling sea;
> Then—only governed by the self-same rule
> Of natural pity—send him not to school."

Now in those days there would have been very much to urge for such a conclusion; and yet, even then, unconvinced by such arguments, many a sober, God-fearing man must have sent his sons to school, not ignorant, indeed, of the risks they ran, not even compelled by intellectual considerations or the necessities of modern life, but because, in spite of all, he thought

that such a course might be morally the best. With
many and many an earnest prayer, perhaps with many
and many a sad misgiving, he would let his son pass
from the quiet vicarage or country house to the Eton, or
Harrow, or Winchester of the eighteenth century, knowing that there he might forget to pray, knowing that he
might learn there to blaspheme and break God's laws;
but knowing also that God's grace, if the boy sought it,
would be sufficient for him; knowing that no power on
earth could make him go astray if he opposed to it a
resisting will; knowing that the innocence of mere
ignorance, and the negative goodness which does but
result from an artificial absence of temptation, is a poor
thing; knowing that however sheltered from every wind
of trial, no human soul can grow up without recognising
in itself the awful power to resist God's laws; knowing
that such an impulse to disobedience must come to
every soul with its complete humanity; knowing, in a
word, that God's will respecting us is this: not that we
should remain wholly ignorant of the very existence of
wrong, but that we should know and conquer, that we
should see and pass it by.

And many a sad experience of many a broken-hearted
parent who followed a different course would have
shown that he was right. For the other method almost
always fails. Often a boy, the child of religious parents,
kept and sheltered by them as the apple of an eye,
brought up it may be by their timid love in some
country parsonage or the calm shadow of some old
cathedral close, going forth, as, sooner or later, he must
go forth, unarmed to meet the shock of the world's
temptations, has fal'en with a more tragic suddenness
into a completer ruin. A great writer of fiction has
drawn such a picture. A youth carefully trained in a

religious home goes to the University, falls into bad company, and gets into habits of intemperance. " Need I," he says, " depict the fine gradations by which he sank; gradations, though fine, yet so numerous, that, in a space of time almost too brief to credit, the clear-browed boy looked a sullen, troubled, dissatisfied youth?" And why? because his religion had been but external, mechanical, artificial. It was a thin veneer; there was in it no heart of oak. His life had never looked up to its source. All that was good in him was good of itself, and not of him. So it was easy to go down—over the edge of the pit. All return to the unific rectitude of a manly life must be in the face of a scorching past and a dark future, and those he could not face.

My brethren, thank God schools are not now what they were when Cowper wrote his *Tirocinium*. I know now—may I not say it in this Holy of Holies of our spiritual temple; may I not say it on this Sunday morning, when the sound of prayers and litanies still rings sweetly in our ears; may I not say it in this chapel, where, morning by morning and evening by evening, you kneel with bowed heads and reverent hearts in the presence of our God and Father; may I not say it at the close of a Half, in which, by God's blessing, there has been so much for which to be thankful, so little to cause pain; may I not say to Marlborough boys?—that your school is to you a kind and gentle nurse, and that it is possible for you here—as it has been to hundreds of right-hearted Christian boys before you—to live innocent and honourable lives, amid a thousand influences for good, none hindering, and many helping you? I know that I may say it; not (God forbid!) in a spirit of boastfulness, but in a spirit of deep humility and gratitude; and yet it remains true even for you, that the life of five hundred boys congregated together—not all, it may be, from good previous influences; not all, it may be, of good and pure dispositions—cannot be so safe a place, so free from all peril and outward temptation to do wrong, as home. Why then do your parents send you here? Why do they not keep you at home? Might not a wise father, in the fewest possible words, tell you in answer that herein he is but following God's appointed method in the probation of a human soul, and that that method is, not to shield it from the possibility of evil, but to encourage and strengthen it in the deliberate choice of good; not to shelter it from all temptation, but with each temptation to provide also the way of escape; not to stop the ears of His children against those voices which call them aside to the right hand or to the left;— but to purge those ears, so that they may listen to the high, authoritative, and tender voice, that still small voice which you hear every one of you, each in the deep of his own heart, which ever reminds you of the one straight path, and ever utters, "This is the way: walk ye in it."

Now, you will be most sensible of such temptations as school life may bring—most inclined to put them forward as a complaint or an excuse—if you have indeed succumbed to them; if on returning home you find that either home is changed or you are changed—

> "And, least familiar where he should be most,
> Feels all his happy privileges lost."

Some change, of course, there must be, but it need not be wholly painful. "On a rock where we landed to fish," says a young emigrant in his journal, "I espied

a harebell, the first I had seen for many years, and with
its meekly-hanging head it told me long and melancholy
tales of times gone by, never to return; not that old
scenes may not be revisited, and the sunshine be bright
as ever, and the flowers blossom as then; but it is he
who revisits them is past and gone—himself and not
himself; the heart that saw them is dead, or worse, is
changed: for that change kills not the memory, the
long lingering gaze after the fading past." What then
is this change? It is nothing less than the growth of
individuality; the full sense of the living free will; the
loneliness, the separation, the distinctness of each soul,
as, "travelling daily farther from the east," it realises
that, like a sphere upon a plane, a human soul can only
touch other souls at one single point; that each human
soul is an island, and that it is surrounded by an
unvoyageable sea.

Now, the infinite importance of this growing individuality is that it is *ourselves*, our inmost being; we
carry it with us wherever we go, not as our shadow but
as our substance. It is wholly independent of our
circumstances; it is wholly independent of our locality.
In a temple it may brand us with the guilt of felons;
in a dungeon it may ennoble us with the holiness of
saints. Depraved and corrupted, it would make a hell
of heaven; cleansed and enlightened, it can make a
heaven of hell. And if it be indeed an island, if it be
indeed surrounded by an unvoyageable sea, must we
not be necessarily miserable if, through our own fault,
the soil of that island bring forth, not the rich wholesome grain whereby man can live, but only the poisonous
flowers of evil passion, or only things rank and gross in
nature—weeds, and thistles, and nettles; the miserable,
starved, ignoble growth of vices with which we will not

struggle, and follies to which, without an effort, we succumb?

Is it not, then, the obvious conclusion of all that I have said that this formation of our character, this making of ourselves, is to us of importance simply infinite; that it is, in fact, the very work of life? Oh take that one thought with you. If you are conscious of a deteriorating life and a wavering allegiance to God, then do not throw the blame upon your circumstances; plead no excuses before the Eternal bar; suffer not thy mouth to cause thy flesh to err, neither say thou before the angel, "It was an error." Think not to lay to your diseased conscience the flattering unction that your sin was the result of circumstance. The first excuse which will be crushed at the throne of judgment will be that which would lay on others the burden of your own blame. Rather recognise on your knees, and with the streaming tears of penitence, the many helps to holiness around you; rather confess humbly that if, in spite of all His love and care for you, you wilfully choose the hard paths of sin, you do so against light and knowledge, and the clear will and help of God. When the waves are calm, when the winds are still, when the charts are certain, when the moon is bright, when the silver mirrors of the lighthouse-beacon, shedding for miles their victorious radiance, warn you off the sunken reef, can it be aught on the pilot's part save wilful negligence or guilty purpose if the gallant ship be cast away? So calm, so still, so certain, so bright, so full of noble and kindly circumstance is your life, whether at home or school. And if, in spite of this, it is an unholy and godless life, whence comes your danger? Is it not from your own will? Is it not from your own heart? Is it not from your own selves?

Let us, then, all ask God our Father to take our hearts and make them wholly His; above all, may we pray that prayer who hope once more to kneel next Sunday, some of us it may be for the last time, at His holy table, in fresh communion with each other and fresh dedication of our hearts to God.

Oh, you who were confirmed four weeks ago, have you indeed borne all this steadily in mind? God grant that you have; but if any impression for good has been growing faint, now and here and during the coming week you may revive it. God grant that you may.

> "Lord, shall we come, come yet again?
> Thy children ask one blessing more:
> To come, not now alone, but then,
> When life and death and time are o'er.
> Then, then to come, oh Lord! and be
> Confirmed in heaven, confirmed by Thee."

June 16, 1872.

SERMON XII.

SELF-CONQUEST.

EPH. v. 15.

"See then that ye walk circumspectly."

I DO not purpose to speak to you to-day about those two least-known apostles to whom the day is consecrated. The Saints' days of the Church are meant far less to glorify the saints by whose names they are called, than to teach us the whole principle of the saintly life—the motives which animated, the methods which trained—above all the example of their Master Christ which inspired those "humble and holy men of heart."

Were I asked to give the briefest possible description of the saints I should say that they were "the heroes of unselfishness." Selfishness—the love of ourselves, the eager passion for our own interests, the grumbling assertion of our own rights, the sinful yielding to our own desires—is the source of nearly all the ruin and misery which devastate the world. Pride springs from it; ambition lives for it; anger leans on it; lust serves it. It is the fruitful source of all disobedience, and of all disbelief; it is a sacrifice of eternal happiness for temporary gratification,—of the divinest interests of the spirit to the basest instincts of the flesh. The law of God says, "Here we have no abiding city;" selfishness says, "Make the world thy feeding-trough." The word of God says, "Be ye holy for I am holy;" selfishness says that "Stolen waters are sweet, and bread eaten in secret pleasant." The law of God says, "Thou shalt love the Lord thy God with all thy heart, and thy neighbour as thyself;" selfishness says, "Forget God; please thyself; despise others; take thine ease; eat, and drink, and be merry;"—aye! and even while the words are being uttered the unseen hand is writing its awful messages on the wall of life, and the awful voice pealing forth those dread tones which only the awakened conscience can interpret, "Thou fool, thy soul shall be required of thee."

But the saints are the heroes of unselfishness; let me on this Saints' day evening call your attention to one of that noble army; I shall not have spoken in vain, if, by God's blessing, I teach but one soul here the lesson which his life mainly illustrates—that without distinct effort there can be no self-conquest. And the lesson is needed. In moral things, certainly, perhaps in all our life, perhaps most of all in boyhood, our great danger is to walk, not as wise but as fools; to live in the most immediate present with no thought whatever of the future; to live as if even manhood, much more as if death, judgment, or eternity were an empty dream. St. Paul says, "See that ye walk circumspectly," or rather βλέπετε ἀκριβῶς πῶς περιπατεῖτε, look accurately how ye walk. There is corruption within us; there is corruption without us. We are swayed by bad impulses; seduced by bad examples; deceived by bad reasoning; over our life hangs a thick veil of darkness which Christ only can remove. The path of life is narrow and uphillward, and unless Heaven's light fall on it one false step may be ruin irretrievable. Wary walking therefore,—as wise, not as unwise,—is essential to our safety.

Now if St. Paul's view of life be true, and it is alone true, then it must be hard to live,— I do not mean to live a living death, but to live a life which is life indeed. Alas! we do not find it so. We live carelessly and at ease; we live full-fed, and indolent, though we are called to the soldier's watchfulness and the pilgrim's toil; we live at random, without plan, without discipline, though bidden to nothing less than the imitation of God. At the best—surrounded with dangers as we are—and often do I wish that I could really reveal, above all to you younger boys and you little boys, how beset with spiritual danger your days may be—we trust to an uncultivated notion of duty for a chance solution of difficulties. You train long for a five minutes' race; you do not think it worth while to train for the race of life. You practise, and practise hard, and endure much to be successful in a game: many of you think it of no importance to practise, or to give up anything which shall enable you to play better the game even of earthly life—much less the awful game on success in which depends the future of your souls. You will be buffeted, and knocked down, and incur danger of heavy blows and broken limbs— (and quite right too in hardy and manly English boys), to win the praise of your house;—why will you think all effort needless to win the praise of God—and to be profitable members of the Church and Commonwealth here, and partakers hereafter of the immortal glory of the resurrection? Do not think that I disparage the physical vigour at which I daily look with interest;

but it is impossible to repress a sigh when one thinks that the same vigour infused also into intellectual studies, which are far higher and nobler, would carry all success and prosperity in life irresistibly before you,—and the same vigour applied also to spiritual things would make you immortal Heroes and Saints of God.

I will tell you a few things about such a hero and saint to-night. You cannot imitate his external life,— any attempt to reproduce that is impossible, and would be ridiculous; but the outward acts speak of an inward spirit, and every one of us may learn—if we care to learn—from the laws that regulated, from the discipline that ennobled, from the hopes that inspired that life.

The third century after Christ was an epoch of intense misery and enormous crime. The Roman Empire had, by its own vices, decayed into rottenness and weakness. The mass of society was degraded, and knew its degradation, and encouraged itself in its degradation; it had reached that worst stage of depravity which willingly fosters depravity in others. Even the salt of religion had in many places lost its savour. We, after eighteen centuries of Christianity, we, for whom it is possible to live the saintly life in the commonest routine of society, can have no conception how enormous was the difficulty for any good man to live holily in that decaying and decadent society. Well, exceptional crises need an exceptional example; and times utterly corrupt demand from the Christian soldier a vaster range of effort, an intenser heroism of endeavour. And God, when He needs such servants, sets them apart with the hands of invisible consecration for this high service of suffering. He called a young boy to the work which should awake a dead and greedy age. His name was Antony. He was born in Egypt, of noble parentage. His boyhood was remarkable for its gentleness and simplicity. In early youth he was left an orphan in charge of an estate, and of a youthful sister. He did his duty faithfully to both, and one day, meditating on the simplicity of the early Christians, he entered a church, and heard in the Gospel the words, "If thou wilt be perfect, go, sell all that thou hast, and give to the poor, and come, follow me, and thou shalt have treasure in heaven." Heroic souls take only heroical explanations; and he had the courage to believe those words, and throw himself as it were on the faith of Him who uttered them. Without hesitation he sold his fair possessions; he entrusted his young sister to the care of some holy women; he began to train himself deliberately for a life, if possible, of sinless and devoted self-denial. What were his methods? First he worked, for he knew the text, "If any man will not work, neither shall he eat;" then he prayed, for he knew the command "Pray without ceasing;" then he sought out good men, for he knew that "Evil communications corrupt good manners." And instead of going about, as we too often do, judging harshly and hardly and arrogantly of our neighbours, he tried to learn from all. He contemplated the courtesy of one, the prayerfulness of another; another's freedom from anger; another's ever ready sympathy. He saw how one watched, how another studied; he admired one for his endurance; another for his meekness; all for their love to Christ and to each other. His fixed object in life was to pain no one needlessly; to make all happy so far as in him lay; above all, and more than all, to be a follower of God. This was his object, his purpose, the settled determination of his life, and, like all who make it their settled object, he succeeded.

Don't think that the youthful Antony had no struggles, no difficulties: he had deadly struggles, superhuman difficulties, long, bitter, terrible. He experienced in his own person that there are some evil spirits which go not out but by prayer and fasting. Now one of the conditions of Antony's mind was that the spiritual world was to him not only real, but the *sole* reality. What others suppose, he knew; what others imagine, he saw; what others saw, he felt. Whatever other men might think, he knew that he was face to face with the Eternal; words of Scripture were to him voices of God; temptations to sin were to him assaults of devils; and therefore never for one moment did he underrate, as we underrate, the grandeur of the conflict in which he was engaged. And so on one occasion it seemed to him that he was assaulted by every temptation at once, love of money, love of fame, love of ease, love of sensual indulgence. With every effort of his reason, with every power of his soul, with watchings, with fastings, with prayers, with thoughts of Christ, he struggled and agonised, and prevailed as against an army of foul and terrible demons. And when he had prevailed,—yet not he, but the grace of God which he had sought, and which was given to him,—he seemed to see before him an Evil Being who said, "I have deceived many; I have cast down many; but now, as in the case of many, so in thine I have been worsted in battle." "Who art thou?" asked Antony. "I am," he answered in a voice of anguish, "I am the spirit of impurity." Then Antony gave thanks to God, and gaining courage said, "Thou art weak, and black of soul, and utterly despicable; nor will I henceforth cast one thought, save a thought of loathing, upon thee."

But Antony having won the victory, still found that

it was only by continued effort that he could maintain it,—and to maintain it—to teach men the awful, infinite value of the human soul—he retired wholly into the desert, there to be alone and face to face with himself and God. And there by twenty years of prayer, and tears, and abstinence, and humbleness, he learnt in his patience to subdue his body, and to possess—or rather, as it should be rendered, to *acquire* his soul. His example was fruitful, as all sacrifice is always: and to all he taught the same lessons—" To trust in God, and to love Him; to keep themselves wholly, sternly, determinedly, from foul thoughts and sensual pleasures; to rule their tongues and their appetites; not to be deceived by fulness of bread; to watch, to pray; never to let the sun go down upon their wrath." So, in the desert, he lived and died. His book was the nature of created things. He saw the great sun rise and set over the granite hills. He saw the great storm sweep the desert, and the great stars look down upon its sands. Working, praying, teaching, meditating, he lived holy and died happy; and let the poor shallow criticism which would sneer at such as he, remember that Athanasius, the glory of the Eastern Church, counted it the highest blessing of his life to have seen him; and that it was by hearing his story that Augustine, the glory of the Western Church, was first won to deliver himself from the trammels of a vulgar, dissolute, selfish life, to become himself a high servant and saint of God.

i. Would to God that you from his life would learn two short but eternal lessons! The one is this—that virtue is not above human nature. God has bidden us be humble, peaceful, charitable, pure; God has not bidden us to do what we cannot do. Most of us seem to act as though the law of God could not be obeyed, or not by us; the soul not saved, or not by us. But we can obey God's holy law; we can work out our own salvation with fear and trembling. Whatever his circumstances, whatever his temptations, whatever his character—aye, even whatever his habits—there is not one boy in this chapel who *might* not be free, and noble, and calm, and pure. Antony was not older than the eldest of you when he obeyed the voice which bade him part with all for God. Benedict was younger than nearly all of you when, in his mountain cave among the Sabine hills, he trained himself by stern self-denial to regenerate his age. Francis of Assisi was still a youth when the spectacle of the Passion burnt upon his soul the lesson, "If thou wilt come after Me, deny thyself, and take up thy cross, and follow Me."

ii. That is one lesson,—that godliness is possible; the other is that it is not possible without effort. Be sure of this—nothing worth anything can ever be gained without paying the price which nature, and man, and God have ordained. If you want physical success, you must work for it. If you want intellectual success, you must work for it. If you would conquer your bad habits, if you would resist your besetting sins, if you would save your souls from sin, and hell, and the death that cannot die, you must work for it. For not, as Dante says—

> "Not on flowery beds, or under shade
> Of canopy reposing, heaven is won."

No man, says another poet—

> "No man e'er gained a happy life by chance,
> Or yawned it into being with a wish."

It stands written in the Koran that, "Under the

shadow of the crossing scimitars Paradise is prefigured:" the prophet meant it of the sword by which he propagated his faith; but we may understand it of the spiritual armour. Yes, under the shadow of the crossing scimitars—yes, in the battlefield against sin and death,—yes, where the fiery darts of the wicked one fly fast and thick—there, in the deadly struggle of internecine opposition against all that we know to be wicked and opposed to God,—there for us lies the only safety. " See, then, accurately how ye walk." If you would win the saint's glory, you must fight the saint's fight:—

> "*They* climbed the steep ascent of heaven,
> 'Mid peril, toil, and pain :
> Oh God, to us may grace be given
> To follow in their train!"[1]

---

[1] For one or two thoughts in this Sermon I am indebted to an unpublished Sermon by Canon Westcott.

St. Simon and St. Jude, Oct. 28, 1872.

SERMON XIII.

THE PERIL OF WASTE.

JOHN vi. 12.

"Gather up the fragments that remain, that nothing be lost."

You have heard these words, my brethren, in the Gospel of to-day. Even in their most literal and obvious sense they are full of instruction. But as the miracles of Christ were more than mere acts of power, so the words of Christ reached farther than their direct significance. And I shall understand these words as warning us against other waste than the waste of food,—as bidding us to gather other fragments than the fragments of a feast. The half-year is nearly over. It has given us invaluable time—that time is drawing to a close; it has been rich in priceless opportunities—those opportunities are being rapidly withdrawn. As regards that time, as regards those opportunities these words warn us against the sin of waste. To myself, and to all of you, I apply this morning the words of Christ, "Gather up the fragments that remain, that nothing be lost."

1. Looking back on this half-year, may we not say that so far it has been by God's blessing a quiet and a happy one? An ancient heathen would never have ventured to speak thus. Before even hinting at any

happiness of his own, he would have thought it necessary to do homage to Nemesis. He would have dreaded lest the mere mention of prosperity should provoke the anger and jealousy of Heaven. The feelings of a Christian are very different. When God has been very good to him, or to the body of which he is a member,—when God has shed the dew of His blessing either on the heart or life,—he looks up to that God, not as to an arbitrary or jealous despot, but as to a tender father, who is pleased with his happiness, who wills his salvation. And so, if, as he walks by the dusty wayside of life, he has drunk of the brook by the way, and plucked some of the sweet and simple flowers which broider it,—very humbly and very thankfully, desiring that God's gifts may make him neither presumptuous nor negligent,— he offers unto God thanksgiving, and pays his vows unto the Most Highest. Well then, thanking God, and taking courage, we may say, I trust, that God has not withholden His blessing from us. No harm has happened to us, nor any plague come nigh our dwelling. We have not been troubled by sickness, nor had to mourn for the stroke of death; nor have we suffered the anguish of worse sorrows than those,—worse, because they affect not the perishing body, but the immortal soul,— the bitter dread, I mean, lest there should be sin flourishing in the midst of us;—lest boys coming among us should be subjected to ruinous perils and cruel temptations;—lest there should be neglected roots of bitterness to spring up and trouble us;—lest bad boys should have more influence here than good;—lest to watch, and to pray, and to seek the love, and to obey the law of God, should be the exception here, and not the rule;—we have had, I say, no cause to indulge such fears; rather have we had every reason to hope the contrary,—to be persuaded better things of you, brethren, and things which accompany salvation. And for this cause we bow our heads, and offer up with thankful hearts our gratitude to God :—

> "Our vows, our prayers, we now present
> Before Thy throne of grace ;
> God of our fathers, be the God
> Of their succeeding race!"

2. But how is it when we turn from the school to ourselves, from the society to its separate members,— from the life of the body to the lives of each individual boy? That must be answered by each for himself. But, though each heart knoweth its own bitterness, I hope —nay, more, I believe—that there are many and many of you who can look back on the past part of this half year without a blush and without a sigh; boys who have been diligent; who have been faithful; who have kept a watch over the door of their lips; who have resisted temptation in their own hearts ; who have, humbly yet zealously, done all they could for the good of others; who, by faith, by prayer, by a sense of the eternal, by seeking and gaining the grace of God, have had a right spirit within them; who, being meek, have inherited the earth; who, being pure in heart, have seen God. These need but a word of gentle and hearty encouragement not to be weary in well doing. Hitherto you have tried to use your time well and wisely: continue to do so, and may God bless you in it! The closing weeks of a half year are often a time of temptation. There is a fear of relaxing vigilance; there is a peril in natural excitement; the moment of putting off the armour may be the moment of a wound. It is a time when all who love and fear God, and desire the welfare of their own souls, and the souls of others, should more than

ever watch and pray against all temptation. It is a time to take Christ's warning to ourselves, "Gather up the fragments that remain, that nothing be lost."

3. But are there not some with whom it is far otherwise? Have not the consciences of some, as they listened, burning with unrepented sins, told them that the picture which I have drawn is not for them? Let me suppose such a one, and let each who is such take my words as addressed in all kindness and faithfulness to him and him alone. You began the term with high hopes and good resolves. You were conscious of serious failings,—but you would resist them. You were apt to yield to special temptations, but you would fight against them. You had one known besetting sin, but, God helping you, now—ere it was too late, ere that sin became inveterate—you would conquer it. In general you had been doing badly at school, now you were determined to do better. Such were the promises you had made to those who loved you, and you meant, or half-meant, or thought that you half-meant, to fulfil them. And such were the promises which, when you came back here, you renewed to us, and at first, in spite of all past disappointments, we almost fancied you would redeem them. But, alas! it is so easy to promise, so difficult, for the weak-hearted, to perform. Why dwell on the old sad failure?—the resolves which proved to be but a house built on the sand,—the goodness that vanished like the early dew? Any interruption, however trivial—any accident, however slight—any passing disappointment, however insignificant—yes, any thistle-down of poor excuse was enough for natural indolence to catch at;—and if there was not even one poor, mean, shuffling excuse to shelter you, then the miserable " I cannot help it" of a weak and enervated

will was enough for you to drug the conscience with. You had learnt a wrong lesson,—you had been unlucky this week,—you had got interested in a novel, and it made you forget your work,—it was hardly worth trying till next week began,—and so on, and so on,—being virtuous only in the future, not in the present; improving only in flaccid wishes, not in strong reality; doing right only in maudlin dreams, not in manly effort; meaning, in some dim, confused, drowsy way to be a good and noble boy, but being, indeed, a weak, feeble, unsatistory one,—until, in fact, you had ceased to care, and were content to be the poor slip-shod character which you knew you were,—always last, or nearly last in everything, never doing anything downright well,—discouraging the efforts made for you, disappointing the hopes formed of you,—even thus early in life preparing yourself to cumber the ground in God's fruitful vineyard —a barren and a blighted tree. And what is the deep moral lesson which this sad, ever-recurring history implies? It is one of the deepest, and one of the saddest of all lessons; it is the moral law—aye, and the physical law too,—which is of all others, the most full of warning—viz., that our to-morrows are shaped with awful force by our yesterdays—that "our days are heritors of days gone by." Nor will it ever be known, I suppose, till the last great day how many men have spent the youth of life in making its manhood almost hopelessly miserable. You cannot learn then too early, by way of most solemn warning,—and I know not whether the lesson be most necessary for the youngest or for the eldest—that he who will but do his duty *to-morrow* does it too late, and is but too likely not to do it all. There is a fatal force of growth in every bad habit,—a fatal continuity in human character,—so that any sin yielded to yesterday returns with more virulent influence to-day, and any sin not resisted to the very uttermost to-day, will return inevitably to-morrow with added insolence to master a weakened slave; until, if God's grace be still resisted—to-morrow, and to-morrow, and to-morrow have made up the tale of a sinful, futile, degraded life, and placed you, reprobate, before that silent, solemn bar, at which each man shall receive the things done in the body, whether they have been good, or whether they have been evil. If such be the state,—if such be even the commencing state of any one of you who hear me this day,—if neither physically, nor morally, nor intellectually, you have been doing your duty,—if, instead of growing better and better, you are steadily and consciously growing worse and worse,—if over your soul is beginning to creep the chill of a fatal apathy, and the past-feelingness of a miserable despair,—then must we not to you *alter* the words of the text, not saying as Christ said to His faithful ones, "Gather up the fragments that remain, that nothing be lost,"—but rather alas! with a more urgent insistency, "Gather up the fragments that remain, lest everything be lost"?

4. For everything is not yet quite lost. If, for instance, every word of instruction which you have heard from this place has been to you but as the sound of the idle wind—if on each Sunday, or each other day, after you have heard truths which so nearly concern the welfare of your soul,—a light word, a profane sneer, a conceited criticism, a recurring temptation, a careless habit, have been to you like those birds of the air in the Saviour's parable which take away good seed of God's Word from the trodden wayside of the hard and callous heart,—if on each Sunday after hearing the truths of God, spoken by His ordinance and in His name, you have but gone to

trifle, to jest, to please yourselves "without one sin brought to your remembrance, without one duty resolved upon, without one thought of your own weakness and Christ's strength,"—only a little more impenetrable than before, only with the hard heart trodden a little harder —if so, then you have one more opportunity to-day. Oh, shall this fragment also be lost? will all of you reject to-day one more appeal of God to the sinful and unrepentant soul? will not one return to His Father? will not one pour into His ear the confessions of a wasted boyhood? will not one, not one, make to Him, in secrecy and in silence, the resolves of a future life?

5. God grant His Holy Spirit to us, that it may be otherwise! Thirteen weeks of this half-year are over; but four still remain. Now I do not mean to conceal that the waste of past time makes all life a sad "might have been." None of you can in four remaining weeks regain the ground, whether moral and intellectual, which you may have lost in the thirteen past. There is no recalling those golden weeks that have gone neglected into the dark backward and abysm of time. The gleaning of the few ears which the hand of the reaper has dropped among the stubble cannot replace the harvest; nor can we repair the lost vintage by gathering the scant grapes left here and there upon the topmost bough. It is the lesson that I have often taught which I must often teach again, that repentance is not innocence, though it is all that stands between the guilty soul and death. And that repentance must be our work, in the time that God yet gives. And when we remember what time is—how short, how uncertain,— then those words of St. Augustine acquire a deeper force, that *Non progredi est regredi*—that, in the spiritual life, non-progress is retrogression. For consider

that awful mystery of Time,—the Future not to be anticipated, the Past not to be recalled, only the Present ours; and that Present, what is it? An island ever encroached upon by the dark and swelling waves—a quicksand which ever swallows the place where last we trod—the flowing water of a river which is already far upon its way to the great sea. Even while we speak, it was and is not. For ever—never. It passes away with every ticking of the clock; with every beating of the heart; with every breath of articulated air. Yet how priceless! In it alone we live. With it alone can we purchase eternity. It perishes and is recorded. And though we waste,—nay, waste is a slight word—though we abuse, fling away, squander, kill it now, may not the hour come to us as to the great English Queen crying in her deathbed agony, " Oceans of money for one drop of time"? Well, though we misuse, though we waste it,—silently, and patiently, whether we will live or die, silently and patiently, to the last,—God gives it us, until (it may be) it shall be suddenly withdrawn. *And then?* And then, for the sin of all waste,—wasted money, wasted hours, wasted affections, wasted health, wasted opportunities, for every wasted boyhood, for every wasted manhood,—we must give account. Then shall the Voice say, "Give an account of thy stewardship, for thou mayest be no longer steward." I gave thee a body full of strength and health,—how is it enfeebled by folly and excess? I gave thee a mind capable of making thee wise and noble,—why is it like the sluggard's garden, full of thorns? I gave thee a life which might have been a blessing to thy fellow men,—why have its powers been guiltily neglected or guiltily squandered? Why is it like grass upon the housetops wherewith the mower filleth not his hand, nor he that gathereth the sheaves his bosom ? Oh when these questions are asked—when the books are opened—when the dead are judged—when thou art weighed in the balances and found wanting—when thou standest speechless before the All-seeing eye of God—when " Mercy has played her part, and Justice leaps upon the stage "—and many glittering faces of the holy and the pure look down upon thy degradation,—?

6. But oh may that great and dreadful moment never be to any of us! In that day may we stand fearless before the adversary, penitent, redeemed, cleansed sanctified, in the white robe of Christ's righteousness. It *may* be so. In giving us time God gives us all. Still God makes the great sun shine upon us day by day,—still, morning, by morning, He causes another day,—a day unstained,—to dawn for us out of His eternity. Still morning by morning His hand holds forth to us a green leaf from the tree of life. Such a day is this. Oh, waste it not! Is there a good impression that you have suffered to grow faint? Is there a holy practice which you have long neglected? Have you an offended friend who is still unreconciled? a temper still unchecked? a besetting sin still unresisted? oh here is work for you to-day. " Watch against that which, in your better heart, with your truer self you desire not to do; watch for the thing which you feel you ought to do;" go back to your life from this sermon, from this warning of God to your souls, a little thoughtfully; and if you find yourself failing in your weakest point, slipping insensibly, were it but in thought into your besetting temptation, kneel at once upon your knees, ask pardon for it, and help to shun it in the future. Make, by God's grace, now—even now and here—a higher purpose, and ask for grace to keep to that purpose;

humbly remembering that you must take the difficulty of the upward path as grave punishment to be patiently borne for going downwards. So gather up the fragments that remain, lest all be lost. Now is the accepted time, now is the day of salvation. Who knows whether for you it may be true even to the very letter that "From this very moment hangs eternity!"

Nov. 17, 1872.

SERMON XIV.

CALLING THINGS BY THEIR WRONG NAMES.

Is. v. 20.

" Woe unto them that call evil good, and good evil; that put darkness for light, and light for darkness; that put bitter for sweet, and sweet for bitter!"

I DID not seek for this text; it comes naturally and prominently before us in the first Lesson of the day. I did not seek it, because it is couched in the language of denunciation and reproof, and I would far rather that you associated the teachings of this chapel with gentler, more soothing, more ennobling influences. It would be my wish that, in future years, Marlborough boys, if they ever recall what was said to them from this pulpit, should connect it with thoughts of peace, and joy, and hope, and the words of Him whose precepts were beatitudes, rather than with the terrors and thunderings of the fiery law. When our first parents were innocent and happy the voice of God, in accents that made them yet happier, floated for them under the trees of Paradise upon the evening wind; and even so would we wish God's messages to come to you. Reproof and denunciation, distasteful as they ever must be, have indeed their office. The Word of God is something more than a very pleasant song; it is sometimes a fire to scathe, a hammer to dash in pieces, a sword to divide the soul and spirit, the joints and marrow; and we should be guilty if we were ever murmuring, Peace, Peace, were there no peace; guilty if, when it were needed, we shrank from ever saying anything which might tend to pierce the slumbering conscience, or agitate the stagnant soul. But I believe—I say it in no conventional or flattering spirit—I feel confident that I am speaking to right-minded and Christian boys; to those whose hearts—amid many sins doubtless, and many failings—are yet not hard, and who will accept the language of kindly warning, with no need for the stern anathema, or the prophetic woe. I would not, therefore, use this text as though I said, "Woe to some of you, for some of you call evil good, and good evil;" but rather would I warn you to beware lest *any* of you should subtly and insensibly slide into the treason of those who do so, and against whom the prophet utters the dread judgment that "as the fire devoureth the stubble, and the flame consumeth the chaff, so their root shall be as rottenness, and their blossom shall go up as dust."

I. What then is this sin against which I would warn each and all of you to be, now and ever, on your guard? It is the sin of disregarding—aye, and even of in the least degree underrating—the eternal distinctions of right and wrong; of putting darkness for light, and light for darkness, bitter for sweet and sweet for bitter; it is, in one word, the sin of viewing things in their wrong aspects, of calling things by their wrong names. "He that saith unto the wicked 'Thou art righteous,'" says Solomon, "him shall the people curse." "He that justifieth the wicked," he says elsewhere, "and he that condemneth the just, even they both are an abomination to the Lord." More even than this, there are some things—as St. Paul tells us—which ought not so much as to be named among those who would live holy lives. To talk, otherwise than sadly and seriously of sin, is sin. "Oh, it was only a light word," you say. Yes, but there are times and states of the human soul on which even a light word may produce an effect which seems strangely and terribly disproportionate. The spark of fire which sets miles of rolling prairie in furious blaze,—the breath of wind stirring the few snow-flakes which before they reach the valley are a roaring avalanche,—these too are light matters: even so the tongue is a little member, but, as St. James impetuously says, "it setteth on fire the whole course of nature, and is set on fire of hell." The evil word—and oh, remember this—is a step, a long step beyond the evil thought; and it is a step toward the precipice's edge. It fixes, it defines, it acknowledges, it embodies, it consents to the inward wrong. The king, in the great tragedy of that our poet, who, of all men that ever lived, saw deepest into the heart of man, *thinks* of murder, wishes to commit murder, has his heart and conscience full of murder, yet dare not commit murder, solely because as yet he dare not utter the word.

"I had a thing to say,
But I will fit it with some better time.
I had a thing to say, but let it pass."

The sunlight prevents him from saying it. Evil deeds are secret, clandestine; they court concealment, they love darkness; "Or," he continues to the man whom he is trying to corrupt,

"Or, if that thou could'st see me without eyes,
Hear me without thine ears, and make reply
Without a tongue, using conceit alone,
Without eyes, ears, or harmful sound of words;
Then would I in thy bosom pour my thoughts,
But ah! I will not."

And when the deed is, as he thinks, done, and only its guilt, and bitterness, and ruin remain,—when he finds that, like all sinners, he has sold himself for nought, and the Furies begin "to take their seats upon the midnight pillow," then he complains of his accomplice, and, so far, complains of him justly, for having been weak, for having met him half-way, for having understood too easily—as weakness does—his guilty purpose.

> "Hadst thou but shook thy head or made a pause,
> Or bade me tell my tale in express words,
> Deep shame had struck me dumb.—
> But thou didst understand me by my signs,
> And didst in signs again parley with sin.
> Yea, without stop, didst let thy heart consent,
> And, consequently, thy rude hand to act
> The deed that both our tongues held vile to name."

Here you see how well our great dramatist recognised the moral phenomenon that vice will always try either to get rid altogether of any verbal acknowledgment, or to hide itself in words which involve a plausible euphemism or a latent jest. The language of vice is twofold:—the one so cynically brutal, so irredeemably depraved, that the merest tincture of education makes it impossible, and its deformed words are heard only in "that common grey mist composed of crime, night, hunger, vice, and falsehood, which is the high noon of the wretched." But this is a kind of hideous shamelessness, which is quenched not by religion, but by culture; and it is perhaps even less dangerous than those ὑποκορίσματα—to use a word for which the truthful genius of the English language has no equivalent—those false words, I mean, prankt in virtue's garb, to which sentimental corruption and cultivated vice resorts. Usually, when it has some wicked thing to utter, or some wicked action to excuse, language, lying in wait to murder truth and righteousness, "disguises itself in the vestibule." Speak of a sin in its true terms, and you strip it of its seductiveness. Call a vice by its real name, and you rob it of half its danger, by exposing all its grossness. The very guiltiest of sinners is he who paints the gates of hell with Paradise, he who supplies to wickedness the mask and the tinsel of such deceptive speech as hides its native and repulsive ugliness. It has always been the characteristic of the worst ages thus to gloze over wicked things by indifferent titles. The great Greek historian, as some of you know, points it out as the surest sign of utter degradation in his own troubled day, that men spoke of virtues as if they were vices, and of vices as if they were virtues. "They altered," he says, "at their will and pleasure the customary meaning of words in reference to actions." They branded prudent caution as mean procrastination; they glorified reckless audacity as social courage; if a man was calm he was taunted with cowardice, and if he were brutal he was belauded for manliness. Yes, strange to say, men are more ashamed of base names than they are of base deeds. And do boys at school know nothing like this? Is there not, even here, something analogous to this? Have you never, for instance, heard a very mild term, a term involving no reprobation, applied to certain forms of taking what is not our own, which a plain man would call "stealing"? Have you never heard jesting names for forms of untruthfulness, which a plain man would call "a lie"? Have you never heard a base, soft, spurious, effeminate fancy arrogate to itself, and degrade by that glozing usurpation, the noble, holy name of friendship? Have you never heard the conduct of a boy, who has acted dishonestly in an examination, described by a word much less unpleasant, far more apologetic, than the true, sincere word, "that he has been *cheating*"?—or again, in the opposite direction, have you never heard names of clear disparagement, names full of the dislike which vice feels to virtue, given to scrupulous honour, to steady diligence, to stainless purity? Oh, beware, then, as the text bids you, beware of ever thus calling evil good, or good evil! If you would be true to yourselves, true to your neighbour, true to God, never suffer yourselves to use one word which sneers at the difficulty of a virtue, or slurs the odiousness of a vice. Even an honest, fearless English boy will cease to see clearly the distinctions of right and wrong, if for the current coin of sincere and truthful language, there be palmed off upon him the false and adulterated counters of those words which come from the devil's mintage. Use true names. Let it be understood that here, and among you,—as pureminded and honourable English boys—the liar, if such should ever obtrude among us—which God forfend—but *if* such should ever obtrude among us, the liar shall be the liar, and the cheat a cheat, and the thief a thief, and unclean unclean. And as a necessary part of this subject let me earnestly warn you against an error into which even good boys might fall—the error of supposing that *ridicule* is a proper engine wherewith to encounter sin.

My brethren, you would shudder if you saw another doing what would maim his body; will you laugh at what may be the headlong destruction of his soul? Believe me, it is wrong to jest at that which you should exterminate, and laugh at that which you should loathe. You who love the Lord, be sure that laughter may be the right cure for *venial* follies, but that it is a reprobation not serious enough for so deadly a thing as sin.

If by a meaning smile, if by a passing allusion, if in mere inuendo, you betray to another your consciousness that he is doing wrong, and do not at the same time make him see your disapproval of the wrong—if need be, your hatred of the wrong, your horror of the wrong, your indignation at the wrong,—your determination, if need be, to expose and put down the wrong—then (be not deceived) you consent to the wrong. For this, if it be not treason, is the scarcely less heinous crime of misprison of treason, against God. You almost become a participator in his wrong doing. Rather abstain from every appearance of evil; rather put away from among yourselves that wicked person: at least, let your language to all be unmistakable in its clearness; at least remember that " By thy words shalt thou be justified, and by thy words thou shalt be condemned."

II. I have spoken of the sin, let me now say a few words about its cause. It is due, my brethren, to a fading appreciation of moral evil; a tampering with it, a destruction of that healthy instinct which revolts at it. It is the very nature of sin, that the more we know of it, the less we know it; the more we are familiar with it, the less do we understand its vileness.

"Oh! he was innocent,"

says the poet,

" And to be innocent is Nature's wisdom."

With what marvellous power is this truth indicated in one of the oldest fragments of the world's history, the third chapter of the Book of Genesis. Our first parents are innocent, and therefore they are noble, they are happy, they hear the Call of God as they sit under the palms of Paradise. But, alas! Eve lingers near the forbidden tree, and near the forbidden tree lurks ever the Serpent-tempter; and then, step by step, little by little, not shocking the soul at once, but alluring it imperceptibly, comes first the subtle insinuation of the doubt, " Yea, hath God said ? " then the bold scepticism, "Thou shalt not surely die," and then the guilty admiration of " the fruit pleasant to the eyes," and then the guilty longing for it as "a fruit to be desired to make one wise," and then the guilt itself—the guilty stretching forth of the disobedient hand, the guilty plucking of the fruit; and then very rapidly the worst, last, most odious, least pardonable consequence, the tempting of others to the same sin; and *then* the sin is over. Yes, the sin is over, but not the issues of it; not the horrible glare of inward illumination; the opening of the eyes; the agony of guilty shame; the Awful Voice; the vain hiding from detection; the conscious nakedness; the feeble, lying excuses, and trying to throw the blame on others; the lost Eden; the pain, the toil, the sorrow; the memory of life reduced to a bitter sigh; the melancholy looking for of ashes to ashes, dust to dust.

> " 'Twas but a little drop of sin
> We saw this morning enter in,
> And lo ! at eventide the world is drowned ! "

Oh, my brethren, now and always let it be your most earnest endeavour to keep your moral instincts right and true. Never let them be disguised by sentiment; never let them be obliterated by self-indulgence, never let them be sophisticated by lies. Do not think that light words and careless thoughts about them will be indifferent, and will leave you unaffected by them. "Character," as is said by our latest moralist, " is not cut in marble—it is not something solid and unalterable, it is something living and changing, and may become diseased, as our bodies do." You learn here, in season and out of season, line upon line, precept upon precept, here a little and there a little,—that obedience, diligence, honesty, truth, kindness, purity, are your duties to God and man. You know that this teaching is right and true, and that, in time and in eternity, your happiness depends thereon. Oh never lose sight of it! Say to yourselves, constantly, that this is good, and that is evil; this the noble course, that the base; this right, that wrong; this your duty and happiness, that your ruin and curse. Oh choose your side in the battle of life, and be not found on the wrong side. Abhor that which is evil, cleave to that which is good.

III.—For, lastly, as you have heard the sin, and its cause, so in very few words hear its punishment. That punishment is nothing less than the failure of all life;— the waste, the loss, the shipwreck of the human soul;—the sapping of every moral force and every vital instinct;— for "as the fire devoureth the stubble, and the flame consumeth the chaff, so their root shall be as rottenness, and their blossom shall go up as dust: because they have cast away the law of the Lord of Hosts, and despised the word of the Holy One of Israel." How powerful is the metaphor! The rose is a glorious flower, yet how often have you seen a rose-tree shrivelled, withered, blasted, producing nothing but mouldering and loathly buds;—why? Because there is some poison in the sap, or some canker at the root. Have you never seen it so? Have you never seen careers that might have been very happy, very innocent, very prosperous—cut short, blighted, in disgrace? And that is sad enough; but alas! there is something much sadder: there is the paralysis of the conscience, the searing as with a hot iron of the very faculty whereby we discriminate between right and wrong. As the Israelites preferred the wretched slavery and reeking fleshpots of Egypt to the manna, which was angels' food; as the pure, delicious water is loathsome to the scorched palate of the drunkard: so do these in their depraved souls learn at last, not merely to call evil good and good evil, but also to put bitter for sweet, and sweet for bitter. "Like natural brute beasts," they have lost the distinctions between right and wrong. That is a powerful and tragic line of the Roman satirist:—

"Virtutem videant, intabescautque relicta."

Let them see virtue, and pine for it, now that it is beyond their reach. But it is a worse stage still not even to see, not even to pine for it; as there is hope for the wound that throbs with agony, but none for that which has mortified to painlessness. And this is death. This is the worst woe that can befall finally those who have learnt to call things by their wrong names—to call evil good, and good evil. "How easy," says a Christian poet, and it may well sum up some of the lessons of to-day:

"How easy to keep free from sin;
 How hard that freedom to recall!
For dreadful truth it is, that men
 Forget the heavens from which they fall."[1]

Dec. 8, 1872.

[1] Coventry Patmore.

SERMON XV.

COUNTERBALANCE EVIL WITH GOOD.

ROM. xii. 21.

"Be not overcome of evil, but overcome evil with good."

You have heard these words in the Epistle of to-day, and you will remember that their first application is to that spirit of gentleness and brotherly kindness, that noble willingness to forget ourselves and to live for the good of others, which, in the long run, triumphs over malignity itself. Take less than your due, St. Paul says; think lowly of yourselves; be not resentful of injuries; if others act wrongly or unkindly, revenge yourselves by a generosity which will win over all but the basest natures, and which, even if it does not win *them*, will ennoble *you*.

But the words of my text have a wider and richer bearing, and believing that St. Paul would be the first to rejoice that they should be accepted in their very fullest significance, I urge you to-day, on this first Sunday of a new term, to take as your wise and constant motto this exhortation: "Be not overcome of evil, but overcome evil with good."

1. "Be not overcome of evil:" those words, you see, contain at once a warning of danger and an encouragement to resistance. They assume, as all Scripture does

—and it is an assumption well worthy of our deepest and most serious attention—that there is such a thing as evil, that it is around us, that contact with it is inevitable, that defeat and ruin by it are not impossible. It would be a shallow and a false philosophy, it would be a treacherous and apostate religion, which should attempt to conceal this from you, or to tell you that the hard, narrow, up-hillward path to heaven is smooth, and easy, and strewn with roses. I know that this is what the worldly wisdom of this age is doing more and more. Men more and more shut their eyes against all that is dangerous and disagreeable, in the thought of righteousness, temperance, and the judgment to come. "Speak to us smooth things," they say, "prophesy deceits." Let your teaching be as a pleasant song which shall not wake the slumber of the soul, or dispel the enchantments of the sense. Boldly bid us trust in the lying words that God will not punish, that redemption is a "boundless infinitude of mercy and reckless obliteration of the work of sin;" or speak to us rather as if there were no sin; as if earth were our only heaven; as if time were the only eternity; as if death meant annihilation; as if pleasure were godliness; as if the body were the soul; as if to think our own thoughts, and speak our own words, and walk in our own ways, were lawful and right, and to eat and drink, for to-morrow we die. And this is especially the fatal sophistry of those who *have* been overcome of evil. It only vexes them to be told that life, if it be true life, must be a fight, a strife, an agony, a service under a captain's banner in time of war, where carelessness is danger, and sleep is death. More gladly would they drug their consciences into stupefaction by believing that there is nothing irreconcilable between the world and Christ, as if the promptings of the flesh and the devil were but in reality the voice of nature and of God. But even the heathen had got beyond this; they knew the eternal distinctions of right and wrong; they knew that there were good and noble things for which men must struggle, and base, seductive things to which they must not yield. They knew that if man could not perish, he must by every effort, and at every hazard, refuse the evil and choose the good. Oh, learn, every one of you, even the youngest, that life is no long holiday, no sunny playing-field. He who has learnt to look without at the fearful phenomena of nature, he who has learnt to realise what agonies of mental and physical torture he himself—aye, every one here present—may in God's Providence be called upon to undergo before death comes; he who from Scripture, or from conscience, or from history, or from experience, has seen what possibilities of infamy, what capacities for crime, lurk, like glaring monsters in the sunless caverns of the human heart—he knows that one of those lessons which God repeats to him with daily warning is, that, to the best and noblest, life is a serious and a difficult thing; but that to the careless, the idle, the sensual, the disobedient, life is a scene of danger in which the soul may sink into present misery and everlasting death.

2. So much, my brethren, as a warning of peril which God would not have us neglect; but now we have the command, which command is itself the most powerful encouragement to resistance. Though physical and moral evil are closely and most mysteriously united, though sin and sorrow walk this world hand in hand, yet in one respect they are wholly separate. Physical evil may crush, but moral evil can alone contaminate. From physical evil we *must*, from moral we need not, suffer. Pain, sickness, bereavement, disappointment,

malice—these we must experience, but not necessarily vice, or guilt, or shame. These if admitted into our nature must be admitted by our own act. The City of Mansoul, if taken, can only be taken by treachery from within. We must meet with evil, but we need not touch it—we must experience temptation, but we need not yield to it—we must be assaulted by wrong, but we need never be defeated by it. We, like our Blessed Lord before us, must be driven into the wilderness of life to be tempted of the devil; but, though he may alter our circumstances, he can never control our will. He can place us on the topmost pinnacle of the Temple, but there he can only say to us, "Cast *thyself* down." *He* cannot cast us down. If we fall, we fall by our own apostasy; and if we stand, as stand we may by faith and prayer, then shall thousands of volant angels bear us down upon their wings, and sing heavenly anthems of our victory.

> "Also it is written,
> Tempt not the Lord thy God : He said, and stood ;
> But Satan, smitten by amazement, fell."

3. My brethren, this warning of danger, this encouragement to resistance, concerns us all very nearly this day. In coming back to school, or in coming, as many of you do, for the first time to school, you are coming to a new scene, and to one which necessarily, and inevitably, and under the very best and most favourable of circumstances, is a scene of greater and more serious temptation than that which you have left. How nearly then it concerns you to know and feel that you will meet with no danger which will really compromise your moral safety, that God will send you no temptation without sending you also the way to escape. Remember, then, that if you fall or go astray, the guilt will be not in your circumstances,

but in yourselves. Never say, "If I had not left home, I should never have forgotten God," or "If I had been somewhere else, I should not have fallen into this or that sin." Perhaps not; but you would assuredly have fallen into others. This is an excuse which is never listened to even before the bar of earthly justice; think you that it will be before His bar who can read the inmost secrets of the heart? God, we may be sure, hates feeble excuses as much as the best men do. Oh, all of you, depend on this, and learn this lesson this morning, for it is as steadfast as the throne of God, that if you,—any single boy among you,—will, in beginning the career of life, listen to the Voice of God, if he will keep himself aloof from the enticement of bad companions, if he will never suffer the inmost shrine of his heart to be darkened by removing from it that holy lamp of conscience which God has placed upon the altar there, if he will steadily, and by honest self-examination, set before him his duties and his dangers, if he will pray to God out of a pure heart fervently, and not walk after his own understanding, then, amid the treacherous assaults of evil, and the fiery darts of opposition, yea, in the very midst of the burning fiery furnace of his enemies, he shall be as safe as though the Wing of God were over him. Such a boy shall not greatly fall, or if, through the weakness of his mortal nature, for a moment he ever fall, he shall say at once, "Rejoice not over me, Satan, mine enemy, for if I fall I shall rise again." Innocence is one thing, virtue is another. That innocence which is but the child's sweet ignorance of evil cannot last; but when the limpid transparence of that fair and fragile crystal is sullied it may be more firmly replaced by the no less clear, but more solid adamant of virtue. Yes, on the one hand, be sure of this,—that were the temptations of any school ten thousand times worse than they are, a good and God-fearing boy may stand unscathed and happy in the midst of them; and that, on the other hand, a soul that is weak, a soul that is bad, a soul that is not sincere may be sheltered all its life long in the sweetest and purest of Christian schools, or even of Christian homes, —may be girt round with an infinitude of care and tenderness, may be placed where the temptations to evil are few, and the incentives to good are manifold,—yet that soul will perish and be ruined, because, anywhere and everywhere, the powers of evil will find their affinities with the weakness and treachery within. To our first parents the school of evil was Paradise itself. Esau was bred in the noble simplicity of the Patriarch's tent; the sons of Eli within the curtains of God's bright sanctuary; Manasses in the pure palace of a royal saint; Judas among the chosen ones of the heavenly kingdom, and in daily intercourse with the Son of God Himself. Yet what became of them? Esau grew into a coarse, sensual hunter; the sons of Eli were sons of Belial; Manasses was a foul apostate; and for Judas, the thief, the traitor, the son of perdition, it were better that he had not been born. So you see, it is God's will that man should be liable everywhere to the possibilities of evil;—but "*resist* the devil, and he will flee from you."

4. The rest of the verse tells you how you may best do this; it gives you the method of victory—"Be not overcome of evil, but overcome evil with good." Aim at that which is good,—cleave to that which is good,— occupy your time with that which is good,—fill your thoughts with that which is good,—and the assaults of evil will have lost half their power. An earnest employment—a steady purpose in life—a diligent use of

time—these are an irresistible panoply against wickedness, these strike out of the devil's hands his worst implements of temptation. You will remember that terrible touch in one of the Lord's sternest parables, about the evil spirit returning to the house whence he came out, and finding it "empty, swept, and garnished," —then goeth he and taketh to himself seven other spirits more wicked than himself, and they enter in and dwell there, and the last state of that man is worse than the first. What does that "empty, swept, and garnished" mean? It means that if your heart is not pre-occupied with good, it will be invaded by evil. Oh, beware of idleness in its every form, idle procrastinations, idle talk, idle habits, idle thoughts, these are the certain ruin of the soul. The labourer who stands idle in the marketplace is ever ready to be hired in the devil's service. The worm of sin gnaws deepest into the idle heart. Never will it be known, till the last great day, how many souls have been shipwrecked on the rock of an idle hour. But pre-occupy your heart with good; pre-occupy your time with honest industry, and you are safe. Whatsoever things are true, honest, just, pure, lovely, of good report, if there be any virtue, if there be any praise, think on these things. Evil can as little encroach on the domain of good as darkness can force its way into the circle of radiance which a lamp flings into the night. Remember that since all sin begins in thought, if your thoughts are safe then you are safe. "When our chalice is filled with holy oil, it will entertain none of the waters of bitterness." When the air is filled with sunlight there is no opportunity for the deeds of darkness. Where the soul has tasted of the bread of life, it cannot hunger for the stones of the wilderness. Where God is all to us, the world is nothing. If any of you have honestly tried, as you think, to encounter evil hand to hand, and have failed, because it has seemed to have you at a disadvantage, now try another and a better way, try now to draw into some innocent and useful channel that life which gives to evil all its strength. The sure way to overcome the evil is to develop, and feed, and fortify the good. In the case of the worst boy or the worst man, there lingers, unextinguished, a spark of heavenly fire. Every one of you has a good, a God-like, an eternal element within you—oh cherish these. The freer life of but one good impulse is the death-warrant to many guilty ones. Counterbalance that which is base, and disobedient, and degraded within you by the opposing weight of that which is holy and divine. Israel overcame the fiery serpents, not by gazing at and struggling with them, but by averting their gaze, and fixing their eyes on the brazen serpent; this was their true deliverance, and our true deliverance will be to consider the Apostle and High Priest of our profession, the life and example of our Saviour Christ. To His service you are dedicated; into His name you were baptized; to Him many of you have renewed, many will this term renew, the vow of their allegiance. Oh, all will be easy to you if you will follow in His steps. In every sense and by every influence—by creation, by preservation, by redemption, by adoption—you are the children of God. God loves you, Christ died for you, the Spirit strengthens you. It is true that without, and still more dangerously within, you, a great battle is going on; Gerizim and Ebal, blessing and cursing, good and evil, light and darkness, life and death are struggling for the possession of your souls. Oh, which shall gain them? If your heart be right with God, if you are humble and faithful, if you watch and pray, you are as safe now, as safe for ever, as safe here, as safe anywhere, as though the whole blue heaven were one great shield held on the Arm of God above your heads. As we kneel down now, at the end of this sermon, let us all pray that so we may live, so die; pray that each and all of us may be not slothful in business, fervent in spirit, serving the Lord,—pray that this place may grow dearer and dearer to everyone of us, because we may feel more and more that God is here,—pray that honest, simple, faithful duty may be the guiding star of all our lives,—pray that we may all be kind to one another, tender-hearted, forgiving one another, even as God for Christ's sake hath forgiven us. Yes, pray each for himself, and each for all—you for us, and we for you—that God may be with us; that His love may ever glide like a fiery pillar before us through the wilderness of life; that whether we have yielded before, or whether we have resisted, henceforth at any rate by His blessing we may not be overcome of evil, but overcome evil with good.

January, 1873.

SERMON XVI.

THINKING OF GOD.

1 Tim. iv. 15.

"Meditate upon these things; give thyself wholly to them; that thy profiting may appear to all."

ALTHOUGH not taken from the Epistle of the day, this text sums up one of its numerous lessons. The Epistle of St. James is intensely practical. It has offended those who confine the Christian religion to a series of beliefs. Even Luther, carried away by passion and prejudice, spoke of it as "a mere epistle of straw."[1] But he who begins with contempt will never end with insight. No Scripture is of private interpretation. It needs for its study at once a large and a humble heart, a heart too large to be taken in by the empty sciolism of much that calls itself criticism; too humble to mistake for the light of heaven the vaporous gleam of those rash and delusive judgments which rise too often from the marshes of an undisciplined intellect and an unspiritual life. No doubt St. James dwells on the value and necessity of holy works, but such works are alike the fruit and the test of faith, and St. Paul, whom St. James is supposed to controvert, would have been as glad to have subscribed to the emphatic utterance of his brother apostle, that "faith without works is dead, being alone," as St. James would have been to adopt

[1] "Ein recht strohern Epistel."

the watchword of the Epistle to the Romans—" We are justified by faith."

The Epistle of St. James is then "a noble protest against laxity of morals," a protest against imagining ourselves to hold the truths of the Gospel while we neglect its principles and violate its laws. He speaks with all the uncompromising plainness of an honest nature, and all the passionate force of a kindling indignation against the sins which were in his days a blot on the character of those who professed the faith. Then, as now, there was a greed of gain, a yielding to the narrow fasciuations of avarice, which made men forget that the life was more than meat, and which, by robbing their characters of all ardour, of all generosity, of all nobleness, tended to give all their labours to the caterpillar. Then, as now, was prevalent the sin and folly of the unbridled tongue, and so far from "speaking with an accent of heroic verity," men fawned, and flattered, and bit, and devoured, and wished other people dead. Then, as now, men deceived themselves into the fancy that a state of sin was a state of grace, that they could do without God, that formalism would be accepted in lieu of fruit; or, if not, that God was a Being of such boundless facility that though He had written alike in nature, and in conscience, and in Scripture, wrath against unrepentant sin, He meant not wrath, but mercy. But all such beliefs St. James denounces as foolish alike and false, and therefore his Epistle, so far from being, as Luther said, "*planè straminea*," is "*verè aurea*." So far from finding it valueless, it seems to me so pregnant in rich truths that even in the few verses of it read to-day there is far more than could be treated of in a single sermon; nor, with all its apparent simplicity, does it offer any exception to the saying of St. Augustine,

"Marvellous, O God, is the depth of Thy utterances; like a great sea their smiling surface breaks into refreshing ripples at the feet of our little ones, but into its unfathomable depth the wisest may gaze with the shudder of amazement and the thrill of love."

This much, however, we may easily see in the Epistle, viz., that every error it denounces has its immediate root in selfishness, that every good work to which it exhorts demands some form or other of self-denial. And herein it will furnish us all with an easy text for answering the infinitely important question,—Am I, or am I not, doing the will of God? Am I, or am I not, fulfilling the purpose of my life? Is there, or is there not, any real connection between the name I bear and the life I lead? Much, for instance, of our life is spent in speech, so that by our words we shall be justified, and by our words condemned. Now no boy can be unaware of the general character of his speech. Is he a profane and habitual swearer? Does he talk of sacred things lightly? Does he love to speak of things whereof it is a shame to speak? Is he for ever complaining, murmuring, defacing, defaming, sneering, backbiting, wounding with his tongue? If so, he is deceiving himself, his religion is vain. Is he, on the other hand, kind and gentle? does he, as the dearest law of his life, desire innocently, wisely, humbly to make others happy? Has he

> "The love
> By constant watching wise
> To meet the glad with joyful smile,
> And to wipe the weeping eyes,
> And a heart, at leisure from itself
> To soothe and sympathise!"

If not, he is yet a forgetful hearer, not a doer of the Word. Or, once more, what is his aim and object in life? Is it noble or ignoble? Is it selfish or generous? Is it to serve God, or to please himself? If it is all selfish and disobedient, then he is deceiving himself, his religion is vain. And how is it that men holding the faith can thus deceive themselves? The apostle gives us the profound reason, on which for the remainder of our time I wish to dwell. It is because his recognition of God's truth is but like the careless glance which a man might give at the dim metal mirrors of those days, going away to forget immediately what manner of man he was, "But," he adds, "whoso looketh into the perfect law of liberty, and continueth therein, he being not a forgetful hearer, but a doer of the work, this man shall be blessed in his deed."

Now what the apostle means is clear, and what he here urges upon us is that very duty, to the neglect of which more than anything else is due the shallowness and imperfection of our lives. He means that a man's nature is insensibly but inevitably moulded by that which is in his thoughts, and that the lives, even of Christians, are often earthly and sensual because their thoughts are not with things above. Tell me about what you think most frequently and most earnestly, and I will tell you what you are. For your thoughts are the invisible influences which give its complexion to your life, even as the insect is coloured by the leaf on which it feeds. "*Abeunt studia in mores.*" What a man desires to be, that he will be. If his thoughts are ever of sin he will be possessed of sin, he will be the slave of sin; but if his thoughts are ever of God and the things of God, then "with open face, beholding, as in a glass, the glory of the Lord, he will be changed into the same image from glory to glory."

If, then, you would live good or worthy lives, you

must not only not suffer your thoughts to become guilty thoughts, but you must not even allow them to be vacant thoughts. You must fill them with all things true, pure, honourable, lovely, of good report. How can we best do this? Best by forgetting ourselves, best by obliterating our own selfish will and pleasure, best by thinking wholly of others and of God; for in the true life there are three factors—God, the soul, and our fellow men; and our duty to ourselves, our duty to our own souls is best summed up in our duty to God and our duty to our fellow men. This is the lesson which I would desire to impress to-day, and it is a lesson for us all, from the youngest boy to the oldest man.

I. Very few of us, I fear—very few even of the best of us—think enough of God. That He is our Creator, Preserver, Redeemer, that He has the sole and absolute claim upon our love and obedience we all know; but oh! if we all knew this in a true and living sense, how different our lives might be! By not thinking of it often enough, or deeply enough, how mighty a safeguard do we lose! "Hear these three things," said a Jewish rabbi, "and thou shalt eschew transgression:—the All-seeing eye, and the All-hearing ear, and that all thy actions are written in a book." How many a life has been kept humble, and happy, and pure, and sweet, by the living realisation of that one truth, "Thou, God, seest me." You know how you are affected, and made better in all your hearts, by the mere presence of some one to whom you can look up as good and true. You know that there are some even among your school-fellows so upright, so innocent, so single-hearted, that to be with them is to breathe a holier and more wholesome atmosphere. Their influence, something which seems to emanate from them and flow in upon your hearts,

surrounds you with the air of heaven as with the perfume
from the waving of angels' wings. Their divine superiority
to all that is impure or sordid seems to run liquid through
your soul, so that you feel that could you always be
with them, you, too, would grow like them. But these,
alas! are rare in this world, nor can you often be with
them; nor even, were this possible, could they save
your souls, or pay your debt to God. No; but there is
a Presence which not only may be always near you, but
which you cannot escape; there is a Love always over
you, which you may reject, but cannot alienate; there
is a Friend always with you, who, even in your loneliest
moments, leaves you not alone. He is a Friend living
and true; nor is He weak as we are, nor is He, as we
are, ignorant of all the secrets of your hearts. That
Presence, that Love, that Friend is God in Christ. Oh
that you would all cling to His hand! oh that now and
ever you would listen to His voice! What would I not
give to impress upon you, as I feel it, that life without
God is not life, but death; so impress it upon you, by
the aid of God's Holy Spirit, that every Marlborough
boy who hears me might feel, for all his after days,
" Much that I learnt at Marlborough I have forgotten:
by much that I might have learnt I never profited; but
this, at least, I did learn, and this lesson, I trust, has so
permeated my soul, so interpenetrated my whole being,
that I cannot forget it if I would, that life without God
is life without joy, without peace, without happiness,
without hope; and that if I would live a life which
shall come to anything—a life which shall not ' be cast
as rubbish in the void, when God has made the pile
complete'—then I ought daily to offer unto God myself,
my soul and body, a reasonable, holy, and lively sacrifice.
I ought daily to pray to God with all my heart that

prayer of St. Augustine, '*Serva me ab homine malo, i. e. a me ipso.*'" You will go forth into the world; your lives will be in outward circumstances very various; some of you will be rich, some very poor; some will be eminently prosperous, some very sorrowful; and all these things are of no real consequence or importance, because all these things are but for a moment: but the difference between the holy and the unholy life, the difference between the life with God and the life without God— that is the difference between the noon of a burning summer and a midnight without stars.

II. But we can only think of God in relation to our own souls. The soul is no measure of God, and yet to us God can be reflected by the soul alone. Now we see through a glass darkly—it is only then that we shall see face to face. "Through the glass darkly," it has been beautifully said; "but except through the glass in no wise. A tremulous crystal, waved as water, poured out on the ground; you may defile it, despise it, pollute it, at your pleasure and at your peril; for on the peace of these weak waves must all the heaven you shall ever gain be first seen; and through such purity as you can win for those dark waves must all the light of the risen Sun of righteousness be bent down by faint refraction. Cleanse them and calm them as you love your life." But how shall the soul be conscious of that Sun if its own mists blot out its brightness? A man may say, with Diagoras of old, that there is no God, or with Protagoras, that he cannot tell whether there is or not; and for him there *is* no God: and he *cannot* tell whether there is or not. For the secret of the Lord is with them that fear Him, and He will show *them* His covenant; but for those who fear Him not there is no secret; and for them whose foolish hearts are darkened no vision; and for those who listen not, no voice. Do you ask how you shall hear His voice? My brethren, you have heard it often, you do hear it daily, you have heard it from your earliest years. "When I was a little boy of four years old," says one who afterwards grew up to be a good and eminent and courageous man,[1] "one fine day in spring my father led me by the hand to a distant part of the farm, but soon sent me home alone, On the way I had to pass a little pond, then spreading its waters wide; a rhodora in full bloom, a rare flower, which grew only in that locality, attracted my attention and drew me to the spot. I saw a little tortoise sunning himself in the shallow water at the root of the flaming shrub; I lifted the stick I had in my hand to strike the harmless reptile, for though I had never killed any creature yet, I had seen other boys out of sport destroy birds and squirrels and the like, and I felt a desire to follow their wicked example. But all at once something checked my little arm, and a voice within me said loud and clear, 'It is wrong!' I held my uplifted stick in wonder at the new emotion, the consciousness of an involuntary but inward check upon my actions, till the tortoise and the rhodora both vanished from my sight. I hastened home and told the tale to my mother, and asked what it was that told me 'It was wrong.' She wiped a tear from her eye, and taking me in her arms said, 'Some men call it conscience, but I prefer to call it the voice of God in the soul of man. If you listen and obey it, then it will speak clearer and clearer, and always guide you right; but if you turn a deaf ear, or disobey, then it will fade out little by little, and leave you in the dark without a friend. Your life depends on heeding that little voice.' She went her

[1] Theodore Parker.

way," he adds, "careful and troubled about many things, and doubtless pondered them in her motherly heart, while I went off to ponder and think of it in my poor childish way. But I am sure no event in my life has made so deep and lasting an impresion on me." Wise mother! happy son! *Your* life, too, depends on heeding that little voice, for that little voice is the still, small voice of God. If you will heed, if you will obey it, you may never hear it but in whispers of tenderness and warning love; but if you disobey it, oh, with what tones of scorn and menace can it speak, what thunder-crashes of wrath and fear can it roll over the troubled sea of the evil soul. Have none of you ever been guilty of mean actions, which you knew to be mean, spoken wicked words knowing them to be wicked, done that which you would fain hide from every eye? Ah! have you never heard it then? Yes, that voice is the voice of God. You may hush it, stifle it, defy it, drown it deep under rivers of iniquity, but all that is good and dear, all that is true and holy, all in your life which can raise man above beasts that perish, depends upon heeding that little voice.

III. But thirdly, and lastly, in very few words, what will it bid you do? Think of yourself? care only for your own soul? No; but think of God, think how you may make your little life a help and blessing to your fellow men. There has been but one perfect life that has ever been lived on earth, and that was the life of Jesus Christ, the Son of God. And what is the briefest epitome of the working of that life? Is it not that "He went about doing good"? And what was the prevailing principle of that life? Was it not "I must be about my Father's business"? Was it not "My meat is to do the will of Him that sent Me, and to finish

His work"? Yes; depend upon it that the path to a righteous and eternal life lies far more in thinking of God as the living source of all our duties, and of the world as the sphere in which those duties are to be performed, than in thinking only, or even mainly, of our own souls. But observe that we cannot serve man without loving God; our duty to the one must flow from, must be aided by, must be mingled with our duty to the other. When a good and wise modern philosopher summed up the law and duty of life in Altruism—*Vive pour autrui*—" Live for others "—he was guided by the same conception as that of the sweet and noble Hillel, the great president of the Jewish sanhedrin. Hillel and Shammai were the two most eminent of the Jewish rabbis in the days immediately preceding the days of Christ, and there is a celebrated story that a Pagan went to Shammai and asked him to tell him the whole law in one sentence and in one minute. Shammai angrily drove the man from his presence, and he then went to Hillel with the same demand. Hillel, with calm and unruffled temper, replied: "What thou wouldest that another should do to thee, that do thou to him; this is the whole law: the rest is but commentary." Yet both these great teachers—the ancient and the modern—said but half the truth. It is quite true that

"The high desire that others may be blest
Savours of heaven;"

but I do not believe that that high desire can either be originated, or purified, or wisely acted on, apart from God and without the aid of God's Holy Spirit, freely given to them who seek Him. To know the whole truth we must go back to the immortal wisdom of the Decalogue, of which the first table comprises the duty to God, as well as the second the duty to man, and we must go to sit at the feet of our Saviour and hear Him explain it, when He says, " Thou shalt love God with all thy heart and thy neighbour as thyself; on these two commandments hang all the law and the prophets." In that rule all is included. God is there, humanity is there; and to love God and to love man is the completeness of life and the salvation of the soul. He to whom God is the living law, he who has no dearer hope than to suffer all and sacrifice all, if thereby he may benefit others, he to whom life is communion, he to whom heaven means principle, oh! there is no fear but his soul will be bound up in the bundle of life, no fear that God will not cherish it in that day when He maketh up His jewels. Go from this chapel with the humble, hearty prayer to God that you may love Him more, and keep Him more in all your thoughts, and that by doing this your lives, more than ever hitherto, may be unselfish lives, and lives devoted to making all about you better and happier; and by doing this you will be looking into the perfect law of liberty, and, not being a forgetful hearer but a doer of the word, shall be blessed in your deed.

May 18, 1873.

SERMON XVII.

THE OMNIPOTENCE OF PRAYER.

1 Kings iii. 5.

"Ask what I shall give thee."

SOME of you will recognise that these words belong to the story of King Solomon. He had recently succeeded to his father's kingdom, and with royal swiftness and dauntless promptitude had crushed and swept away the guilt and opposition of dangerous schemers. Then, the moment that his throne was established, he went with Oriental pomp to the high palace of Gibeon, and after many a prayer and many a hecatomb for the future of that realm, whose fairest fields and cities he saw from that sacred hill, he retired to rest. And in the night he dreamed a dream, and knew that this dream was a reality. The God whom he had been worshipping came before him and said, "Ask what I shall give thee;" and Solomon, reflecting the yearnings of the day in the visions of the night, asked God to give him a wise and understanding heart. He was but a boy—according to the Jewish historian he was but fifteen years old—and yet he was king over a great nation. He prayed for God's grace that he might govern them aright. And God, approving the petition, gave more besides. Solomon had asked for wisdom, and God gave him besides riches, and long-life, and victorious success. And why was Solomon's prayer so acceptable to God? First, because to Him every true and faithful prayer is so acceptable; and next because of all prayers He loveth best those that are wholly unselfish, those in whom all thoughts of self are absorbed and annihilated in thoughts of Him and of our fellow men.

"Ask what I shall give thee." Had any man ever so splendid an opportunity? It is not only all the kingdoms of the world and the glory of them, but it is that at no price of iniquity; it is that with no concurrent sorrow; it is that with God's peace besides. There is no commoner field for the exercise of fancy than this; and the tales of every land and age have imagined what man would desire if the powers of good, or the powers of evil, offered him a boundless choice. And it is one universal moral of all these tales that unless the choice come immediately from God, it were far better to make no such choice at all. Over and over again, in classic in mediæval, in later stories men are supposed to sell themselves to the Evil Spirit, and it is the object of everyone of those tales to show the crushing ruin and overwhelming bitterness of such an attempt to gain earth at the cost of heaven. The story of Midas, who wished that all which he touched might turn to gold, and was compelled in the agony of starvation to entreat a withdrawal of the gift; the story of Tithonus, who asks for immortality, and pines away to nothing and utter misery, till he too is relieved of his foolish prayer; the story of Gyges, whose ring, which makes him invisible, turns him from an innocent shepherd into a guilty king; the story of Faust, and all the lonely anguish and haunting dread which rise from the satiety of wrong desires—how beauty becomes the curse and ruin of one—and intellect the delusion and snare of another—and power the death and corruption of a third—all these have made a commonplace of the vanity and folly of chance desires,—all a comment on the deep words of the poet,

> "Evertere domos totas optantibus ipsis,
> Di superi."

Yes, all gifts, save the spontaneous gifts of heaven, are like the fairy gold that turns to dust. It is God who weaves the little thread of our destinies, and He weaves it for our best happiness, unless our rude folly mars His plan. The granting of our prayers, even when they are not granted as they sometimes are, in anger, is not always for our immediate happiness. The priestess of Juno asks the goddess to give her choicest blessing to her two duteous boys, and next morning she finds them lying in the temple with a smile upon their faces, but lying in the dreamless sleep of death. All these stories are the echoes of the same sad experience—they are the pagan forms of the Scripture lessons, "Set your affections on things above." And herein too Scripture history and secular history agree. Tiberius, lord of the world, who exhausted earth to gratify his luxury and lust, is known by his own public confession to be the miserablest of men.[1] Abderahman the Magnificent, prosperous in peace and magnificent in war, dreaded by enemies and adored by friends, leaves it upon record that in all his life he can count but fourteen happy days. Solomon, king of Judah, the beautiful, the successful, the renowned, the loved, whose name in all the East is a synonym of magic, magnificence, and splendid ease, has nothing to say of it all, but that saddest of all weary sighs ever breathed by disappointed humanity, "Vanity

[1] Plin., *H. N.* xxviii. 5; Tac. *Ann.* iv. 6.

of vanities, all is vanity." The very worldliest have come to the same confession. One of themselves, even a poet of their own, has said,

"There's not a joy the world can give like those it takes away;"[1]

and another,

"This world is but a fleeting show,
For man's illusion given,
The smiles of joy, the tears of woe
Deceitful shine, deceitful flow,
There's nothing true but heaven."[2]

II. He then whose heart is set—above all if it be inordinately and selfishly set—on earthly joys is not wise. There is, indeed, nothing wrong in praying for such earthly blessings as are simple and innocent; and even if God, in His higher wisdom, does not grant our prayer for them, He will grant us sweeter and better things instead. "Seek first the kingdom of God, and His righteousness, and all these things shall be added unto you." God does not grudge to any of His children the loftier and nobler elements of earthly happiness. Do you think that this glorious offer made Solomon the most favoured of mankind? Do you wish that God would do the same for you? do you think with rapture of what you might ask if He gave to your young lives the same royal choice? Are you certain that you could never neglect so enormous an opportunity? My brethren, the offer comes to you all; it has come in part already, is coming now, will come hereafter, but most decisively now, in these the days of your youth. We were not born assuredly for nothing: it was not for waste, or for wretchedness, or for annihilation—nay, but for happiness, for immortality, for life with Him, that God gave us so many grand faculties. It is true that

[1] Byron.   [2] Moore.

thousands of lives *do* fail, and are wasted; but that is not of God. It was not for this sad fate that God sent us into a world of large air and abounding sunshine; not for this that He encircles our infancy with tenderness, and our youth with care; not for this that Scripture is rich with wisdom, and conscience bright with intuition; not for this that Christ died, and the Holy Spirit came. If all men do not receive those gifts which are God's richest and most priceless blessings, it is not because God will not give them, but because men will not ask for them. St. James, whose blunt, practical directness I pointed out to you some Sundays ago, may well exclaim, "Ye ask, and have not; ye have not, because ye ask not. Ye ask, and receive not, because ye ask amiss." And yet to every one of us God says, "Ask what I shall give thee." To every one of us is the promise true, "Whatsoever ye shall ask the Father in My name He will give it you." Yes, he of you who wills may ransack the very treasures of heaven. The insolent and the faithless, the wilful and the disobedient, cannot enter there; but it opens with heavenly facility to them who will use the golden keys of sincerity and prayer.

III. Let us then apply these thoughts; let us see how they are true, first of things earthly, then of things heavenly.

1. I say that even of things earthly God says to each of you, and most clearly now, "Ask what I shall give thee." Do you not see for your own selves the simple fact that your lives may be very much what you choose to make them? Do you not see that what makes the chief difference between man and man, boy and boy, is not so much diversity of powers as force of purpose, clearness of aim, decision of character? Every day of your life repeats the question, "Ask what I shall give

thee." Every day comes to you like the Sibyl of old to the incredulous king, offering you priceless opportunities of wisdom, and, as they are rejected, tossing them into the flame, and passing away in sorrow or contempt.

"Muffled and dumb,"

says a modern poet,

> "The hypocritic days,
> And marching single in an endless file,
> Bring diadems or fagots in their hands.
> To each they offer gifts after his will—
> Bread, kingdoms, stars, and heaven that holds them all.
> I, in my pleachëd garden, watched the pomp,
> Forgot my morning wishes, hastily
> Took a few herbs and apples, and the day
> Turned and departed silent: I too late
> Under her solemn fillet saw the scorn." [1]

Of course you will see at a glance that asking God for these gifts at the hands of time or opportunity does not mean *mere* asking; that he who asks must, if his prayer is to be listened to, be sincere in his petition, and if he be sincere, will naturally and necessarily take the means which God appoints. God only helps those who help themselves. Were it not so, if vice could, with a wish, yawn into being the rewards of virtue; if sluggishness could, at a touch, appropriate to itself the gifts of toil: then prayer would corrupt the world. But God will not listen to a prayer that is not a prayer; nor will He regard as a prayer the drawling formula of the sluggard or the sly falsehood of the hypocrite. Action, effort, perseverance: these are the touchstones that test the pure gold of sincerity. Pagans saw something of the truth. "To the persevering man," says the Persian poet, "the blessed immortals are swift;" and one of the most vigorous of the Roman emperors died

[1] Emerson.

with the grand word "*laboremus*" on his lips. And labour may do much.; but if we add the *oremus* to the *laboremus*, then the two are simply irresistible. The race is not to the swift, nor the battle to the strong, but to the diligent and to the prayerful. As for vulgarer and purely earthly ends, any one who chooses to obtain them *can* obtain them. If any of you cared to make to-day so poor a vow, as that you would die rich, there is no doubt that you could die rich. If any of you willed to-day to force your path to power and distinction, there is no doubt that you could so force on to power and distinction. Nature will give you nothing for nothing. She offers you her gifts clenched tight in a granite hand, and before you can have them you must force that hand open by sheer labour. Say what you will have, pay the price, and she will give it you; she will give it you, although she warns you beforehand, that if rank, and wealth, and fame, and ease, are what you long for, these, without God's blessing, are apples of Sodom filled with bitter dust. But take a better case—the case of many of you. You are here at school; certain studies are set before you, certain opportunities given you, certain rewards offered. Your interest and your duty coincide in urging you to use these advantages, to work, to do your best. Your interest,—because every term wasted now may mean a year of sorrow and anxiety; and every year wasted now may mean ten years of disappointment and hope deferred hereafter; and a school life wasted now may mean a man's life of useless mediocrity and repining struggle. And your duty,—because in this are involved the intense wish of your parents, the gratitude you owe to friends, the earnest hopes of your masters, the honour of a school you ought to love, the distinct indications of the voice of God. Now, if neither interest

nor duty move you, you must be of poor natures. None
but bad influences are on the other side. Idleness
pleading the charms of sloth; conceit inflating with a
silly self-satisfaction; despair saying "I cannot;" pride
saying "I will not." It is the lotos-fruit, and the
charmed cup, and the siren song, set in competition with
the voices of heaven; and you may think the lotos-
fruit delightful, but it means exile; and the charmed
cup sweet, but it means degradation; and the siren
song enchanting, but it means death and shipwreck on
the desolate and loathly shore. Oh yes, this is all more
or less possible, and the outcome of it is a life wasted
for want of humility or want of purpose. But I say—
for I have often and often witnessed it, and prophesied
it, and been true in my prophecy—that any boy who
steadfastly resists those evil influences, any boy who
works and denies himself, and prays to God to bless
and help him, may win if he will. Whole-heartedness,
manly determination, noble resolve, above all, the
humility which always accompanies true worth,—I
would rather possess these a thousand times, and I
should feel certain that, even for worldly success, they
are infinitely more valuable than the mere flash in the
pan of a conceited cleverness. The "modesty of fearful
duty" is more blessed of God, and more beloved of man,
and more valued even by the world, than the raw
presumption of a shallow quickness, and the crude
self-confidence of an ignorance which takes itself for
knowledge. I say that these things will succeed; but
even if they do not—and of success we all think far too
much—they at least involve that holy self-control, that
contentedness of heart, that capacity of service, which
are more golden than earthly gold, and are the success
of heaven itself. So that to the youngest and most

self-distrustful boy here I say, My child, doubt not, only believe; cast your bread on the waters, you will find it after many days. God says, "Ask what I shall give thee." Ask in faith, nothing doubting, and do your duty while you ask, and then not only have you no need to envy the gifts of any living man, but the very angels up in heaven—even those nearest to the throne, *lucentes et ardentes*, the shining spirits of knowledge, the burning spirits of love — might, with no sigh, exchange their lot with yours.

2. And though I believe, nay, though I know, this to be true of earthly things, it is ten times more indisputably true of the better and the heavenly. Oh, covet earnestly the best gifts, and you shall have them. Here God says to you with yet more earnest insistency, "Ask what I shall give thee." Dost thou love uprightness? Ask it, *will* it, and thou shalt be upright. Dost thou love purity? Ask it, will it, and thou shalt be pure. Dost thou feel the high ideal of moral nobleness? Ask for it, will it, and thou shalt be noble. Were an angel to glide down upon the sunbeams, and offer you anything which you sincerely desired, would you not think it at once ungrateful and senseless to refuse? Is it less senseless to refuse when God offers you an immortality of blessedness, and garlands that cannot fade? Perhaps you have lost the wish for such blessings, as the drunkard, loving only that which is destroying him, loathes the pure water of the springs. Well, God can restore you the moral and the spiritual taste yet undepraved. Let the "sorrow rise from beneath," and the "consolation will meet it from above." He offers it you again to-day. Pointing to the fair fruits of the Spirit which grow upon the Tree of Life; pointing to the river of the water of life, clear as crystal, flowing out of the

throne of God and of the Lamb ; pointing to the heaven of radiant peace which shines in every cleansed and forgiven heart; pointing to the peace which passeth all understanding, and which man can neither give nor take away, He has said to you often from your childhood, He says to you once more in this sacred place to-day, "*Ask what I shall give thee.*" He said it to Solomon in the dim visions of the night, He says it to us by the voice of His Eternal Son. "Ask, and it shall be given you; seek, and ye shall find; knock, and it shall be opened unto you: for every one that asketh receiveth; and he that seeketh findeth ; and to him that knocketh it shall be opened."

June 15th, 1873.

SERMON XVIII.

SOWING AMONG THORNS.

JER. iv. 3.

" Thus saith the Lord, Break up your fallow ground, and sow not among thorns."

LAST Sunday I spoke to you of the first part of this text, and tried to urge upon you as its message that you should, with all your hearts and all your souls set yourselves to the fresh duties which now, at the beginning of another term, devolve upon you here. The second half of the text seems appropriate for to-day; it dwells, not on the need for labour, but on a danger which, if neglected, would render that toil unfruitful. It warns you that it is not enough to break up your fallow ground, nor even to sow good seed; but that the ground must be a clean fallow—that it must be free from pre-occupations—that there must be room for the good seed to grow.

The metaphor must be clear to the youngest boy. The field is the human heart; the seed is the word and the will of God; the harvest is your sanctification. When the heart is simple, and innocent, and free from wrong, there are no thorns there; it is as Paradise before Adam fell; nothing grows in that heavenly garden but the golden fruits of the Spirit and the fair flowers of grace. But when man fell, the ground was cursed;

thorns and thistles grew in it; only by the sweat of his brow could man wring from it the bread of life. Even so it is with all of us. When, in growing years, we pass forth out of the Paradise of our early innocence, the soil of the heart is more or less encumbered; the seeds and roots of evil things are in it; those evil things must be cleared away, must, at the worst, be utterly kept down, or the good seed will produce nothing but barren and blighted ears.

You will all remember the Parable of the Sower. There some of the seed falls upon ground so bare that it will not grow at all, and the fowls of the air carry it away; just as there are some natures so callous, so past feeling as to seem incapable of even a good impression. And other seed fell on stony grounds, on natures so thin, so shallow, so poverty-stricken, that the seed appears only to wither, scorched by the first sun, because it has no strengthening root. And other seed fell among thorns. Not, observe, on full-grown thorns—no sower would be so senseless as to sow seed there—but on thorn-roots lying under the surface, hidden, unnoticed, of which we are afterwards told that they sprang up. Yes, the soil looked good enough, but roots of bitterness were in it, and under it. The fallow had been broken up, ploughed it had been and harrowed, but not deeply, not resolutely, not faithfully enough; and so when the sunbeams fell on it, and it was watered from above with the gracious dews of God, the seed grew indeed, but the thorns grew also, and stronger and more rapidly, and the more they grew the more they robbed the good seed of heat, and light, and moisture, and so absorbed into their own evil nature the whole strength and energy of the soil, that the green blade could never become the ripened ear, and at last, as you looked upon the field, you could hardly tell that there had been corn in it at all;

> "Things rank and gross in nature
> Possessed it merely."

Now I think that in this part of the Parable, and in our text, there is a special lesson, because the facts of which it warns us are specially common. Hard and trodden soils—dull and heavy as the fool's heart—there are; thin and shallow soils, on which only hunger-bitten and blighted harvests grow, there are; and, thank God, there are also soils rich, and good, and deep, which bring forth fruit to perfection; but commoner perhaps than any of these are those soils in which the tares and wheat grow side by side, and the crisis of time and of eternity depends on *this*,—whether we suffer the tares or the wheat to prevail. Do not many of you feel it to be so? Do you not, as I speak, recognise within you this duality of nature? Do you not at some times feel yourselves capable of sinking to almost any depth of folly and of degradation, while at other times the grace of God seems to be stirring sensibly within your heart, and everything sweetest, and noblest, and even saintliest seems naturally within your reach? Have you never felt with St. Paul, "the good which I would, I do not; the evil which I would not, that I do"? Yes, I am well assured that you all feel that there is an Adam, and there is a Christ within you all, that "the angel has you by the hand and the serpent by the heart," and that you, like the great King who heard the preacher dwell on the new man and the old man within us, feel ready to exchaim, "I recognise those two men." Now the thorns of the parable, and of the prophet's metaphor, are that evil nature, these evil impulses; the wrong which struggles within you, and which, if not suppressed, if not to the utmost of your power eradicated will render it impossible for the good to grow. This is one of the sternest, strongest, plainest lessons of life. There are in every man, said the Jewish rabbis, two impulses, the good and the evil impulse,[1] and he who offers to God his evil impulse offers the best of all sacrifices. Yes, this self-sacrifice is one of the most excellent as well as one of the necessary lessons. He who has not understood the lesson which all nature tells him, "you must abstain," "you must give up,"—or, as our Lord expressed it, "you must sell all that you have," "you must deny yourself," "you must take up the cross,"—has as yet learnt nothing of life's meaning. He has not yet learnt what every good man must learn, that life is a battle, a struggle, the cultivation of a stubborn soil, a service in an enemy's country in time of war, where carelessness is danger, and sleep is death.

I hope then that you will understand something of what is meant by this warning, "And sow not among thorns." To sow among thorns will be to render the harvest of your lives impossible; to make the soil of your hearts a wasted spot in God's garden; unfruitful, rank with poisonous berries and pernicious weeds; "the miry places thereof, and the marishes thereof shall not be healed, they shall be given to salt." If then you are in earnest, beware that there be not—hidden deep under the soil of your heart—any sins and tendencies, any desires or passions, any vanities or lusts, which you have not as it were stubbed up, but which remain as a source of special danger; looking diligently lest any of you fail of the grace of God; lest any root of bitterness springing up trouble you, and thereby many be defiled.

[1] *Jezer tôbh* and *Jezer ha-ra*.

And to fix this warning more deeply in your hearts, let me ask you whether even the experience of this week since your return may not have put for you a real emphasis into the words, "Sow not among thorns ?" All of you I am sure returned here with the simple and sincere *purpose*, or at the lowest, *wish*, to be better and to do better than before. Has that resolution been for any of you as the morning cloud, and as the early dew? Have you found yourself slipping insensibly, and unchanged, with fatal facility, into the old faults, the old errors, the old sins? Perhaps last term you had been an idle boy; you had made no real progress; you had wasted the term in games, in frivolities, in amusements; you had not made it a help for you in the future; you had only grieved your parents in it and disgusted yourself: it was a year that the locust had eaten. Well, you came back prepared for one more effort: you would do better; you would avail yourself of this fresh chance; you would turn over a new leaf; you would not be deaf to what, on this matter, conscience said. But as the old temptations begin to surround you, the old amusements to turn you aside, the old indolence to creep over you the old claims of gossip, procrastination, half-heartedness, self-indulgence, to make themselves heard, have you not already begun to succumb? Alas! he who has once fed on the lotos-fruit of indolence too easily craves for it again ! Or perhaps your temptation was quite different;—it was to irritability of language, violence of temper, headstrong want of consideration for others, a tendency to unjust hatreds and bitter words. And you had meant when you came back this time to keep a watch over the door of your lips, and some control over the passion of your heart. Yet when something you did not like was said or done, have you not yielded perhaps already to the old fault ? Alas, "*lucerna recens extincta, levi flatu accenditur;*" when a candle is but just extinguished, how does a mere breath make it flame again! Or, once more, your temptation—and it would be a foolish and fatal hypocrisy to assume the absence of such temptations—had been to desecrate the temple of your soul by dwelling on forbidden images and impure desires; but, knowing the stain and the shame and the curse of this, you meant now to be more watchful, more temperate, more prayerful, that yours, by the aid of God's Holy Spirit, might be the clean heart and the right spirit within you; but there came some wicked suggestion, some neglected prayer, and out of your heart have proceeded evil thoughts. Alas! he who has lifted to his lips the poisoned chalice finds it hard to resist its brutalising power. And so it may be that many of you have even already experienced the truth, which must come to the unbeliever with despairing force, but which should only stimulate the Christian to more hopeful effort, that, save for God's special grace on your own efforts, your destiny has been already decided by yourselves; you have increased your own perils, diminished your own force. If this has been so with you,—if in any way, in spite of resolutions which were all too feeble, you have realised already your own infirmity,—and if, recognising it, you have sought to find its cause, then you will know why the prophet says to you, "Break up your fallow ground, and sow not among thorns." He says it because no harvests can grow on the half-cleared soil. What must you do to those hidden thorn-roots? You must do what the husbandman does. Have you never seen how he deals with some hard, stubborn fibrous root which he finds in the ground? He dashes it to pieces with his pickaxe, he stubbs it up with the spade and hoe; he tears it out with main force; he burns the vicious weed out of the soil with fire. You must do the same; you must —Christ Himself has said it—give up; cut off,—rather than perish, rather than yield yourself the willing slave of sin,—you must cut off the right hand, pluck out the right eye.

As the outcome, then, of all that I have said, I would urge upon you two thoughts, which, stated in simplest and plainest language, may be good for you to take to heart.

I. First, then, make your choice now, and for ever. In the field of your life, which shall grow, wheat or tares? that is, shall it be death or life? shall it be good or evil? shall it be light or darkness? shall it be shame or peace? shall your life be pure or debased, useful or pernicious, selfish or devoted? Some men have died, and have left the world better for them; their goodness has fertilised the ages as with a refreshing stream, and, "having planted many a rose of Sharon, and made their little portion of the desert smile, they departed in the faith that the green margin would spread as the seasons of God came round, till earth ended with Eden as it began;" and other men have died, whose memory and whose wickedness have been as a taint in the pure air, and a poison in the crystal stream. To which class will you belong? The decision of that question will probably depend in large measure on these schoolboy years. Oh, make your choice now and for ever! Make your choice? Nay, it is made for you,—by every fact in your life from the cradle until now,—by your birth in a Christian land, by your education in a Christian school, by your baptismal admission into the Christian

Church,—you have been signed, and sealed, and chosen for God, you have seen His face, and His name is on your foreheads. For this He made you; for this His Son died for you; for this the Spirit pleads with you. I cannot say to you, How long halt ye between two opinions? If the Lord be God, follow Him, but if Baal, then follow him. For God is your God, and every hymn you sing in His praise, and every morn and eve you meet in this chapel, and every Sunday that you worship, and every Holy Communion of which you partake, and every time you kneel "by the altar of your own bedsides," you acknowledge your allegiance to Him, you say, or profess to say, "Oh God, Thou art my God, early will I seek Thee." But the choice must not only, my brethren, be made for you, but made by you; it must be a choice made not only with your lips, but in your lives, it must be a choice more earnest, more conscious, more determinate. Your life must be a life in earnest; a life not from hand to mouth; a life not of easy yesterdays and confident to-morrows; but as a pilgrim's journey—as a soldier's battle—a toil as of the faithful husbandmen from summer to summer and from dawn to night. Oh that ere you leave this chapel there might be on some of your minds at least an inflashing of this truth, and that when you kneel down, as you all will do, you would offer up yourselves, your souls, and bodies to your Heavenly Father, and say, "O God, my heart is ready, my heart is ready; by the blood of Christ, oh cleanse it; by His Spirit strengthen it; for His sake, oh accept it, make it Thine."

II. And the second lesson is, Let the choice be absolute. No lukewarmness—neither cold nor hot; no backward glance at the guilty city. No tampering with the accursed thing; no truce with Canaan; no weak attempt to serve two masters; no wretched and wavering wish to grow both tares and wheat. Oh do not, my brethren, fall into that fatal and desperate error which maims the usefulness and mars the peace of so many lives,—the error of supposing that you can keep your sin and your Saviour,—that there can be any compromise in your heart between good and evil,—that good and evil may dwell in that heart side by side without being forced to wrestle in deadly antagonism till one has the undisputed sway,—that you can be a child of God, and yet, each time the temptation comes upon you, can reject His mercy and break His law. "When any one says I will sin and repent afterwards," says an ancient Jewish book, "and does this a second time, and again does the same, no more strength for repentance is granted him." For this is *willing* sin; it is to sell yourself to work wickedly. Therefore, as Israel was bidden to exterminate the guilty Canaanites, or they would be corrupted by them, so you must destroy the sins you best love, or they will destroy you. Take then the Cross; as our fathers smote with sword and battle-axe to free Palestine from Paynim feet, so do you be brave and dauntless in the great crusade for the Holy Land of your soul. Fight, and fight hard; strike, and strike home for God.

My brethren, believe me, in conclusion, that there is nothing doubtful about what I have said. It is certain. It is the truth of God. You must not sow among thorns; and to dig out the thorns is not easy. But one word, let me add, lest any of you be discouraged. If you fall into a sin of weakness, repent indeed, and humble yourself before God, but do not despair; say indeed it is mine own infirmity, but remember the years of the right hand of the Most Highest. A good man may sin, and when he sins God will not spare him; but —when he falls,—then from the earth which his knees have touched in prayer, he rises, Antæus-like, with tenfold strength, and says with a voice whose resolution no sobs can choke, "Rejoice not over me, Satan, mine enemy, for when I fall I shall rise again." It is said of the best riders that they know how to fall. Do not think it beneath the dignity, I had almost said the awfulness of my subject, if for the encouragement of those who are helpless because they fail so often in the effort to do right, I draw an illustration from common life. I would say then to every Christian boy, as was said by one of the most famous of modern hunters, you must expect a fall sometimes, but with a fall you may get over anything. He himself had been thrown no less than seventy times in his life, but the end was that he could ride anywhere. He rode at the most tremendous leaps, and never even cast a glance back at them. And what was his secret—"Fling your heart over," he used to say, "and your horse will follow." I take the everyday illustration, and I say to you, In spite of hindrances in the present, in spite of difficulties in the future, in spite of obstacles from the past, press forward in God's service, press forward in your Saviour's strength, *fling your heart over*, and nothing shall stop you in your heavenward course.

September 28th, 1878.

SERMON XIX.

HOW TO KEEP GOOD RESOLUTIONS.

2 KINGS x. 15.

" Is thine heart right ? "

THE words, my brethren, are a fragment: I have dissevered them from their context; I have made them subserve to a meaning not quite identical with that in which they were spoken. But still they formulate a solemn question, well suited for this day. Imagine that the guardian angel of your life and destiny—nay, imagine that the God and Father who created you, the Saviour who died for you, the Holy Spirit who dwelleth in the temple of all undesecrated hearts—is asking you here and now this short question: "*Is thine heart right?*" and let your consciences answer in the silence, and answer clear and true.

The answer of him to whom the question was addressed was, "It is."—"If it be, give me thine hand. And he gave him his hand; and he took him up to him into the chariot. And he said, Come with me, and see my zeal for the Lord." Let the rude fragment of a cruel history serve in some sort as a symbol or allegory of nobler things. Whatever were the sins and errors of these, who thus drove forth to trample upon idolatry and deal retribution upon crime, let us at least be like them in this, that, with united efforts, with earnest zeal, with unswerving purpose, we set forth once more to-day to fight, in our own hearts and in the world around us, the battle of the Lord of Hosts. Whether we can do this—whether we are on the Lord's side at all, or in the ranks, secret or open, of His enemies—depends on the truth with which we can answer this question: "Is thine heart right?"

And I do not doubt that most of you would answer with Jehonadab the son of Rechab, "It is." Sitting here in God's holy place, now on the first Sunday of a new, and what may be, I trust, please God, a happy term—now so shortly after the confirmation of many of you, now before the Holy Communion of the supper of the Lord—you would scarcely hesitate, any one of you, to answer—in different tones, indeed, and with very different degrees of earnestness and sincerity, but still to answer—"Yes, my heart is right; my mind is set upon righteousness; I do think, or wish to think, the thing that is right."

Yes, my brethren, but what I want to make you see and feel this morning is, that there is all the difference in the world between the different ways in which this answer is spoken; and that there is only one way, only one meaning, in which it can be indeed spoken honestly, as before God, from the ground of the heart.

1. There is, for instance, the careless, indifferent, frivolous answer; the answer of those who have hitherto resisted the grace of God, and who, finding that they can sin as yet with but little sorrow, neither know nor really care what religion means. It is the answer of the gay young prodigal ere the famine has come, and

while in the genial flush of youth and pleasure he sits at the lighted banquet, and does not dream that there lurks in the winecup a deadly poison, and that those bad friends, with their false caresses and the lie upon their smiling faces, are but a wretched company of the living dead. Untrained as yet in the meaning and discipline of life; ignorant as yet of what may be its fatal import; not believing as yet that the sunshine of youth is but a transient gleam, and that the blue heaven from which it falls is the heaven of eternity; such as these would give the answer very carelessly. "Is my heart right? Yes, I suppose so. I have still some fragments of memory about things which I learnt when I was yet a child, and these serve me as a sort of religion. I have not quite forgotten what my mother taught me when once, more innocent than now, I lifted my little hands in prayer. I do not love evil for its own sake. There are some wrong things that I would not do. I am not worse than he, or he, or he. If I am not particularly good, neither am I entirely bad," and so on, and so on. One knows too well the hollow ring of words like these. Ah, my brethren, do you think that this is enough? that this answer will do? Alas! such an answer means nothing, or worse than nothing. Do not deceive yourself with the notion that it implies the faintest effort. To Him indeed who readeth your heart, to Him before whose eye all your real thoughts lie naked and open, it has a meaning, but it is an evil one. In your yes He reads no. In your "My heart is right," He reads that it is "deceitful above all things, and desperately wicked." To Him your answer means nothing more nor less than this: "I will continue in sin," "There is no God," or "Tush! if there be, He is far away, and careth not for it." And if this be indeed the real meaning of any answer, then if the word "beware" were in the thunder's mouth it could not speak too loudly: for this is the beginning of the fatal history of every lost and ruined soul, it is the slope of the smooth bright river, as in broad, unbroken sheet it rushes in silence to the cataract. "Every man is tempted when he is drawn away of his own lust, and enticed. Then when lust hath conceived, it bringeth forth sin: and sin, when it is finished, bringeth forth death."

II. 1. Let us take another answer, not like the last, wholly hollow and insincere, but too impulsive, too confident. "Is thine heart right?" "Yes," another will say, "I do sincerely dislike what is bad, and I do rather despise myself for the weakness with which I have yielded to it. And I mean to be quite different now. Last term I had such and such a companion, such and such an excuse, such and such a hindrance; I began badly, and could not break off from a false start: but this is a new term, I will do better; I will be less idle, or less passionate, or less self-indulgent," or less whatever his special fault has been. You will? his guardian angel might say to such a one; but for how long? and in whose strength? In your own strength, and only until the next temptation comes? You will? and do you know what this answer involves? Do you know that it means not merely a weak wish, but a strong desire; not only a strong desire, but a resolute effort; not only even a resolute effort, but an intense and absorbing purpose. It means the girded loin, and the burning lamp, and the race continued though the feet totter and the breath sobs. Alas, it is so easy to be good when there is no temptation near. The man or the boy, for instance, who, with thankful heart and weakened frame, rises from the bed of long and dangerous sickness—who, perhaps, in the lonely hours of imminent death has thought with shame and sorrow over his sinful life—that man or boy thinks it cannot be but that henceforth he shall be a changed character; but is he so always? When the voice of the siren is loud again, when the full tide of blood runs in the healthy veins, have you never known cases in which he has only risen from the bed, well-nigh of death, to be an open backslider, worse even than before? My brethren, a weak resolve, a half resolve, a mere verbal resolve, a resolve made in your own strength, of what value is it? Have you never heard, or have you never understood, the deep-sighted proverb, that "Hell is paved with good intentions"? Let me take no very bad and grievous case, no case of shameful degradation or deadly sin, but a common every-day case of a life not strong in duty—a life that not a few, perhaps, among you may recognise as your own especial danger—a danger to be overcome. Such a boy at the beginning of this new term has formed, or thinks he has formed, a sort of half-resolution to improve, and not to waste yet another of his few precious years of happy life and golden opportunity. He begins well for the first few days; he springs up cheerfully and manfully in the morning in good time, with no lazy self-indulgent lingering; he says his prayers humbly and reverently; he kneels punctually in chapel; his lesson has been honestly prepared; he succeeds, and thinks that he is entering on a better state of things, and that this term *at last* is going to be a well-spent, and faithful, and honourable one. It goes on for a few days. But it hardly needs even a temptation to make him fall away; if a temptation does come, however trivial, his good purpose slips into instant ashes, like tow at the very breath of fire. But even if no special temptation comes, there is no perseverance, no solidity, no manly consistence in his brief improvement. One morning all is done a little later; the rising begins to get hurried and slovenly; the morning prayer first slurred over, then shortened, then neglected; unprepared, he meets the temptations of the day; the work is put off or done anyhow; the playtime unduly lengthened; the novel not laid aside; the duty forgotten or neglected. He sinks lower and lower, the esteem of his teachers is lost, his self-respect is wholly weakened, and so, little by little, ever little by little, the old story is renewed again, and the new term is wasted like the old; and, like the waves of a silent river, irrevocable time flows on, and the careless boy enters the hard struggle of life an irresolute, ignorant, half-armed man. Yes, little by little, irrevocable time flows on; the twenty-four hours of the day seem a long time, and yet it is the second hand that does it; it is all traversed, as has well been said, by tiniest tickings of the clock. And life is but a day like this, and the days are its seconds, and the terms its hours; and the morning of its boyhood, and its manhood's noon, soon merge, merge insensibly, into the chill grey evening and darkened close.

> "To-morrow, and to-morrow, and to-morrow,
> Creeps in this petty pace from day to-day
> To the last syllable of recorded time;
> And all our yesterdays have lighted fools
> The way to dusty death."

2. I have purposely chosen a minor instance; but how is it when things are worse? where the temptation is more serious? the fall more heinous? How is it when Satan, having for a time cunningly forborne to startle his victim with any great sin, with any glaring or violent

temptations, suddenly confronts his biased will and his
nerveless heart, and pushes him with all the dead weight
of reiterated weaknesses into some sin of a moment
which is the curse and anguish of a life? Has there
not been a fearful answer then to the question "Is
thine heart right?" and has not that answer been quite
other than that which some of you may quite honestly
think that you are giving now? And are such warnings
vain? Would not the experience of past terms empha-
sise them to some of you? Have you not on the first
Sundays of other terms meant well, and yet not done well,
and the idle been idle, and the weak weak, and the unjust
unjust, and the filthy filthy still? And of the hundreds
and hundreds who have sat before you on those same
benches, have none gone through the same life history?
have none left the school after a career ungrateful, discreditable, wasted, having only pained the hearts of
those who loved them? And have not others sat on
those benches as new boys, hopeful perhaps and happy,
who yet grow up to be false, and treacherous, and to set
shameful examples, and to do the devil's work, and to
carry with them through life the extreme malediction
which lights and shall light upon those who, in their
selfish depravity, have wilfully led others into sin?
Few, thank God, very, very few; but still some; and
let those some be to some—yea, to all of you and of us
—a warning deeper than death. I have seen the tears
of mothers over their dead sons' grave; but the anguish
of bereavement melts soon into the golden light of a
faith full of immortality; and all of you who have the
spell of home affection in your hearts, remember this—
that less salt and less bitter are the tears which wet a
mother's cheek, and less envenomed is the agony which
lacerates a father's heart, over a dying child than over

a child that causeth shame; and many and many of your parents would echo with all their souls the saying of Queen Blanche, the mother of St. Louis of France, that she would rather see her son a corpse at her feet than know that he had committed a deadly sin.

III. "Is thine heart right?" Let us take one more answer: some may answer carelessly; some presumptuously; but will not many of you—yes, I am very sure you will—answer in a deeper, humbler, sincerer, more serious spirit? "Yes," you will say, "I am weak, I know, and sinful; and bitter experience has taught me that my own good resolutions are as the morning cloud and as the early dew. They have been so because at former times I have not watched enough or prayed enough, or listened enough to the voice of conscience, and of God's Holy Spirit within my soul. But I am sorry—though my life has not been always right, yet I hope, I trust, that my heart is right—it is not hard. I do hate the thing that is evil; I am not blinded by self-conceit and sin. And God, I know has not forsaken me. Here, like a green leaf fresh-plucked from the Tree of Life, He gives me now a new term, a new hope, a new chance; and even now will I offer to Him a silent prayer, and will cry to Him, Oh, my God, my Father, lead back to Thyself thy sinful and wandering child. Here is my wilful, sinful heart; make it humble, and strong, and faithful unto Thee. Here is my poor stained and feeble life; take it, and make it pure and noble. My own strength, O Lord, is perfect weakness; my own wisdom is utter folly; my own righteousness is utter sin: but I lift up mine eyes unto the hills whence cometh my help, "Make me to do the thing that pleaseth Thee, for Thou art my

God. Let Thy loving Spirit lead me into the land of righteousness."

This, my brethren, this is the tone and spirit of the answer, which, would to God we all might make; because, if any resolve in this spirit, God will help him. He will lift up the hands that hang down, and strengthen the feeble knees. Fear not thou who canst answer thus. The ocean of life is large, and thy little boat is small, and there has been many and many a terrible and disastrous shipwreck on those rough waves; but though the great winds blow and the angry billows roll, God shall keep fast thy feeble hand upon the guiding helm, and thou shalt reach the safe haven where thou wouldst be, and out of the gossamer threads of thy weak and wavering will, He will forge the iron cables which shall moor thee safe to that everlasting Hope, which is an anchor of the soul.

With such thoughts, with such prayers, with such purposes, with the determination more and more earnestly to make our hearts right before God—humble, earnest, watchful—let us kneel at the Holy Table of the Lord. Nowhere can we better consecrate our hearts than there. Oh, let every one of us kneel there, meaning indeed to consecrate ourselves,—our souls and bodies, this term and all the rest of our lives—to Him who created and Him who died for us. Let it be to us an Eucharist, a feast of deep thankfulness to God for His many mercies to us and to our school; let it be to us a Communion, to bind us all more and more closely together in the bonds of Christian fellowship, eager to stand by one another, to wish each other prosperity, to do each other good; above all may it be to us a memorial of our Lord and Saviour Jesus Christ. If we follow the footsteps of His blessed life, they may lead us indeed, at times into sad and lonely places, and there may be times when we, like many of earth's noblest, may have to tread them with bleeding feet. But what matters it? If we walk in those footsteps, we shall see God's face, and His name shall be in our foreheads, and they shall lead us at last to the realms of everlasting joy.

May 10th, 1874.

SERMON XX.

THE OBJECTS OF SCHOOL LIFE.

1 KINGS xix. 13.

" There came a voice unto him and said, What doest thou here ?"

I ISOLATE these words from their splendid context, upon which I am not going to touch. To-day the Voice comes, not to Elijah in the wilderness, but to us in this chapel; and, in answer to its appeal, we must try to understand our position, here and now, in all its definiteness. We lose by not reminding ourselves of our special duties; we lose by not going up into the tribunal of our own consciences, and setting ourselves before ourselves;[1] we lose by laying to our souls the flattering unction of general professions, and not rigidly bringing them to bear on daily acts. We should do our work, I think better, I am sure we should deceive ourselves less—if we asked ourselves, "Am I, day by day, doing my day's task in the little corner of the vineyard which God has given me to cultivate? and am I doing it, not perfunctorily, but faithfully, not discontentedly, but humbly, not with eyeservice, but in singleness of heart?" If we can put those questions to ourselves very searchingly, and still answer them with a clear conscience, it is enough. Sloth, discontent, disobedience, disloyalty to duty,—

[1] St. Augustine.

these torture and scourge the souls of those who yield to them; but, whether others count a man fortunate or unfortunate, and whether the elements of earthly happiness be largely or but very sparingly within his reach, yet the world,—were it "one entire and perfect chrysolite"—were all too little to give in exchange for that deep peace which God sheds into the inmost soul of that man who has simplified every other end and hope in life to this:—to do God's will from the ground of the heart,—to show that we love the Father whom we have not seen, by loving, by serving, by helping in the holy life, our brother whom we have seen.

I. To-day, then, if we will hear God's voice asking us "What doest thou here?" let us not harden our hearts. What, for instance, does the Lord require of *us* who are set over you? To feed the flock of God which is among us; to bear every labour, to make every sacrifice; to be instant in season and out of season; to reprove, rebuke, exhort; to remind ourselves often how deep and wide are the interests entrusted to us, how strict and solemn is the account which we must one day give before the judgment seat of Christ:—are not these *our* duties? It may be that, like all duties in any sphere of life, they may be often irksome and discouraging; it may be that we may see the tares springing up in rank growth among the good seed which we have sown; it may be that childish frivolity, that subtle impurity, that want of dignity, and want of loyalty, and want of gratitude, may often make us sad at heart: but results are not in our hands, efforts are; and what God requires of all of us is effort, not result; and the very best efforts of the very greatest and holiest men have often been exactly those which, from the Cross of Christ downwards, have often seemed to fail the most; so that all we have to do is to work on always, undiscouraged, in the unalterable conviction that, in the course of duty, failure can never be more than apparent, and that to the end of time, because God is God, evil things shall perish, but " good deeds cannot die." [1]

II. But if these are *our* duties, what are *yours ?*

(a) In the first and most everyday sense, you are here to be taught, to learn, *i.e.*, to store and to enlighten your minds, and to be saved from that low and dangerous ignorance which is at once a misery and a disgrace. *What* you are taught is not altogether a matter of choice, either for us or for you. In all its main outlines, at any rate, it is dictated to us by the wisdom of past experience in many ages, and by the exigencies of that which is immediately needful for you in this. Yet it is only the very shallow, or, which is much the same thing, the very conceited, who can fail to see that the range of subjects to which you are here introduced is sufficient to last you for a life. History, the story of nations, so inexhaustible in moral interest, so rich in spiritual lessons ; Divinity, the study of our relation to God, and of the deepest utterances of His Eternal Spirit to the heart of man ; Science in all its branches whether it deal with forms and numbers, or with those laws which God's own hand has written on the stars of heaven and the stone tablets of the earth ; Language, the common instrument of every intelligent being that lives and thinks ; Antiquity, with its immortal lessons of many races, and specially of "the beauty which was Greece and the grandeur which was Rome;"—there is not one of these studies which might not with profit occupy the intellect during a well-spent and serviceable life ; not one which may not be, to the holy and the humble, " a sunbeam from

[1] Tennyson, *The Princess.*

the Father of Lights." And to profit in any one of these you must begin early. There are some things which, if you have not learnt thoroughly before the age of twelve, you will hardly learn thoroughly at all; there are many others which must, in their elements, be mastered before you are seventeen, or you can never succeed in them. You may wish hereafter that you had done so, " but it will be too late, and your wishes will not give you back the power that is gone."[1] Now even the lowest ground for diligence in these studies cannot legitimately be despised. That lowest ground is that, for by far the most of you, your future will be affected very decisively by your present; that on the way in which you work now will depend largely the opportunities of earning your daily bread; that even one year's idleness now may make to you all the difference hereafter between a life reasonably prosperous, or heavily clouded by poverty and struggle. When the great Napoleon visited his old school at Brienne, he addressed these words only to the assembled boys, "Boys, remember that every hour wasted at school means a chance of misfortune in future life." Now these considerations alone would make gross laziness and selfish sacrifice of duty to pleasure in a boy's life a flagrant folly; but the higher ground, the loftier motive, the consideration which should appeal most strongly to the clearest and noblest souls among you, is that it is not only a flagrant folly, but a dangerous sin. For the true end of knowledge is not curiosity, is not vanity, is not profit, but it is that we may build up others—and that is charity; it is that we may be built up ourselves—and that is wisdom.[2] *Sursum Corda*,

[1] Bishop Templo.
[2] Sunt namque qui scire volunt eo tantum fine ut sciant; et turpis

lift up your hearts. Let none of your motives fall short of the highest. Be diligent in order that by the habits in which such diligence will train you, if by nothing else, you may grow up to be, not a curse and a burden to your fellow-men, but "a profitable member of the Church and Commonwealth, and hereafter a partaker of the immortal glory of the resurrection." So then I trust that on this ground all of you—alike the little boys who have just joined our body, and the eldest of you who will have your last chance this term of paying your θρέπτρα to Marlborough by showing yourselves worthy sons of the School which has trained you—will, as part of your answer to the question "What doest thou here?" reply distinctly, "I am here to be taught; I am here to learn."

(β) For indeed teaching is but *a part* of the reason why you are here, and, as a higher end, you are here *to be trained*. It is only the few who are gifted; only the few whose abilities and whose power of will can win them a foremost place; only the few whose names can be recorded in our annals as having done intellectual honour to the teaching they have received. But I do hope that not the dullest boy here will ever think that, because he is dull—because he can never repay what he owes to Marlborough by making her name more famous—that therefore he is less dear to her, or his interests less sacred to those who love her. When I recall the memories of those Marlburians whom for their virtue and their manliness I honour most—of those who

---

curiositas est. Et sunt qui scire volunt, ut sciantur ipsi, et turpis vanitas est. Et sunt item qui scire volunt, ut scientiam suam vendant, . . . et turpis quæstus est. Sed sunt quoque qui scire volunt, ut ædificent, et charitas est; et item qui scire volunt ut ædificentur, et prudentia est." *St. Bernard*, Sermon xxxvi. *Super Cantic.* p. 608.

have ever seemed to me the worthiest, the noblest, and the truest—of those whose names I believe to be written in heaven—it is not always of the ablest that I think, or of the most successful. The boys who leave us modest and manly, loyal and grateful, affectionate and courteous, humble and pure—and God grant that there may be always many such!—do us infinitely more honour in its highest sense than they could have done by any amount of that cleverness which is not dignified by seriousness and by character; and Marlborough is doing to the country a transcendently higher service if she can fill every grade and office of our national life with honourable, well-mannered, serious-minded, pure-hearted boys, than if we could be ever so pre-eminent for producing graceless capacity, conceited worthlessness, or brilliant vice. To train you to speak the truth always, to take Christ for your captain, and to do your duty to all the world; to bring you up in the knowledge that your bodies are temples of the Holy Ghost, and that those temples must be kept pure and holy; to set before you God's will, and that this is the will of God even your sanctification; to make you rather die than lie, rather cut off your right hand than steal, rather pass through fire than betray into vice and wickedness a soul for which Christ died; to make you feel how divine is the blush of modesty on young human countenances,[1] how sweet is humility, "that lily of the valley which blossoms only in the Christian heart;"[2] to inspire you with an honour so sensitive that it would feel a stain like a wound;[3] to help you so instantly; and so constantly to direct your lives by the high eternal law of duty, that you should ask about every act, not is it easy,

---

[1] Carlyle, *Frederic the Great.*   [2] Archbishop Leighton.
[3] Burke.

or is it popular, or is it pleasant, but Is it *right?*—that is the education we most desire for you, it is in *these* things that you come to Marlborough to be trained. Oh try, on this first Sunday of another summer term, to set them distinctly before you in answer to the question, "What doest thou here?" If this term passes without *intellectual* progress, it will so far be wasted and will be to you like an enemy in the rear; but if it pass with no *moral* progress, with no strengthening of noble principles, no conquest over sinful tendencies, no subordination of the senses and the passions to law and to reason, then it will be worst than lost, worse than wasted, for then it *will* be a source of future difficulty, it *may* be even of future condemnation. It will be a fountain of bitter waters. It will be the creeping premonition of paralysis to come.

III. So important is this period of your life. It is often spoken of as a *preparation* for life, but its main solemnity lies in the fact that it is not only a most momentous preparation for life, but also a most momentous *part* of it. Every day—we might almost say every hour, every moment of our mortal life has its own importance; for on any day of it death may come, and on any hour of it eternity may hang. But these days and hours are most important of all, because on them so many future days and hours may depend; because the whole oak lies in the acorn; because "fruit is seed."[1] It is a mysterious thing—one could almost weep to think of it—that the house of a young boy's soul is built as it were in the midst of enemies, on the edge of a precipice, on the ashes of a volcano; and that the assaults upon constancy and upon character seem so often to have shaken it to the very foundation or

[1] George Eliot, *Romola*.

sapped it at the very base before the constancy is established, before the character is formed. But we cannot alter the fixed conditions of life; and if to parents and to teachers this thought be full of misgiving and of sadness, there is another which is full of encouragement and hope, which is that God is nigh unto all them that call upon Him, even all such as call upon Him faithfully; that no one can make another do wrong; that the life and the death of each soul is in its own power; that in the case of the youngest boy, nay even of the weakest child, God never suffers any one to be tempted above that which he is able, but will with the temptation send also the way of escape. But, oh, if you have indeed realised all that I have been saying, how awful is the responsibility which these circumstances entail! You who are Prefects and Heads of houses, oh, let these thoughts help you to feel the meaning of an office which gives you more opportunity of doing good than you may have in many after years, and which consists far more of high duties than of special privileges. And you who are in the higher forms, who are older than the majority, who know more of the dangers and difficulties of life and of school life, how much of the happiness or the misery of your fellows depends on you! And you who are Captains of class-rooms, of dormitories, of the Upper Schoolroom, who live in the very midst of your fellows, who know—what we cannot always know—which of them are good and which bad, which weak and which strong, which trustworthy and which treacherous—you, without whose cognisance either no bad influence can be exercised at all, or at any rate not for long—oh do not betray your trust! There is one evil which neither the eye of man nor angel can detect—it is hypocrisy. Your parents, your masters cannot even profess to be never deceived in you. *I* do not know, perhaps none of those set over you may ever know, what this or that boy is— what a corrupt heart may lurk under the smiling countenance, under the fair semblance what a bad, mean souL But does *no one* know? does not *God* know? If I could, here and now, name any thoroughly wicked boy, if such there be, by name; if I could bid him by name stand up in his place; step forth into the presence of this congregation; if there I could convict him of any evil he has done; if I could flash and brand upon his quivering soul a sense of the enormity of that evil; if I could deliver him as St. Paul did the offender of Corinth to Satan, because he has done the devil's work; if it were given to mortal man to look on the hardened sinner with that eye, which, reading the inmost secrets of the hearts, "strook Gehazi with leprosy and Simon Magus with a curse;"[1] if, further, as he stood there, the power of life and death were ours, and we could raise our arm, and in the uplifted hand were such thunder as could hurl him blighted to the earth;—if we could do this, would not disobedience, would not corruption be an awful thing, and might it not be that there may be here some guilty soul which would die away within it, and shiver as the last dead leaf of autumn shivers in the frosty wind? *We* have no such power. But *God* has; He knows you; His eye is ever on you; He has witnessed the worst actions of your lives; He hears at this very moment every thought of your imagination, and every beating of your heart. The depths of trackless forests, the curtains of blackest midnight, cannot hide you from Him; nor does He need any lightning for the punishment of apostasy; a touch, a breath, the germ of an animalcula, the sporule of a lichen, the

[1] Milton.

microscopic seed of a pestilence, the invisible blight of an evening wind—these are enough to be the potent ministers of His awakened wrath; and a child does not crush more easily the petal of a flower than He at a touch could dissolve into dust and ashes not only the insolent, guilty, polluted soul, but the very race to which we belong, the very globe we live on, the very universe which He has made.

IV. Only let us remember for our comfort that this God, that this awful God, who made, who knows us, in Whose hands are the issues of life and death—that this God Whose will we may have rejected, Whose law we may have disobeyed—is also our Father. He has sent His Son to die for us, and to reconcile the world unto Himself. At morning and evening by your own bedsides, and all day long in the thoughts of your hearts you may seek Him, and here in this chapel you may hear His voice, and see His face. Oh! seek Him here. Oh! seek him early; seek Him while there yet is time; seek Him for your own sakes; for Christ's sake; for your brethren and companions' sakes: and let every one of us who *may*, at yonder Holy Table consecrate to Him the labours and efforts of this term—consecrate to Him ourselves, our souls and bodies, a reasonable, holy, and lively sacrifice.

May 9th, 1875.

SERMON XXI.

EXCUSES TO MAN AND TO GOD.

LUKE xiv. 18.

"I pray thee have me excused."

THE parable which you have just had read to you as the Gospel for the Day, might well be called the Parable of short-sighted folly, rendered more glaring by impotent excuse. Asked to the palace of a great man, the guests of course accept,—not only because they are bound by gratitude and allegiance, but because it is an honour and a delight. And yet when the hour comes, and, as is still usual in the East, the messengers go round to announce that all things are now ready, they all avail themselves of excuses, civil indeed, but as final as they are inadequate. One has bought a piece of ground, and is very sorry, but he must really go and see it. Another has just purchased five yoke of oxen, and is just starting to try them. A third has married, and thinks his narrow, absorbing, and selfish domesticity an adequate excuse for any possible neglect. Not deigning to notice their paltry excuses, in just scorn and just anger, the great man cancels his invitation, and sends for other guests. In vain, later on, haply shall these long to enter the lighted hall. Their chance is over; other guests are seated; the door is shut; and as they shiver without in the cold and in the darkness, their own consciences can but echo the burden of their own rejection,

"Too late, too late, ye cannot enter now."

I. 1. Before we consider the subject of their excuses, let us first consider the sin and folly from which these excuses were the pitiful refuge. For the behaviour of these guests may well strike you as strange, absurd, improbable. Yes, but that is one of the very points of the parable; for yet more incredible, yet more absurd, is the conduct of which that refusal is the illustration and the antitype. What is that? It is that God, the great King of all the earth, invites our souls to the palace of His heavens, to the banquet of His love;—to all things that are noble and eternal; to the heavenly manna, and the fair fruits of the Tree of Life, and river of His pleasures, and an eternal home and an unfading crown. And the soul refuses, delays, turns aside—for what? To feed on ashes; to eat the dust all the days of its life; to pluck the crumbling bitterness of the Dead Sea apples; to rusted treasures and broken cisterns; to guilty joys which, after brief madness, end in famine, and degradation, and hopeless death. Is it, then, that the soul does not believe in those good things which pass understanding, which God promises to His faithful children? Yes, it does believe them; but that faith is without works, and dead. Why? Because of the strong sorcery of the present, the fatal fascination of the near; because, when it has once admitted the slavery of sin, to the soul—as to the beasts that perish—the here and the now are more than the eternal and the unseen. Put the future, if you will, wholly out of the question; suppose for the moment that there is no heaven, no hell, no immortality beyond the grave, but that nothing more awaits us after this poor life save "the intolerable indignity of dust to dust." Yet even then the voices of all men in all ages—the guilty no less than the innocent—have declared aloud,—the one in their full beatitude, the other in their wild despair,— that vice is always misery and sin—always death—and that holiness is the only joy or peace. And not even the veriest and most headstrong fool can disbelieve this, for it is the unanimous experience of all the world. How is it then that men do follow vice, and live in daily disobedience to God law ? It is for the reason I have already given, and which all life illustrates.

2. Two youths once started together on a way which led over the desert to their father's house. At first their road lay by fountains, and by groves of orange and pomegranate, with which one as he passed stored his scrip and filled his water-skin, while the other, though gently warned, went forward without a thought and without a care. Together they reached the desert; and soon the great sun was flaming over them,—and the burning heat, and the scorching thirst, and the weary toil pressed most on him who was worst provided. At last they saw more and more distinctly before them the sight which many a traveller sees. A bright city seemed near them in its green oasis—with palms and palaces and runnels of silver water—while voices of strange fascination lured them there. But amid those tempting calls they heard continually a still small voice, sounding like the voice of their father from afar. "And look not," it whispered, "and listen not; that enticing loveliness is the deadly mirage; those sounds are the voices of the evil spirits in the wilderness, and they who listen to them return no more." And one of them knew that

it was so in his miserable heart, but more and more after those alluring voices, and more and more towards that gleaming falsehood which faded and fled before him, he turned aside into those haunted solitudes. And when the twilight came with its dew and stars the one was resting in his father's happy home; and they who with heavy hearts followed the wandering track of the other, saw only a dead body on the sands,—heard only the flapping of the vulture's wing. Alas! what is this but the transparent allegory of ten thousand lives; the wilderness—the temptation—the wandering—the warning voices—the delusion—the self-deception—the agony of vain remorse—the despair of unrepentant death. And it all comes from the refusal of the soul to resist the influences immediately around it, and to listen to that loving call which summons it from the ruinous treacheries of the world and of the senses to the glories of its Monarch's banquet, and the holiness of its Father's home.

II. But leaving this aspect of the parable, let us turn now from the refusal to the excuses that followed it. "They all began with one consent to make excuse."

To make excuses, my brethren, seems inherent in our nature. It rises from our pride. We rarely see ourselves as others see us, or even as we see others. We are so full of self-love that it seems like a miracle of grace when a man frankly, humbly, penitently admits and confesses himself to be in the wrong.

> "Come now, will the doer at this last of all
> Dare to say I did wrong, rising in his fall!"

No! in nine cases out of ten he will not. He will make excuses. No one can be placed in a position of authority without seeing daily instances of the habit; which, being all but universal in little things, is yet more fatally so in great. Suffer me to illustrate it in the words of another. "Excuse-making," says one who knew boys well, "is the scourge of boyhood and of school. I might venture, perhaps, to refer even in this place to a very common and familiar form of excuse in which one of you being late for a school-engagement pleads that his watch was wrong; perhaps it was, and yet several things may go to make this a mere excuse; perhaps he knew beforehand that it was wrong; perhaps he might have prevented it from being wrong; or perhaps he had other means of information within reach had he used them, but refrained from doing so that he might keep his excuse. And when any obvious duty is neglected, each of those who is thus failing has his excuse—his excuse to himself, to his parents, to his masters; his excuse varying a little with the day, but substantially the same each day, capable of modification or reproduction at pleasure, and sufficient at all events to palliate self-reproach, if not to inspire confidence. And thus there are those who never can be surprised into a frank confession. They are always armed against blame. The fault was not theirs; they were interrupted; they were tired; they thought they knew it; they thought they should have had time; they had meant to get up early; they had learnt every part of the lesson but that one line; they could have answered everything except that one question; they were only just late; they forgot;—anything in fact and everything but a frank admission of fault; and so on through a labyrinth of pleas and evasions—in one plain word excuses—till a miserable habit is formed, and all room for the operation of a candid self-judgment is precluded and barred. And when special pleas are exhausted they find an excuse in their very failings; they are so indolent, they say, constitutionally; they are so weak, so irresolute, so procrastinating; in the tone it may be of regret or evasion, but still with the effect of apologising for the less fault by the greater, for the particular by the general, of escaping censure for the fault by the help of the failing."[1]

This is, perhaps, enough to show you, by simple instances, and mainly in the words of another, the commonness of excuses; but I want you now to consider with me their hollowness, their meanness, their self-deceiving character. And this is implied by the very language of my text: "I pray thee have me excused." ἔχε με παρατηρημένον—hold me as an " excused "; treat me obligingly just this once; kindly make a special exception in my case. The very phrase shows the misgiving of the speaker; and scripture—in its plain and simple narratives—will show you better than ten thousand volumes of sham philosophy and would-be profundity, the radical falsity of this self-deceiving spirit. Take one or two excuses from the Bible—how hollow they are, how mean they are. Take Eve in her sin and shame; is there, even at that dread moment—when the awful voice speaks to her, and the sounding footstep is heard amid the garden trees—is there any frank confession of that deadly disobedience? No; but the usual subterfuge—a weak laying of the blame on others. "The serpent beguiled me, and I did eat." Does Adam come any more nobly out of the trial? No; but with ungenerous complaint and sullen recrimination. "The woman whom Thou gavest to be with me, she gave me of the tree, and I did eat." I choose cases, observe, in

---

[1] The substance of this paragraph is borrowed from an admirable sermon by Dr. Vaughan.

which there is no chance of denying the fact. If there were, is there not too much cause to fear—since there is so near an affinity, so undeniable a resemblance between excuses and lies—since, in fact, excuses are but the younger, and as yet less hardened, children in the great family of falsehood—must we not fear that the self-conscious pride which holds up against blame the wicker shield of excuses, might otherwise snatch at the sevenfold shield of lies? "Whence comest thou, Gehazi?" asks Elisha of his servant. The man does not know that he has been seen, that he has been detected already. And how smoothly, how unblushingly, though a prophet's servant, he slides at once into the glib and blank denial. Whence cometh he? whence should he have come? "Thy servant went no whither," he says, looking up with a plausible air of injured and innocent surprise. For him no after excuses were possible, for on him at once, with that "*went not my heart with thee?*" the white leprosy fell like blight. But in the case of the unhappy Saul we have both the prevenient falsity and the subsequent excuse. The great ban has been laid upon Amalek. False to his plighted word, he has violated and evaded it, and going to meet Samuel, smoothly says, "Blessed be thou of the Lord: I have performed the commandment of the Lord." "What meaneth then this bleating of sheep in mine ears?" is the stern and brief reply. "Oh! that is only what *the people* have done; they have kept the best of the sheep and the oxen—forsooth—to sacrifice unto the Lord; and the rest (yes, all the vile and all the valueless) we have utterly destroyed." And even then, when plainly reproved for his sin, his excuses are not over. "Yea, I *have* obeyed the Lord, and took Agag, but *the people* (again) took of the spoil," as though he had said (and oh how like it is to what we often hear!) I *did* do my duty; it was the people that did not do theirs; and even they did do theirs, only they kept some of the oxen, and even that was to sacrifice." "Behold, to obey," says the indignant prophet, tearing away the cobwebs of his hypocrisy and emptiness, "to obey is better than sacrifice, and to hearken than the fat of rams." Then, at last, when it is quite worthless, when there is no nobility and no manliness left in it, comes the reluctant confession, "I have sinned;" but even when this has been wrung from him, then once more comes the mean habitual recurrence to self-excuse and the blame of others. "I have sinned: because I feared *the people*, and obeyed their voice." The scene is very instructive to show us how persistent excuses are, and how utterly selfish, and how meanly self-deceptive; yet there is one more excuse in Scripture which in its sheer imbecile futility is even worse, and is wholly unsurpassed. Yet, perhaps, we may see our own tendencies immediately reflected in it, for it was a great man, a great priest, who made it. Moses is alone on Sinai, and in forty days the people have forgotten all, and want a visible idol, a low base idol, whom they can serve with sin and shame. Aaron, in his weak complicity, agrees. He carefully and elaborately makes them a gilded calf, and they serve it with vile and sensual worship. Then, in hot anger,—shattering in his wrath the granite tablets of the yet unpromulgated law,—like a messenger of doom, and with the glory of holy indignation on his countenance, comes Moses, striding down the hill, and flings into the dust their wretched idol, and stamps it to powder, and strews it on the water, and makes the children of Israel drink it, and then turns in his fury upon the trembling Aaron, and asks him, with bitter upbraiding, how he could have brought this great sin upon the people. "Oh, my lord, let not thine anger wax hot: thou knowest *the people*, that they are set on mischief," and so on. "And I said unto them, Whosoever hath any gold, let them break it off. So they gave it me: then I cast it into the fire, and there came out this calf!" "*There came out this calf!*" Can the force of imbecile fatuity go farther? In no passage of Scripture is there a larger or more cutting irony, yet the irony is not too bitter or too broad, nor the smile on the lips of the sacred historian too entirely scornful, for the utter folly and craven feebleness alike of Aaron's excuses, and, alas! of ours.

And alas! if these excuses do not even deceive ourselves, can we think that they deceive God? No. God has laid down a law that cannot be broken. It is all in vain for the sinner to stammer out, "I was surprised into it," or "I did not think," or "Only this once," or "It was only just," or "I was not the only one who did it," or "It was the fault of my school, or of my companions, and not mine." No; this is all useless. Nature is one name for the material laws of God, and Nature may reveal to us something of His will. Does Nature take excuses? Is there weak pity, is there relenting good nature in her? Or does he who violates her law suffer, suffer always, suffer inevitably? does not the fire always burn, and the water drown, and the lightning fall, and the pitch defile? Does nature spare the drunken man? does nature spare the dissolute youth? or does she stamp her brand upon his forehead, and strike her paralysis through all his frame? Stern as necessity, inexorable as death, does she not proclaim that he who transgresses her decree, be he the very favourite of the world, shall suffer for it, and that she does not swerve aside from her inevitable course? May not Nature thus teach us to fear nature's God? Excuses will never cease on earth; never cease till we stand at the solemn bar of God. Then they will. Then "every mouth will be stopped." Then each self-deceiving apology will sound too blasphemous, each miserable excuse too ridiculous to utter. Were it not better now to anticipate the revelations of that day? to judge ourselves that we be not judged? to make no excuses to ourselves, none to our fellows, none to our God now—to humble ourselves under the mighty hand of God—to lay our mouth in the dust, if so be there may be hope.

Hope—for *though* in the physical world there be no forgiveness of sins, in the spiritual world, for the penitent, and only for the penitent, there is. Where can it be found? In Christ, and in Christ alone. If we find it not in Him, we cannot find it anywhere. There is no other name under Heaven whereby we must be saved. Oh, not with excuses; not with any fancied palliation or fancied merit, but with deep penitence, with utter self-abasement, with absolute confession to Almighty God,—so let us come to Him, for so alone can we acceptably seek Him.

> "Just as I am, without one plea,
> Save that Thy blood was shed for me,
> And that Thou bid'st me come to Thee,
> O Lamb of God, I come.
>
> " Just as I am, and waiting not
> To rid my soul of one dark blot,
> To Thee, whose blood can cleanse each spot,
> O Lamb of God, I come."

June 14th, 1874.

SERMON XXII.

THE TEMPLE OF THE GOD OF TRUTH.

2 CHRON. xxxvi. 23.

"And he hath charged me to build him an house in Jerusalem, which is in Judah. Who is there among you of all His people? The Lord his God be with him, and let him go up."

You have just heard these words in the Second Lesson of to-day, and the thoughts which they suggest seem applicable to the present position of us all. The Israelites were returning to their home. Difficulties and dangers on every side encompassed them; but whatever those difficulties and dangers might be, their one duty, their one ambition, their one purpose, their one hope, was to build a temple to the Lord their God. It was to be for them an effort, at once strenuous and sacred, at once united and individual.

I. It was to be a material temple that they were to build. This is the first conception which men always form of the habitation of God—places set apart to His honour, hallowed by the associations of His worship; places like the chapel in which we are met to-day,—the outward beauty of which we desire to make a symbol of the love and honour which we owe to God, but which, I trust, every one of you will still more earnestly desire to honour with love and reverence—to hallow by seriousness and godly fear. God may be near you in every place; but nowhere nearer to your boyhood than in this your school-chapel. If daily, as you enter, each of you will kneel low on your knees before God's footstool, entreating Him to banish from your cleansed soul all low desires, all dreamy reveries, all guilty thoughts, that the words of your mouth and the meditations of your heart may be acceptable in His sight;—if you determine, from the first, faithfully to fulfil the simple duty of joining with your own lips in the hymns and responses, and by the Amen of serious hearts, making each prayer your own,—then here most assuredly, to the infinite help and blessing of your lives, will you be enabled day by day to see more and more brightly the Face of God; and pure Faith and meek Charity and every "hovering angel girt with golden wings," will here take you by the hand and waive off each baser temptation, till, in your own earthly lives, you have found a place for the temple for the Lord, an habitation for the mighty God of Jacob.

II. But though you may best seek Him here, you may find God everywhere. The Most High dwelleth not in temples made with hands. This great glorious world is His. The sky is His, with its driving clouds, with its sunset colourings, with its overarching canopy of stainless blue. The trees of the forest are His, with every moss and lichen that inlay their gnarled boughs with silver and emerald, and the flowers that nestle at their feet, and the birds that sing among their branches. This long summer which you have all enjoyed is His, and the autumn with its raiment of gold and purple;—and the sea is His, and He made it, and all that moveth therein. What you see around you is not—as the obtrusive ignorance of fancied wisdom has often so arrogantly proclaimed to us—

is not dull, dead matter, not blind and formless law, but the translucence of a divine energy, the work of Him who layeth the beams of His chambers upon the waters, and maketh the clouds His chariot, and walketh upon the wings of the wind. The darkened and unspiritual intellect, wise in its own conceit, may distenant creation of its God; but the fact that there are blind eyes does not disprove the reality of the light. The proof of that Light is simply that it shines; nor does it need other evidence save its own existence. The materialist may proclaim to us that to him all is darkness, but the senses are not man's only teachers, and the humble and the spiritual-hearted shall feel in this universe of God no dead combination of chance atoms, but a

> "Sense of something far more deeply interfused,
> Whose dwelling is the light of setting suns,
> And the round ocean and the living air,
> And the blue sky, and in the mind of man;"[1]

and that something is none other than the presence of the Lord his God.

III. But though to all who know and love Him God is the Soul of the visible universe, and we "climb by these sunbeams to the Father of Lights," He hath a nearer and a truer temple still. The earth hath He made, indeed, for the children of men, and it shines with His handiwork; but it is spirit only that can know spirit, and God's truest temple is the upright heart and pure. I look around upon you all—upon these youthful bodies into which God has breathed the breath of life, and which so have become living souls. I look around me, and I say—Some may be neglected, some desecrated; in the shrines of some there may be secret idols,

[1] Wordsworth, *Tintern Abbey.*

worshipped with the flame of strange fires and the smoke of unhallowed incense; but even of the most ruined it is true now—and God grant that it may be more and more true hereafter!—that the temple of the Lord, the temple of the Lord, the temple of the Lord are these! What? Know ye not, every one of you, that your bodies are temples of the Holy Ghost, who dwelleth in you,—temples which you ought to be raising now and to the end,—temples which God has given us all charge to build and hallow, and of which I ask you, "Who is there among you of all His people? The Lord his God be with him, and let him go up."

IV. For in striving to hallow in your own mortal bodies a house for God's habitation, you will all be joining to build yet another temple—God's last, best, truest temple,—a Church, that is, a society of God's children;—in this instance the society of a great English school, rising invisibly and silently to God's honour—a school in which God wishes and loves to dwell—a school "with Christ for its one foundation, while those for whom Christ died are the materials of which it is composed." And this is an eternal temple. The day shall come in some far-off time when our chapels and our schools shall be in ruins, and the stones of them shall have crumbled into dust; but when that day comes, we, as living stones in that spiritual and eternal structure, may long have been fitly framed together and grown into a holy temple which time effaceth not, and where God continually dwells. This—the temple of God in a Christian school—this is the temple which God specially charges every one of us, from the least to the greatest, to build for Him to-day. It was no easy task of old for Israel; it will be no easy task for us. They did it in anxious labour, and amid many perils, and so must we. Their enemies came scoffing. "What do these feeble Jews?" asked Sanballat the Horonite. "If a fox go up, he shall break down their stone wall," sneered Tobias the Ammonite. But they went on, because the people had a mind to work. And when their enemies conspired by force to hinder them, they did as we must do. They set a watch against them, day and night; and each of the people had his spear, and sword, and bow; and each as he builded with one of his hands, with the other he held a weapon, and so, sword on thigh, toiled at the high labour from the rising of the sun till the stars appeared. And so must we build;—all of us unitedly;—all of us prayerfully;—all of us from morning till night;—all armed and watchful;—all working with a will. For God has charged us to build, and the work is great and large. Will even one of you be such a traitor as to join with scoffing opponent or conspiring enemy? Will even one of you be such a caitiff as to be idle himself, and to spoil the work of his brethren? Arise! and build for God! "Who is there among you of all His people? The Lord his God be with him, and let him go up."

V. But what kind of a temple does God require? On what condition will the Lord our God who is so high, deign to dwell in the house we build? I will mention one condition.

God is essentially and before all things a God of truth. If God is to be with us there must be truth here, and by truth I mean not only truthfulness, which is a part of it, but reality; not merely that absence of falsehood which is its first element, but absolute sincerity. What a grand thing it is in a human life—what hope it gives that a boy will grow up worthily to that virtue which is nothing but perfect manliness—when everything that he is and does is built upon the large basis of sincerity; when we know that, whatever his faults may be, there is no sham about him, no thievish corners in his character, no subterranean jealousies, no smouldering malignities. He may strike the downright blow, but he will not use the poisoned dagger; and if he smite it will be by broad daylight, and in the face, not at the back and in the dark. His character may not be perfect, but at least it is transparent; his countenance may not be winning, but at least he does not wear a mask. If we know that we may trust his honesty and his straightforwardness; if we feel that he would rather die than lie; if his worst enemy yet might fearlessly appoint him a judge and arbiter: then I say that, having clean hands and a pure heart, he who hath not lift up his soul to vanity nor sworn to deceive his neighbour, this man shall receive the blessing of the Lord, and righteousness from the God of his salvation.

a. Since, then, this school must be built up into an habitation for the God of truth, let us see to it that we be true. We must be true first to one another. Not one of us stands alone. We are bound together by common hopes, common interests, common duties, common affections. If we be true to one another we shall not seek our own; there can then be no treacheries, no falsities among us; no influences that subtly corrupt, no lies that secretly undermine; but in word and deed a nobility and a loyalty which renders all baseness impossible between man and man. We who are set in authority over you must be thoroughly loyal to you; loyal to you by never forgetting how solemn is our responsibility for those your interests which are entrusted to our care; loyal to you by considering your welfare more even than our own; loyal to

you by seeing that, in whatever other way you may lose
or fail, you shall never lose by one hour of our idleness,
or fail by one carelessness of our neglect; loyal to you
by never allowing a like or a dislike, an offence or
an impatience, to deflect for one moment the even scale
of our impartial justice ; loyal to you by never allowing
an impulse of anger or a thought of popularity to
divert our judgment by one hairsbreadth from what is
right; loyal to you, therefore, by often doing, not what
you like, but what you need,—not what might please
you for the moment, but what will be best for you in
the end. God forbid that I should shrink from setting
before you our duties as masters no less frankly and
faithfully than yours as boys; and these are our duties
—to meet all your wishes half-way when they are good
or innocent, but never to indulge them when they are
unwise or wrong; to make the path of labour, and of
knowledge, and of self-denial as smooth before you as
God permits, but to do our utmost, at any cost, to check
your feet when they would stray into the paths of
death, or the steps that take hold on hell. All this you
know, and I feel an entire confidence that here, if anywhere, the ruled and the ruling are one in heart. For
as we to you, so must you be no less loyal to us; loyal
to us even when we ask you to do hard things and to
make great sacrifices; loyal to us even when you do
not yet see why certain restrictions are necessary, or
certain studies desirable; loyal to us, even if in all
honesty, we have failed to understand your character,
or failed to appreciate your efforts ; loyal to us for having
tried faithfully to serve you, even when you cease to be
under our authority. For your gratitude we ask not;
from the noble it will come spontaneously, from the
ignoble it never comes at all, nor does it even enter into

our calculations. Enough for us if, whether grateful or ungrateful, we can help you a little on life's hard and thorny road. But more than this, you must be loyal not only to us, but to one another. When you daily meet in the school, in the classroom, in the dormitory, in the playground, cherish in your hearts not only a holy charity for one another, but with it a deep reverence for the awfulness before God of your common nature and your common immortality. Yes! be true to one another. Behold how good and pleasant a thing it is, brethren, to live together in unity. In lowliness of heart let each of you esteem others better than himself. Bear ye one another's burdens, and so fulfil the law of Christ. Oh, you, who are elder, while you lessen each other's trials by a friendship full of manly and mutual honour, make it your highest common duty to shelter the young, the weak, the inexperienced, so that neither cruelty, nor thoughtlessness, nor, worse than all else, the deadly curse and plaguespot of impurity inflict on their souls an irreparable harm. Build God's temple in kindness, by seeing that there be no such thing as a bully to vex, unhindered, the life of his fellows; build it in manliness, by seeing that no one elder or younger boy be allowed, unchecked, to profane the sacred name of friendship by corrupt and spurious fancies, which, beginning in effeminacy and vanity, end in shame and degradation. Yes; if you would build the temple of the Lord you must be true to one another.

β. But remember that you cannot be quite true to one another unless you are true to your own selves. As our great poet says:—

> "To thine own self be true,
> And it shall follow as the night the day,
> Thou canst not then be false to any man."

And to be true to yourselves is to be true to your

higher nature—true to the aims and purposes of an immortal soul, created in God's image and redeemed into His adoption. He who degrades God's high ideal for his mortal life—he who sows to the flesh and not to the spirit—he who prefers the death of sin to the life of righteousness—he who to the impulses of his lower nature sacrifices the inspirations of his higher and eternal nature, as Adam did when he flung away his Eden of innocence for the forbidden fruit, as Esau did when for one mess of meat he sold his birthright, as Saul did when he suffered one raging envy to poison his whole existence, as David did when he debased his soul to be trampled in the mire by one evil lust—such a one is a traitor to himself. It is sometimes said of a man that he is his own worst enemy; but this, alas! is true of many a man in a sense far *deeper* than that in which it is ordinarily used. An enemy might injure for a time, but what enemy, short of Satan's self, would destroy another with a subtle, everlasting, irremediable destruction, as he who sells his soul for nought? To be true to yourself you must take as the one law of your being that only which is best, and purest, and likest God.

γ. For as you cannot be true to one another without being true to yourselves, so neither can you be true to yourselves if you are not true to God. He has made your heart His dwelling-place; you must be true to Him by not defiling it with idols. He has made the fortress of your soul strong for Himself: you must be true to Him by not betraying it to devils. He has given you talents and opportunities: you must be true to Him by employing them in His service. He has entrusted to you, as a labourer, the vineyard which His right hand hath planted: you must be true to Him by yielding Him its fruits of increase. Oh! strive to be

true to Him by obeying His commandments; to be true
to Him in your daily prayers by bringing Him real sins
to be pardoned, real wants to be supplied; to be true to
Him in this His house, coming before Him with meek
heart and due reverence : by coming here not to dream,
or to sleep, or to smile, or to trifle, or to look, or to be
looked at, but to praise and pray; by listening to the
messages He sends you here as to words addressed to
your individual souls. And one such message He is
speaking to all of you now. The elder of you—the
Prefects, the Heads of Houses, the Captains of Class-
rooms and Dormitories—He bids you protect the weak,
punish the wicked, put down with a strong hand all evil
doing, support and countenance whatsoever things are
pure, true, lovely, and of good report. And no less to the
younger—even to the youngest new boy amongst us—
He says, Be strong in the Lord, for moral weakness is
very nearly akin to active wickedness. You, too, must
help us to build God's temple. "Who is there among
you of all His people ? The Lord his God be with
him, and let him go up."

Sept. 20, 1874.

SERMON XXIII.

DRIFTING AWAY.

Heb. ii. 1.

"Therefore we ought to give the more earnest heed to the things which we have heard, lest at any time we should let them slip."

ONCE, in the safe harbour of a great bay, amid scenes not specially beautiful or circumstances wholly delightful, yet sheltered from every serious and fatal storm, there was anchored a little boat, which contained three youths. They were brothers, and had been bidden to wait there till towards the sunset, when a vessel would come to fetch them away; and they had been carefully warned that the bay was less safe than it looked, and that beyond the harbour-bar the sea was perilous and vast. One of these three youths, who, although the youngest, had the air of an altogether nobler race, felt a deep and instinctive horror of disobeying the command. The second of the three was a twin brother, a little older than this one,—attractive, brilliant, and capable of the highest things, but so apt to be misled by self-will and blinded by delusion, that when he grew wise in his own conceit, "there was more hope of a fool than of him." The third, though in every respect inferior to his brothers and base in aspect, except only when his features reflected some family resemblance to theirs, yet being the eldest, and physically the strongest, was constantly trying to control and master them. Capable of admirable usefulness when he submitted to their guidance, he was so violent and headstrong that there had never been any instance in their lives when he took the lead, in which all three had not been more or less injured or disgraced; nor was it without misgiving as to the result, that a father who loved them had left them together in the boat to-day.

But during the early morning hours nothing went wrong. They amused themselves innocently, each according to his own bent. Now and then, as he passed by, some passenger upon the shore, or sailor in another boat, would talk with them, and seeing that they were but boys, would sometimes remind them that they must be careful. To such words the youngest always listened respectfully, even when the elder brother would hear them impatiently, and the second with a conceited smile. But an hour or two had barely passed by when the eldest boy got weary. Indolent and ill-conditioned, he let the time hang heavy on his hands; and at last, in an evil, idle moment, stepped to the boat's prow, and gazed long and earnestly towards the forbidden sea. It did not look dangerous—only the lightest breeze appeared to ruffle it; and as he gazed on its magic sparkle, and listened to the light laugh of its waves upon the shore, a longing, yearning curiosity flowed into his heart as with a siren song. The longer he gazed the more passionate grew his desire to sail away; and nothing checked him but an indefinable misgiving, as long as one brother faintly dissuaded, and the other warned and entreated him from his purpose. And soon the second, who was much under his influence, began to waver and hesitate. Perhaps after all it did not matter much. The warnings of peril might be only old wives' fables, as in his selfish depravity an enemy who wore the mask of friendship had subtly hinted to him. The more he wavered, the more he got to share and to support the bad longing of his brother. Under such united pressure the youngest failed to hold out; his half-remonstrances were first, imperiously overruled, then contemptuously neglected, At last he hardly checked his brother's hands when, after long handling and trying the rope, they flung to the winds all that had been told them, knit their minds to the desperate resolve, slipped the hawser from the shore, tugged up the heavy anchor from its hold, hoisted the light sail, and the boat swung free.

Their course at first was not quite smooth; though pulled up from its hold, yet the anchor was of massive iron. Here and there it dragged along the beach, giving the boat a troubled motion; here and there it caught upon the rocks, pulling the boat up with a sudden shock. More than once they were reduced to seriousness, and half determined to listen to their younger brother and to stop; and all the more because they did not feel quite happy or at ease. But the eldest urged that, having once slipped anchor, it was a pity to have committed that fault for nothing; and the second was confident that no harm would come of it after all; and even the youngest, corrupted by his brothers, began to share that guilty longing for the sea. For soon they felt a kind of delirious exultation as the new scenes sped by them, bathed to their imagination in the colours of enchantment. Once indeed they were imperilled on a sandbank. Once they were met by another boat, hastily returning, with frightened, outwearied rowers, and strained and broken oars. And when they reached the harbour-bar there was a great roar of waves, and the boat was almost swamped. But they were caught just then in a sudden gust, and their sail was up. Almost unconscious of what they did, they shot over the seething bar,—and then they were in the open sea.

And there, when gradually the sunlight began to fade from dark and heaving expanse, and the seductive treachery of the placid waters to be flecked with angry foam, and the blackness of clouds which had been slowly gathering over them to burst into rain and storm, the youngest brother, who had often turned homewards his timid glances, did pluck up courage, and by his tears and entreaties prevail on them to strike sail, and begin to row back. But alas! that rowing back was a desperate effort!—the wind was against them; the waves broke over them; their arms were weaker than once they were; their very wills seemed to have been smitten with paralysis: and, worse than all, they found that they were now in the fatal grasp of a powerful current, against which they thought it in vain to struggle, and fear and shame would not suffer them to make signals of distress; and in the last glimpse of them which was seen from far by those who loved them, the two elder were seated in sullen defiance at the prow, and the face of the third was hidden in his hands, as he sat apart in stupefied despair. And what happened to them could only be conjectured by the wreck that had befallen many another boat on those fatal waves. Of these all which was known was that some had been seized by pirates; and some foundered in the deep sea; and some been shattered to pieces on rocky headlands or sunken reefs;—but one sad hope was left —because some, aided by merciful change, of wind and tide, *had* struggled, bruised and weary, into other and bleaker harbours, where, by painful endeavour, their anchor would just hold out; and some, even at the last moment of desperation, had been saved by the lifeboat, destitute and shattered, and with the total loss of all.

The youngest of you will have seen that those things are an allegory, and will perhaps guess something of those moral laws to which the allegory points; but only a few of the elder of you will know that it is simply an expansion of my text. "We ought to give the more earnest heed to the things that we have heard, lest at any time we should let them slip;" for that word "let them slip," is in the original μή ποτε παραρρυῶμεν, lest perchance we should *drift away from them*. In the Greek usage, water, any brook that disappears, is said παραρρεῖν, but anything which is borne along on the surface of that flowing wave—any boat, for instance, which is loose upon its current is said παραρρυῆναι, to float, or drift away. And the writer bids us not drift away from the things we have heard. For he has begun by telling us that of old God spake to our fathers πολυμερῶς καὶ πολυτρόπως, "at sundry times and in divers manners" or, with more accuracy, fragmentarily and multifariously; fragmentarily, as in the Old Testament, now revealing God's unity, now man's immortality, finally man's redemption; and multifariously, now by dreams, now by Urim, now by prophets; and of these prophets sometimes a king, sometimes a shepherd; now an exile, now a gatherer of sycamore leaves. But in these last days, in this new dispensation, not fragmentarily, but in one final whole; not multifariously, but by one divine, eternal Voice, hath He spoken unto us by His Son. Τετέλεσται, it is finished; the revelation is finished now, the vision sealed, the Son Himself has come to His labourers in the vineyard; and through all history we hear a Voice from heaven saying, "This is my beloved Son, hear Him." Never can the race of man, never can the soul of man be nearer to God than Christ has brought them: nor since Him hath there been, nor hath there needed to be, one further ray of moral light, one brighter gleam of spiritual illumination. Yes; the last Voice from heaven has spoken: be deaf to it, and you will hear it indeed no longer—not a whisper of it shall stir the air, not a murmur of it echo in the ear; but you will hear no other. Hate that light, and you may then conscientiously deny it, for you will cease to see it—it will exist to you as little as if you had been born blind; but besides its quiet shining you shall have no other. Jesus may become to you a peasant-prophet who died in Palestine; God may become to you dead matter and formless law: yet, for all that, the truth remains, and it is the blood of Christ that alone cleanseth from all sin, and we must all stand before the judgment seat of God. But all of you have heard and have learnt the truth. A vow was made for you at baptism; that vow was repeated in the sight of God at your confirmation: therefore you ought to take the more earnest heed to the things which you have heard, lest at any time you should drift away from them.

Drifting away;—try to fix that word in your minds. There is a moral and there is an intellectual drifting away of the soul from truth; and very often the moral is the cause of the intellectual, so that a man does not know God's doctrine, because he will not do God's will; and very often the moral is the result of the intellectual, so that, as St. Paul says, he who has become vain in his imaginations, and his foolish heart is darkened, professing himself to be wise becomes a fool, and giving himself up, as did the heathen world, to uncleanness, changes the truth of God into a lie. But it is of the moral drifting away from the truth, not of the intellectual, that I would speak now.

Drifting away; how much there is in that mournful

word! If the very picture it involves had not led me insensibly into allegory, exactly the same moral truths might have been expressed in simplest fact. Is not your mortal life that frail shallop, in which you must wait in the little harbour of Time, till you are summoned to that world where the eternal is also the visible? And in that life are there not the three influences, of the body, the intellect, the spirit; and the command that all three receive, is it not the moral law? And that anchor of the soul, sure and steadfast, which, if you will not tamper with it, or tear it from its hold, will grapple you safely to the shore—is it not your conscience? And is not the history of many human lives exactly this—by the allurements of the world, or the lusts of the flesh, or the wiles of the devil, you are tempted to loosen that anchor; to assert a spurious freedom; to disobey the moral law of God: and is it not the worst and eldest brother—the flesh, the body, the temporal within us—which first is stirred; and then the intellect is perverted; and then, by the joint infatuation of the passionate body, and the poor, vain, darkened, perverted sophisticated intellect, the spirit youngest born of God within us, is encarnalised and depraved; and do we not thus force conscience from its anchor-hold, and begin the bad career? At first conscience drags a little; and the sinner, not yet quite happy in his disobedience, might then easily be saved; but if this be neglected—if the last barriers of moral scruple be surpassed—if every spiritual instinct within us be sedulously silenced—if each faint short effort be suffered to become yet shorter and yet more faint;—oh, then it is that we drift and drift and drift, and the shore lessens behind us, and the sunset fades from the God-forgetting soul, and the false smile vanishes from the treacherous temptation, and the smooth surface becomes a sweeping current, and strong tide, and roaring sea! And when I say this, am I not tearing a page from ten thousand life histories? from your life history, and yours, and yours? And what remains for these? One thing only: return, repentance—to be won at all hazards, at the cost, if need be, of the very life—repentance even through agonies and energies—or a certain fearful looking-for, and to stand naked, ashamed, guilty, speechless, before the just and inevitable bar.

"Drifting away." He who wrote that expression knew something of the human heart; he knew that the soul does not leap at once into absolute apostasy; he knew that the beginning of sin is as the letting out of water; he knew that, as the proverb says, the mother of mischief is no bigger than a midge's wing; he knew that by almost invisible deflections we arrive at almost infinite distances. We read of vessels separated from their consorts at evening by a few yards, which yet, caught by the stealthy flow of some invisible current, have in a single night drifted a hundred miles away. And do you ask me "How are you to know whether you are drifting away or not?"—that, as your own hearts will tell you, is an idle question. You cannot walk the dim borderland between vice and virtue without knowing it. You cannot drift from heedlessness to indifference, from indifference to disobedience, from disobedience to rebellion, without being well aware of it. You cannot be swept along from the thought to the wish, from the wish to the word, from the word to the act, from the act to the habit, from the willing habit to the penal necessity, without being well conscious of it. Drifting away from the truths of God and of your father to the lies of those false friends who are your worst enemies; from home to a hungry and barren land; from innocence to a stained and evil life: oh, you cannot thus drift from the safe shelter of childhood into the strong currents of youth, into the dangerous seas of temptation, into the awful gulf and cataract of death, without, at the first stages, being only too well and fatally aware of it. There is not one of you who does not know whether, with him, at this moment, the anchor is holding firm and fast, or whether it is dragging, or whether his little boat has already rushed over the harbour bar and is in the sea. It is only late in the career of impenitence that words of warning fall on the ear no longer; that if the scorner hopes it is a hope without an effort, and if he prays it is a prayer without a change; and the twilight becomes the evening, and the evening the black, dark night; and grey hairs are upon him, and he knows it not; and "the eye of the soul has grown dull, and the heart waxed fat, and he is least afraid when most in peril."

And what is the remedy? It all lies in the one word, "Take heed." If you take heed to that which you have heard, neither man nor devil can slip the hawser or shake the anchor of your soul. How well Moses knew this when he bade the Israelites bind God's law as a token upon the hand and as frontlets between the eyes. How well David knew it when he said, "Wherewithal shall a young man cleanse his way? even by taking heed thereto, according to Thy Word." How well Solomon knew it when he said $υἱὲ\ μὴ\ παραρρυῇς$—"My son, drift not away from my commandments; keep them as the apple of thine eye; bind them upon thy fingers; write them upon the table of thine heart." My brethren, be not deceived. Attention to the moral law of God and the awful truths of religion is an act of the will. Show me the boy who is living from hand to mouth; in whom the impressions of holy reverence are being worn away; whose life is frivolous, weak, thoughtless; whose nominal prayers are no prayers at all; who kneels daily in this holy place, but kneels dull, and mute, and heavy, and with wandering, and often guilty, fancies, but never kneels to praise and to worship; who has forgotten the lessons which he learnt as a child at his mother's knee, and neglected the advice which his father taught him when he parted from his home; show me the boy who rose this morning late, and sluggish, and prayerless; who has spent the time since chapel in aimless idleness, or in frivolous gossip, or in reading his trashy novel or his sporting newspaper, without one thought of duty, or eternity, or God; without once confessing his sins to his Father in heaven, or making holier resolutions for the week to come;—show me this boy, and I will show you one who is drifting away. Therefore if you would be safe, take heed. You, whose boat is still anchored to the shore, since the temptations of boyhood will assuredly steal upon your security and assault your inexperience, take heed to these words, that you may be faithful and watchful to the end. You who are drifting away, take heed to them, while there yet is time, as to the warning voice of one who calls to you from the shore. Let us all take heed to them, not as a subject for vain, empty criticism or fool-born jest, but as one more message of our God and Father to these souls of ours, to be despised, indeed, and rejected at our pleasure, but also at our peril. Oh, set in the midst of so many and great dangers, rarely or never do we take heed enough. Therefore, in the repeated language of Holy Scripture, I say to you, to all: Take heed, let the fear of the Lord be on you. To the younger: take heed, regard not iniquity; take heed that no man deceive you. To the elder: take heed that ye despise not one of these little ones; take heed what thou doest. To the abler and more advanced: take heed that the light in you be not darkness; take heed of an evil heart of unbelief. To all—to every one of you: take heed how ye hear; take heed of the things you have heard, lest perchance you drift away from them.

September 4, 1874.

SERMON XXIV.

THE HISTORY AND HOPES OF A PUBLIC SCHOOL.

Ps. cxxii. 8.

"For my brethren and companions' sake, I will wish thee prosperity. Yea, because of the house of the Lord our God, I will seek to do thee good."

LAST Sunday I spoke to you of the temple of God in a Christian school, and tried to show you that it must be built on the broad foundation of truth, and that we, if we would be builders therein, must be true to ourselves, true to one another, true to God. It seems no unnatural sequel to such a subject if to-day I speak to you about our school itself. You will pardon me if, in the inadequate attempt to say even a little of what might be said on such a theme, I unwillingly detain you a moment longer than usual. I am persuaded you will not think the topic useless. Anything that raises us to the full consciousness that we are not our own, but members one of another—anything that deepens in us the conviction that God has placed us in this His world not to seek our own pleasure, or think our own thoughts, or speak our own words, but to do His work in our own hearts, and for our fellow-men—this must be good for us. Many a sin and many a baseness will be destroyed or weakened if we can thus kill within us the perverted love of self. Since, then, on Tuesday next we keep by a religious service that commemoration day which reminds us that Marlborough College has now, for thirty-one years, taken its place among the Public Schools of England, let us to-day look backwards and forwards—backward to its past history, forward to its future hopes—in order that we may love our school still better, and the more heartily feel, and more vigorously follow our path of duty in its present circumstances.

I. I need not do more than remind you of the associations which surround us in the place where our College stands,—yet even they have their deep significance. That Druidic mound which faces our chapel door is but one of the links which associate us with the past. Strange but humbling fact, that the most permanent memorial which man can rear is just a heap of the soil on which he treads! In that mound we have the most ancient monument in the possession of any English school. Once the tumulus of some great British priest or chieftain, it is the relic of a worship of which the very deities are forgotten, At Rome the stupendous ruins of the Colosseum strike us with wonder; but that mound was reared before one stone of the Colosseum had been laid—before the herald angels sang from the midnight sky—before, over the fields of Palestine walked those blessed feet, which

> "Eighteen hundred years ago were nailed
> For our salvation to the bitter cross."

it stood, in all probability as now it stands. And thus for two millenniums has it been the silent witness of that sacred light by which God "shows all things in the slow history of their ripening." When it was reared England was a country of waste and morass and moor, like Labrador; wolves howled in her forests, wild boars wallowed in her fens. Then came the "drums and tramplings" of successive conquests. Roman discipline subjugated barbarous disunion; Saxon, and Dane, and Norman each triumphed in turn over the enervation of their predecessors. Then our mound became the keep of a Norman castle. In the days of the Plantagenets English princes lived on it, and English kings have dated their charters from it. Through the long lines of Lancaster, and York, and Tudor, and Stuart, it continued. In the civil wars its castle was dismantled. Then these grounds became the home of a noble English family, and in the reign of Charles II. our old house was built by the most famous architect of his age. How in those days it became familiar to poets, nobles, and statesmen—how then it became one of the most famous inns in England, and, as a resting-place between London and the West, was visited by many of England's greatest worthies, and among others by the most splendid and powerful of her Prime Ministers—you may read elsewhere. Then came that change which makes it so memorable to us. Thirty-one years ago, on August 25, 1843, the first Marlburians walked with considering footsteps about the place which was to be the new home of their boyhood, and to which, as time passed on, some of their sons were to follow them. Some of you who sit on these benches to-day are sons of some of those 200 who, thirty-one years ago, first entered this place as Marlborough boys; and of their traditions, of their influences, of their characters, of the motives brought to bear upon them, of the manner in which they yielded to those motives—so far-reaching are the pulsations of our moral life—all of you are the heirs. The sound of their boyish laughter, the echo of their happy voices has died away, and many of them have passed away from the life of earth. In a body so large as this many die as the years pass on. I remember the first boy who ever entered my room as a pupil here nearly twenty years ago. He lies now under the deep sea-wave. I remember the first head of my form here —that memorial window records his character. Yes, we die; but not the effect of our deeds. All other sounds

> "Die in yon rich sky,
> They faint in hill and field or river;
> Our echoes roll from soul to soul,
> And live for ever and ever."

If you be living weak, miserable, effeminate lives, then let it be a warning and an awful thought; if you are living true, manly, righteous lives, let it be an ennobling, an inspiring thought, that your lives too will live, in their moral echoes, for coming generations of Marlborough boys.

II. And another fact reminds us that these thirty-one years, which are a generation of human life, have passed over this young school. It is that our first founders, our first benefactors, those who first worked, and toiled, and thought for us, are fast passing away. A wise impulse in this age, as in the days of Elizabeth, led to the foundation of many new schools. After the long and dreary slumber of a corrupt and atheist century, waked by the trumpet voices of Wesley and Whitfield, the clergy were beginning to shake off their apathy, and in every parish of England to practise those lives of stern self-denial and honoured poverty of which they now set so happy an example. There was a widespread desire to help them in furnishing their sons with an education as good as that of the proudest noble in the land. It was while that thought was in many minds that a clergyman, afterwards Dean of Manchester,[1] whose bust is in the hall, was walking about these grounds with a gentleman[2] who then resided here; and, struck with the prospect of the river, the valley, the forest, the downs, and with the quiet, the green fields, the healthy air of the place, he exclaimed, " What an excellent site this would be for a great school !" Those words, which we may well regard as a *Bath Kôl*—a providential voice—led to the foundation of Marlborough College. He enlisted others who felt an interest in the same cause. Some were men of eminence, but most of them were simple English gentlemen, who with great zeal and self-denial carried out their noble purpose. That clergyman died last year ;—the grandsons of the gentleman to whom he spoke, and of another,[3] who also died last year full of years and honours, and who has often been called the father of the College, are sitting among you now; and he to whose well-judged munificence you owe the inestimable boon of the Adderley Library,[4] which adds so much to your advantages,—the most generous and the most faithful of all the friends of the College,— he too lies on the bed of sickness. And as I speak I recall the names of others, and younger men, who could not enrich Marlborough with their worldly goods—because they had them not—but who, working here as earnest, and faithful, and zealous masters, or living here as high-minded, and pure, and noble boys, enriched it with the more golden legacy of manly memories and Christian lives. I recall the names of some in past days and some in these—of Edward Lawford Brown, and Thomas Harris Burn, and Edward Colquhoun Boyle, and Herbert Edward Booth, and Walter Ernest Congreve—who being

---

[1] Dean Bowers.
[2] Mr. Halcomb.
[3] Christopher Hodgson, Esq.
[4] F. Alleyne McGeachy, Esq.

dead, yet speak, and who have not lived in vain. Yes, year
by year the old generous benefactors, the old munificent
friends, the old self-denying labourers for Marlborough
College are fast passing away, and leaving us only
the heritage of those good deeds which cannot die.
We need others to take their places; and I trust that,
by God's blessing, we shall find them in her sons. We
shall find them, I trust, in some of you. You will arise
and call her blessed. You will hand on undimned to
others the lighted torch of bright enthusiasm and
honourable tradition, which was put into your hands.
You will continue and extend for others the blessings
from which you yourselves have gained. Some of you,
when you grow up, may become rich and prosperous
men. If you do, remember that in a greedy age you
were taught at your school, as a lesson drawn from
the good deeds of its founders, that, as there is nothing
more absolutely vulgar and despicable than selfish and
grasping riches, so you can adopt no surer means of
ennobling your wealth, and thereby ennobling your own
souls, than by aiding those institutions which have
been founded for the welfare of mankind. And for a
wealthy man I cannot think of any means of using
gold more fruitful in usefulness, more likely to preserve
an honoured memory, than to support sound learning
and religious education by becoming the benefactor of
some great school.

The College then was founded; and they who had
laboured and given their substance for it, won thereby
a grace and a blessing which nothing else could have
given them.

But how did their work prosper? At first not well.
Let us bear in mind that in those days it was a great
and wholly new experiment: and some hundreds of

boys, all strangers to one another, collected in one building—without a past, without unity, without traditions—fell at first into many rough and discreditable ways, which seemed likely at one time to make the name of Marlburian a byeword and a hissing. It must have been a bitter thing for those who then worked for our school to bear; but they who sow faithfully, though it be in tears, shall reap in joy. Yes, *laborare et orare* were (as in one way or other they always are) successful; and the first master of Marlborough[1] has lived to see that he was doing a work which, though different from that achieved by others, has yet been granted to few. For to those days of trial, and greatly to his work, we owe that organisation which has since been imitated in its minutest particulars by later schools. And what was still wanting it was granted to his successor to achieve. It is something for every Marlborough boy to know that when he looks at that portrait of Bishop Cotton which adorns our hall, he is looking at the likeness of one of the best men whom this generation has produced. It was God's special blessing to a new school that sent him here. He was not great as the world counts greatness. When he came here he was but little known beyond a narrow circle of attached friends. Nor was it at once either in numbers, or in intellectual successes, or in improved finances, that Marlborough began to flourish. Yet, undoubtedly, it was Bishop Cotton who saved the school. He was here but six years; and great as was his work as Bishop of Calcutta and Metropolitan of India, before that disastrous fall into the waters of the

---

[1] The Rev. Matthew Henry Wilkinson, D.D., Prebendary of Salisbury and Vicar of Melksham. [Obiit. March 4, 1876.] As a slight memorial to the name of a good man, to whom scant justice has been but tardily rendered, I venture to append to this sermon some lines which I wrote while returning from his funeral.

Indian river after which he was seen no more, it is yet with this place that his name will be most identified. It was my own deep happiness in those days to know him, to love him, to work with him, and in daily walks and intercourse with him, as afterwards by letters, until he died, to learn what manner of man he was. And how did he save Marlborough, when it might any day have disappeared, unhonoured and unregretted, from its place among the public schools of England? My brethren, it is well for you to know—it is a valuable lesson for anyone to know : it was not by the genius of the thinker; it was not by the brilliancy of the scholar; it was not by that burning enthusiasm, and personal ascendency with which Arnold of Rugby had done his work. Such gifts were not his; but it was by those fruits of the Spirit which are in the reach of all, and by that heavenly grace which is given in even larger measure to them that seek it. The lesson of his life for you and me is that it is a thing dearer and better in God's sight, and more fruitful to our fellow-men, to be entrusted with but one talent, and to use it faithfully than to have a hundred, and use them ill. A calm hopefulness, a cheerful simplicity, an exquisite equanimity of temper, a humility which made him a learner to the very end, a genuine, self-denying love for Marlborough, and for those boys whom God had here entrusted to his charge—these were what gave to his life that mysterious power which is always granted to the unselfish purpose and the single eye. And this was the type of character—God grant that it may long be stamped upon some of the sons whom this school shall train!—which he produced among his pupils and his colleagues. I shall never forget the spectacle which the Marlborough of that day presented. Something was due, no doubt, to the fact that it was a day of adversity, which often brings out all that is noblest and sweetest in human lives. But certainly the few here present who remember that time will bear me witness that it taught us all a priceless lesson. We all felt that it was a struggle, first, whether Marlborough College should live at all, next, whether it should live in honour or obscurity. We won no great successes; we were beaten in every game; there was much that was mean in our surroundings—much that was trying in our arrangements—much that was still coarse, and rough, and unintellectual in the habits of the place. And yet how we all loved it! How boys and masters alike worked for it! What a pride they felt even in its humility! what a thrill of delight we all felt when one succeeded! How ready they were, some of them, even to the permanent surrender of better prospects, to serve Marlborough and work for her. And verily they have their reward; they have their reward, that is, if the highest price which life can offer is clearly to see what is best, and resolutely to do it. And is there anything better than this? Life is not the mere living. It is worship—it is the surrender of the soul to God, and the power to see the face of God; and it is service—it is to feel that when we die, whether praised or blamed, whether appreciated or misinterpreted, whether honoured or ignored, whether wealthy or destitute—we have done something to make the world we came to better and happier—we have tried to cast upon the waters some seeds which, long after we are dead, may still bring forth their flowers of Paradise. The seed dies, but the harvest lives. Sacrifice is always fruitful, and there is nothing fruitful else. Try, then, to fix in your hearts one lesson, to register in your prayers one vow, this morning—the lesson that life consisteth not in the abundance of things that we possess, but in the good and honest work we do—the vow that you, too, will live, not to lade your soul with the thick clay of earthly riches—not to daub your lives with the untempered mortar of human praise—not to waste your labours on those gains of the wilderness, which can neither satisfy the soul's hunger nor quench its thirst; but to live for what is best and greatest, to take Christ for your Captain, and do your duty to all the world. For those efforts succeeded, as such efforts always will; they raised Marlborough from adversity. Bishop Cotton was summoned to other work; but under a successor, whom many of you still love and remember—a pupil of Arnold, as Bishop Cotton had been his friend and colleague—the name of Marlborough rose into brilliant reputation.[1] In spite of its youth, in spite of its struggles, in spite of the fact that it had neither royal founder nor rich foundation, it took its place decidedly, and unless you, its sons, degenerate, took its place permanently among the leading schools of England, striving, not unsuccessfully, to be second to none in the training it could offer, in the distinctions it could win, in the affection it could inspire, in the honour it could reflect. This prosperity you inherit; but, my brethren, do not lose sight of that fact—which all history has shown so forcibly—that the day of prosperity is the day also of peril. The very qualities which lead to glory and eminence are but too apt, when they have produced it, to merge into the weakness, the luxury, the effeminacy, the neglect, by which it is as inevitably undermined. It has been said of nations, and it is no less true of schools, that "in their perplexities, in their

[1] The Rev. G. G. Bradley, D.D., Master of University College, Oxford.

struggles for existence, their infancy, their impotence, and even their disorganization, they have higher hopes and nobler passions. Out of the suffering comes the serious mind; out of the salvation, the grateful heart; out of the endurance, the fortitude; out of the deliverance, the faith. But when the violent and external sources of suffering cease, worse evils seem arising out of their rest—evils that vex less, but mortify more—that suck the blood, though they do not shed it, and ossify the heart, though they do not torture it." Yes, in every prosperous institution there is danger that "enervation may succed to rest, apathy to patience, and the noise of jesting words, and the foulness of dark thoughts, to the earnest purity of the girded loin and the burning lamp. About the river of human life there is a wintry wind, though a heavenly sunshine: the iris colours its agitation—the frost fixes on its repose. Let us beware that our rest becomes not the rest of stones, which, so long as they are torrent-tost and thunder-riven, maintain their majesty, but when the stream is silent and the storm passed, suffer the grass to cover and the lichen to feed on them, and are ploughed down into the dust."

To sum up, then, in one last word—it was the duty of others to found, it is ours to build on their foundation; of others to rescue Marlborough from adversity, it is ours to preserve and to ennoble her prosperity; of others to mould our institutions, it is ours to see that those institutions, year by year, train every grace and virtue of boyhood into the strength of Christian manhood, and send forth, in the high service of God and man, Christian scholars and Christian gentlemen to be the hope and glory of our land. Love your school with an unselfish and loyal devotion. Feel how disgraceful it would be to wound, by worthlessness or wickedness, the breast of that mother who thus nurses your early years. If you work for yourselves, feel it a yet higher thing to work for her honour; covet for Marlborough College a high career and a more and more distinguished name; covet for her yet more earnestly the best gifts of a pure and manly tradition, a vigorous and happy life. To her, and not to another, is your faithful allegiance, your chivalrous devotion due. *Spartam nactus es, hanc exorna.* You are not at a tutor's to be crammed, as isolated units, for some purely selfish competition: from the necessarily vulgarising influences of such an absorption in a merely personal end you are saved by the vigorous and varied life of an English public school, which, if a boy's heart be not quite eaten out by selfishness, is enough, one would think, to ennoble the meanest nature with the thought that his life does not affect himself alone. Throw a stone into a still lake, and you will see the rings of its ruffled surface widen and widen till they die away upon the farther shore: even so, in the concentric circles of their ever-widening influences, do the lives of every one of you leave their trace in the common life of your companions. From this school many an old Marlburian has gone forth, year by year, not only with well-earned laurels, which they have won for us by manly self-denial and diligent resolve; but—what is better still—carrying with them into the world's life high lessons which they have learnt in this place—lessons of earnest purpose, of unresting diligence, of childlike and gentlest modesty. It is these who, by the grace of God, have created for Marlborough a not ignoble past. Marlborough boys of to-day—you whom God has placed here for the most intellectually difficult, the most morally important years of all your lives—sons of Marlborough College, all of you, and, most of all, you who will kneel with us in Holy Communion at the Supper of our Lord—determine, in God's name, that you too will heedfully follow the very best and truest of those who have gone before you in the footsteps of our Master Christ; vow that, like them, as the worthy sons of a common mother, you will strive here to be profitable members of the Church and Commonwealth, that with them you may partake hereafter of the immortal glories of the Resurrection.

September 27, 1874.

IN MEMORIAM M. M. WILKINSON, D.D.
First Master of Marlborough College. Died March 4, 1876.

Aye, they are o'er—his pain and his endeavour,
  Our scant acknowledgment, and frequent wrong;
Hushed are all tones of praise or blame for ever,
  For those who listen to the angels' song.

He sowed the seed with sorrow and with weeping,
  Barely he saw green blade or tender leaves;
Yet in meek faith, unenvious of the reaping,
  Blessed the glad gatherers of the golden sheaves.

But we,—when reapers unto reapers calling
  Tell the rich harvest of the grain they bring,—
Shall *we* forget how snow and sleet were falling
  On those tired toilers of the bitter spring?

And yet of him nor word nor line remaineth,
  Picture nor bust, his work and worth to tell;
And though nor he nor any friend complaineth,
  We ask in sadness—'Marlborough, is it well?'

Enough! he murmured not!—in earthly races
  To winners only do the heralds call;
But oh! in yonder high and holy places
  Success is nothing, and the work is all.

So—since ye will it—here be unrecorded
  The work he fashioned and the path he trod;
Here, but in Heaven each kind heart is rewarded,
  Each true name written in the books of God!

F. W. F

SERMON XXV

THE NEED OF CONSTANT CLEANSING FROM CONSTANT ASSOILMENT.

JOHN xiii. 10.

"He that is washed needeth not save to wash his feet, but is clean every whit: and ye are clean, but not all."

I. IT was at the Last Supper of the Lord. Jesus and His apostles had taken, for the last time, the familiar walk from Bethany to Jerusalem, and had entered the upper chamber for their final gathering on earth. Even at that supreme moment the petty jealousies of life had not been exorcised, and the twelve had had an unseemly dispute which of them should be greatest. Jesus listened in pained silence, and wishing to teach them a lesson infinitely more significant and more touching than any rebuke, knowing that His hour was come to depart out of this world unto the Father, having loved His own, He loved them unto the end. They had walked along the hot and dusty road over the shoulder of Olivet; on entering the chamber they had indeed taken off their sandals and left them at the door; but still the dust of their journey was on their unsandalled feet. To have their feet bathed before the meal was cooling, cleanly, and refreshing; but in their little mutual jealousies, no one had offered to perform the menial office. And therefore, when supper was ready—

for so the words ought to be rendered,—Jesus, as the scene in all its minute details had impressed itself on the memory of the Evangelist of love, rose in perfect silence, stripped off His upper garment and tunic, took a towel, girt it round His waist, poured water into a bason, and began to wash the disciples' feet, and to wipe them with the towel wherewith He was girded. The example of so infinite a humility kept them dumb with deep shame, until Jesus came to Peter; but the warm-hearted, eager apostle starts back with almost indignant surprise. "Lord," he exclaims with his usual irrepressible emotion, "Dost *Thou* mean to wash *my* feet?" Thou the Son of God, the King of Israel,—Thou that hast the words of eternal life,—Thou who camest forth from God, and goest to God, perform a slave's office for Peter's feet? It is the old strange mixture of self-conceit and self-disgust,—the self-conceit of old, which under the shadow of Hermon had called upon him so stern a rebuke when he had said "That be far from Thee, Lord; this shall not be unto Thee;" the self-disgust which of old, on the Lake of Galilee, had flung him to his knees with that great cry wrung from his yearning heart, "Depart from me, for I am a sinful man, oh Lord." "What I do," said Jesus—and His words apply to all our mortal life, in which the lamp of faith can alone fling a little ring of illumination amid the encircling gloom—"What I do thou knowest not now, but thou shalt know hereafter." Unconvinced, he impetuously cries out, "Never, never, till the end of time shalt Thou wash my feet." "If I wash thee not," said Jesus gently, revealing to him the profound significance of the act, "thou hast no part in Me." "Little as thou mayest understand it, yet it is I, even I, who must wash thy feet, and no other. Thou canst not do it thyself. I alone can do it. Reject it indeed thou canst, for it depends on thine own will. I wash no man who prefers his stain. But to reject My cleansing is to reject Me. Therefore if I wash thee not, thou hast no part in Me." Then the deeper meaning of it all flashes in upon the conviction of the passionate apostle. "No part in Thee! oh forbid it, Heaven! Lord, not my feet only, but also my hands and my head." "Purge me with hyssop, and I shall be clean; wash me, and I shall be whiter than snow." But no: once more he is too impetuous; once more he has failed to catch the meaning of Christ. This total washing was not needed. The spiritual baptism for him was over. In that laver of regeneration he had been already dipped. Nothing more was needed than the daily cleansing from minor and freshly-contracted stains. The heart, the inward being of the disciples—these were already washed, were cleansed, were sanctified; but the feet, soiled with the clinging dust of the daily walk, these must be ever cleansed in daily renovation. "Jesus saith to him, He that hath been bathed (ὁ λελουμένος) needeth not but to wash his feet." And so, in His deep humility, in His abounding love, the Saviour washed His disciples' feet; washed— and surely there is something awful in thinking of it —bent over, with His sacred head,—touched with the tenderness of His cleansing hands,—even those feet of the traitor, which the foul dust of their murderous mission was soiling still.

II. Even from this brief explanation you will see at once that what Jesus did was an acted parable of deep and many-sided significance. Its easier and more obvious meanings—those which Jesus afterwards explained—were the unfeigned humility needed from all who would come to His sacred ordinance, and that duty of mutual love and helpfulness which makes of that ordinance a true communion. "If I, your Lord and Master, have washed your feet, ye ought also to wash one another's feet." Instead of these miserable heart-burnings and jealousies, ye, who are My children, love one another; do for one another all gentle acts of kindly courtesy; above all, wash one another's feet by that best, sweetest, kindliest service of all, which is that each should help his friend or his brother to draw daily a little nearer to God—to triumph daily a little more over human temptations and human infirmities—to leave the broad, dusty, trodden roads of iniquity and toil up the narrow, rocky, up-hillward path, which may make the feet bleed, but defiles them not,—even until that day, when,

> "Envy and calumny and hate and pain,
> And that unrest by men miscalled delight,
> Can touch us not, nor torture us again,"

because at last

> "From the contagion of the world's slow stain
> We are secure, and then can never mourn
> A heart grown cold, a head grown grey in vain."

But not dwelling now on these more obvious lessons of personal humility and mutual charity, as essentials for the Lord's Supper, and indeed for every means of grace, let us rather for a few moments think on the deeper spiritual significance of this washing of the feet by Christ, as pointing to our need, all through life, of the daily renewal of daily purifying grace.

III. To whom does it apply?

"Ye are clean," said Jesus, "but not all." And if this were true even of the chosen twelve, must it not, alas! be true also of every Christian congregation?

We have all indeed been baptised, all bathed in that laver of regeneration; but have all kept the white robe of their baptismal innocence? Ten, thirteen, fifteen, eighteen years ago, have the parents of you all stood, with some who loved them, at the holy font, in many a church near and far away, in England or beyond the sea, and while yet you smiled in unconscious infancy, you were admitted into the fold of Christ's Church, and signed with the sign of the cross in token that hereafter you should not be ashamed to confess the faith of Christ crucified, and manfully to fight under His banner against sin, the world, and the devil, and continue Christ's faithful soldier and servant unto your life's end. Many at that time were their hopes and prayers that their child might lead the rest of his life according to this beginning; and in old days it was customary to hang up the white robe—the chrisom robe of baptism—in silent memorial to each soul of the holiness which becomes Christ's house for ever. But that baptismal vow, have you all kept it? That white robe, has it received no fatal stain? Have you all fought, and manfully, under that banner? You have entered upon various paths of life. You have all passed from the sacred shadow of home to the society of other boys, congregated, it may be, from very different homes, and subjected, it may be, to very different influences. You have met with temptations. You have become familiar—some alas! how early— with the existence of evil, of disbelief, of disobedience, of dishonour, of wicked words, of corrupt communications. Into these temptations have none fallen,— first wilfully, then willingly, then greedily?—learnt to despise God's sabbaths, learnt not to mind grieving their parents, learnt to take God's name in vain, learnt to indulge in evil thoughts, learnt to hate and annoy their fellows, learnt to say that which is not true, and learnt to desire that which is not right; and, which is a yet deeper downward step, not only to do these things themselves, but to promote these things in others, and to have pleasure in those that do them? And if so, is it not true even of this young congregation—" Ye are clean, but not all ?" And if so, what shall we say to these ? Bathed indeed again they cannot be. Baptism, confirmation, which is the completion of baptism, can be but once; but the renewal by repentance of the grace of baptism, yes ! that can be for all time. For those who are not clean, who are bad boys and not good—servants and agents of the devil, not of God—for these there is no *earthly* remedy; their brother cannot save their souls, or pay their debt. Abana and Pharpar, rivers of Damascus, will not wash away their guilt; but there is a spiritual Jordan, wherein they may wash and be clean; there is a fountain opened for all sin and for all uncleanness. Only they must come to it of their own free will. God promises these forgiveness. He cannot promise them the repentance on which forgiveness alone depends; that must come from within; and whether they will hear or whether they will forbear, whether they will turn and repent, or whether they will wander farther and farther, and wax worse and worse—there is for them but one voice, and it cries : " Wash you, make you clean ; put away the evil of your doings from before Mine eyes ; cease to do evil ; learn to do well."

IV. But our Lord said: "He that is washed needeth not save to wash his feet," and " Ye are clean." And surely this is true of the vast majority of you. Surely the state I have described can be the state, if of any, yet only of a very few. Is not the condition of most of you rather this? You have indeed sinned; you have gone astray and done wickedly; you have sometimes offended with your tongue; the thoughts of your heart are sometimes very evil; you are but too conscious of many weaknesses, many transgressions. You know that you are not yet what you should be, what you might be, what you yet hope to be. But, while you acknowledge all this, you acknowledge it with shame and penitence. Your heart, though unfaithful, is not hard; your will, though biassed, is not corrupt; your rebellion, though manifest, is not absolute. You have not yet forgotten God, you have not yet ceased to struggle; you yet bow your head and kneel upon your knees and pray in sorrow and in sincerity to the Father whose love you often grieve. Careless you have been, cowardly, all but mutinous, but never an open traitor; falls you have had, disgraces, weaknesses, but you have never quite deserted your ranks, never been found fighting among the enemies of God. Though not good, you are at least trying to be good; though you have not done good, you have wished to do it, and at leas you have not got the blood of others on your soul. Well, my brethren, this is a very common state; and to you I say, that if you be sincere, if you be growing better, be it even but a little better, if, though not yet victorious, you are beginning to gain ground, even a little in an honest struggle against sin, then be assured of this, "God will not break the bruised reed, or quench the smoking flax." Come to Christ your Saviour, come with humble penitence, come with honest purpose, and gently, even as He longeth to do, will he wash each stain from those weak and wandering feet; he will cleanse from your repentant souls this daily assoilment of daily but unwilling sin; he will strengthen you to contract it less and less as years go by.

V. Only if, indeed, you be sincere you will not fail to recognise the mercy, the necessity of this daily cleansing. Alas! we may all sin, and we do sin, from human infirmity, and because we do not, as we might, seek strength where it can be found; but a little sin ceases to be little if, knowing it to be a sin, we yet think it little. Are these sins light, are they little? Consider against whom they are committed: against God; consider by whom they are committed: by you, a redeemed, a created, an adopted child of God—and you will not think them little. Weigh them, not with the false weights of self-deception, but in the unerring balance of the sanctuary, and you will not think them light. We walk in a muddy world, and Satan will not suffer even the saints of God to reach heaven with stainless feet; but as the feet, even of apostles, must be washed before they could sit at the Supper of the Lord, so must every stain be constantly washed from our souls before we are in any way fit to come into the presence of God. If we do not repent of these sins, if we defend or excuse them, if we try to cheat God and to cheat ourselves by making only a sham effort to get rid of them, that is like saying "Never shalt Thou wash my feet;" and then to us the answer will be still the same. "If I wash thee not, thou hast no part in Me."

a. For only think, if we do not seek this constant repentance, this constant purification, if, habitually, even in what we dare to think light things, we go wrong, and make no use of God's appointed means of grace to get rid of these daily sins, how vast, how terrible in their aggregate do they become! Walk into the forest and learn this lesson from the falling autumn leaves. Dead leaves fall one by one: how small, how light a thing is a dead leaf. But when they lie together in putrescent multitudes, how dense, how miry do the forest paths become! "*Si ea non times*," says St. Augustine, "*quando ponderas, time saltem quando annuneras*,"—if thou fearest not when thou weighest them, at least fear them when thou numberest them ; and "*Si non nocent ut fulmine, nocent saltem ut grandine*,"—if they lay not waste the vineyard of the soul like the single thunderbolt, they lay it waste, no less terribly, like the many hailstones.

β. And, then, consider too that however little such sins may seem, they always, inevitably, if unrepented of, lead to great ones. Does not every sinner begin with little sins? Was not every furious tempest which has battered and drowned the soul in destruction and perdition,—was it not once a little cloud no bigger than a man's hand?

γ. And consider, lastly, that God will have no reserves. He says, "Son, give Me thine heart;" and less than the whole heart He cannot and will not have. He does not say "Give Me thine heart, but one dark corner thereof thou mayest hide away from My light, and there thou mayest keep some secret idol to be worshipped with unhallowed incense and strange fires." He says, "Thou shalt," and "Thou shalt not,"—not "obey Me in this, and then in some other thing thou mayest disobey." Fared it well with Ananias and Sapphira when they kept back part of the price? Oh! how many men would be Christians if God would make but one exception in their favour, give them one indulgence, forgive them the retention of one bosom sin.

Ah, no! God would have none of His awful holiness, the moral law would have none of its unspeakable majesty, if this might be; and what God says is not this, but rather is "Pluck up the roots of bitterness. Make no truce with Canaan. Cut off the right hand; pluck out the right eye."

VI. I dwell on all this because I do so feel the importance, and want all of you to feel the importance of the lesson that a state of sin—of willing, of constant, of deadly, of habitual sin—is not, cannot be a state of grace. The one thing which is insisted on in the Mosaic law of sacrifice is that the victims offered at God's altar must be faultless victims—victims without blemish, and without spot. The ancients, sometimes when they offered to Jupiter a victim which was not quite white, would chalk over its coloured spots, and so try to pass it off as white, and, as it were, cheat their gods into an acceptance of that which was imperfect. But think you that the Allseeing God will thus be cheated into the acceptance of a soul of which the voluntary, the self-contracted stains are but smeared over and hidden under the white chalk of self-deception, of hypocrisy? Nay; but rather take that soul to Him all stained as it is, and ask Him to wash away its stains, and accept its wretchedness for the Great High Priest's sake, and to wash it white in His precious blood. This He will accept; this He will do; this fitness—if you pray for it with all your heart—He will give you.

Either praying—if only it be sincere praying—"will make us leave off sinning, or sinning will make us leave off praying." Either love of self will make us forget God, or love of God will make us forget self. But neither prayer, nor the Holy Communion is a charm; neither will benefit us—any more than they benefited the traitor Judas—if they be not approached in the right spirit under the right conditions. But if they are, how high, how infinite a blessing! Then they will tell on your daily life. These chapel services at which all, even the youngest of us, daily kneel—these Holy Communions, of which all who have reached the more difficult years of life are privileged to partake—will send us on our way refreshed, rejoicing. After each of them, if you have an enemy, you will at once forgive him in your heart, and try to be reconciled with him in your life ; if you know of one immoral boy who is doing mischief to others, and above all to his juniors, you will denounce him, make him tremble, check his bad career ; if you have one bad companion, you will amend him or cast him off; if you have left one duty shamefully neglected, you will go and do it ; if you have fallen constantly into one particular sin, you will nerve the whole force of your conscience to resist it. Thus will you go from strength to strength; these will be the vows which you will pay to the Most Highest; thus will you wash your hands in innocency, and so come to God's altar ; thus will you offer from your inmost heart that prayer which many a time has been offered in deep sincerity and penitence by many a Marlborough boy —many still living, some who are among the dead—before you;

> 'Then, gracious Lord, prepare
> Our souls for that dread day ;
> O wash us in Thy precious blood,
> And take our sins away."

November 5, 1874.

SERMON XXVI.

SOBERMINDEDNESS.

Tit. ii. 6.

"Young men likewise exhort to be sober minded."

So wrote St. Paul to Titus, the Bishop of Crete. The one thing which he most wished to impress upon the youthful members of his diocese was sobriety of mind. Let us herein follow his guidance; and though the subject is too large to be treated otherwise than fragmentarily and slightly,—though to a stranger, speaking among you solely out of respect to the wish of others,[1] many ways of treating it are precluded,—yet, since "great is the effort, great, and not so easy as it seems, to be good, and not bad," let us pray to God, to Him who can make even the grains of sand a barrier against the raging of the sea, that even a thing so poor and weak as a single sermon may, in its small measure, help us in the difficult daily strife to abhor that which is evil, to do that which is good.

But what is this σωφροσύνη, this sobermindedness to which you are thus exhorted? The word, as some of you may know, is one of the most suggestive in an almost perfect language. It is derived from σῶς and φρὴν, and means that moderation, temperance, integrity, soundness, in which consist the preservation, the safety

[1] This Sermon was preached at Eton College.

of the mind. "There is a way," says Solomon, "which seemeth right unto a man, but the end thereof are the ways of death." That way is the path of self-indulgence, of wilfulness, of intemperance, of excess. That path is the destruction of all nobleness, of all wisdom, of all life. It is the very dissolution of the immortal soul. The Greeks therefore called it χαλιφροσύνη, ἀκολασία, ἀσωτία, looseness of mind, absence of self-restraint, a condition that cannot be saved; which, in one direction, makes the soul soft and vulnerable, in another headstrong and profligate; in both cases loose, wandering, unapt for noble efforts, enslaved by base principles, prefering the senses to the spirit, the appetite to the reason, the death of sin to the life of God. The Greeks represented its effects in the grand legend of the Odyssey. The sailors of Ulysses, greedily drinking the poisoned cup of Circe, are smitten by her wand and changed to swine. Not so their chief; he confronts the sorceress; when she smites him with her wand he disdainfully draws his sword and drives her to her knees. Why? Because Hermes has given him a spray of magic herb, which is sovereign against these sorceries. What is that magic flower? It is σωφροσύνη—it is sobermindedness. It is a thought followed by a resolve, a resolve followed by an action, it is an action matured into a habit. It is the sovereignty of law and duty. It is the bridle of passion. It is the basis of integrity. It is the safeguard of all noble dispositions. It is, as one of our poets sings,

> "To sit, self-governed, in the fiery prime
> Of youth, obedient at the feet of law."[1]

It is the one effectual foundation which no insidious

[1] M. Arnold.

current at the basis of our being can ever sap or wash away. In one word, "it is the life of God in the soul of man."

Now, in exhorting you to sobermindedness, I might treat the subject in many ways. I might show you the necessity, I might show you the difficulty; yet, in spite of the difficulty, I might show you the possibility of its attainment. Yes, it *is* possible for those between whom and the fires of youth the Spirit of God has drawn His sevenfold veil—it is possible for those who listen to the voice behind them saying, "This is the way, walk ye in it," when they turn aside to the right hand or to the left. Life, it is true, is a struggle of conflicting elements, a contest of opposite tendencies, a law in the members warning against the law of the mind. Reason and temptation, duty and impulse, right and wrong, are ever striving for the mastery in the battle-field of the human heart; and, as when an archer would shoot an arrow, he draws the bowstring with one hand to his shoulder, and pushes from him with the other the curving wood, and then the string twangs, and, driven by the opposite motions, the swift arrow whizzes to its mark—such an arrow is the soul of man. In one direction the senses and the passions strain the quivering string; but the conscience, like the tough and curving wood, must restrain their tension, and the strong hand of the archer must guide and aim the arrow's flight; must, like the young Sun-God pierce the Python of corruption, must grasp the silver bowstring, and send the arrow hurtling into the monster's heart.

Let me then, as one slight fragment of the subject, ask you to think of one or two only of the directions in which you may strive after the acquisition of this high virtue. Let me point you to one or two only of the lowest rungs of that ladder of sunbeams, at the summit of which is the Son of God—one or two of the first steps on that path of righteousness, which is indeed no primrose path of dalliance,—which must be trodden often, as many of earth's noblest have trod it with bleeding feet and aching brow, but whereon "law and conscience will attend you on the right hand and on the left, walking by your sides with steadfast countenances and measured steps, and making you feel that you may not deviate or stop, lest they should turn upon you their intolerable looks of calm and awful condemnation."[1]

I. Now foremost among these most essential means of attaining to this chief glory of the youthful character, I would place *seriousness of mind*. And when I say this, do not for a moment think that in bidding you be serious, we would bid you be other than happy. Let not the Evil One, or those who do his work, let them not persuade you that seriousness is sadness, or righteousness depression. Religion is no " haggard necromancer " to be driven away, but a noble and loving friend, to be nobly welcomed. Innocence, so far from being the foe to true happ'ness, is her twin sister. Guilt is her foe. Innocent happiness, yes, that is within the reach of you all ; but guilty happiness, there is no such thing. Guilty pleasure there is ; it is " delusive and envenomed pleasure, its hollowness disappoints at the time, its poison tortures afterwards, its effects deprave for ever." But guilt and happiness—between these there is so deadly a repugnance that never can they even join hands. In bidding you be serious, God does not forbid you to be bright. Let the web of your youthful days be shot through with gold, and woven, an God will, of crimson in the grain. That web of life, hereafter, will quite inevitably be

[1] Whewell, *Sermons*, p. 8.

dimmed; for the most prosperous of you, misfortune will rend it; for the most innocent, sin will stain it; for the most fortunate, the dust of disappointment will gather and lie upon it: for all, thick and heavy the ashes of the churchyard will fall over it at last. But ere those days come, and those years draw nigh, the brighter it is the more blessed is it. But do you not think, or rather, do you not know, that it will be brightest of all for him whose brow is open, whose heart is innocent, whose conscience is clear, who is trying, humbly and heartily, to work in himself, and for his fellows, the work of God ? Will endless amusement, will wasted opportunities, will abused privileges, will stolen waters, and bread eaten in secret, make up to anyone for the loss of virtue, the loss of manliness, the loss of self-respect ? Will the laughter of fools, which is as the crackling of thorns under a pot—will the riotous living in a far-off land make up to him for that inward misery, when

> "The powers, that tend the soul
> To help it from the death that cannot die,
> And save it even in extremes, begin
> To vex and plague it ?"

There is a seriousness which is anguish; but this is the seriousness of retribution, and differs far from that holy and happy seriousness, that earnest, sober, reverent thoughtfulness at quiet moments on bended knees, to which God invites you, and which alone can save life from sin and shame. And you cannot escape from its needfulness. You have a dial on your chapel terrace, you have a clock in your school turret. You may squander time, you may determine to take no account of it; but can you hinder that creeping of the shadow on the dial which marks out our destinies ?—can you silence that ticking of the clock that beats out the little lives of men?—can you obliterate that inscription which warns you that, *Pereunt et imputantur?*

When will you who hear me die? In one sense it may be in a few short years; but in another sense never. The sun may be shattered; and the moon and stars rolled in one common fire with the heaven in which they shine; the solid earth we tread on may crumble into dust; but *you* shall live. The sinful body may die, but not the soul; and therefore you shall never die; for your souls are you. And therefore, make time for serious thoughts. Let no day pass without some memory of solemn things. Each morning as you rise, remind yourselves that " God spake these words and said"; each evening as you lie down to rest, let God's angels close the door of your heart on thoughts of purity and peace. The soul that has never lived face to face with eternity is a vulgar soul; the life that has never learnt the high law of holiness is a ruined and a wasted life.

> " Who never ate with tears his bread,
> Nor, through the long-drawn midnight hours
> Sate weeping on his lonely bed,
> He knows ye not, ye heavenly powers."

II. And next to seriousness, as a first step to sober-mindedness, be not surprised if I place obedience. That high virtue—the true school of empire—has two applications—a narrower and a wider; but the two are essentially connected. In the narrower sense it means the opposite of vain presumption, of spurious independence, of self-asserting importance; it means loyalty, humility, modesty of character and of demeanour, cheerful submission to just authority : in its wider—to which the narrower leads—it means the law of duty

cheerfully accepted as the law of life. Let us take the
narrower first. As the principle of the forest lies in the
acorn, so does the germ of every duty spring directly
from the thought of God. Now from our earliest years
God delegates some of His authority to our fellow-men—
first to our parents, then to all set over us. And therefore respect for authority is a sacred duty, as it is also
a divine command. Never has there been an age where
that command has been violated which has not become
a corrupt age. Never a country where it was neglected,
which has not been a despicable country. In the
loyalty, in the humility, in the obedience of youth—in
their reverence for their parents, in their respect for all
their elders,—have ever rested a nation's hopes. You
thirst for honour—you do well; but before honour is
humility; and without humility there can be no true
obedience. And this is the rule of every great society,
as it is, in truth, the rule of the universe of God.
Wherein lay the sole greatness of Sparta? Was it not
revealed on that epitaph over the Three Hundred at
Thermopylæ—

"Go, tell the Spartans, thou that passest by,
That here obedient to their laws we lie!"

Wherein lay the true majesty of Rome? Was it not
on the solid bases of filial and of national obedience
that she built the magnificent superstructure of universal
power? If you would know why Rome was great,
consider that poor Roman soldier whose armed skeleton
was found in a recess near the gate of Pompeii. When
on that guilty little city burst the sulphurous storm, it
would have been easy for him, as for so many, to escape.
Why did he not? Because to escape would have been
to abandon his post, and so—the unnamed hero—rather

than disobey, he just dropped the visor of his helmet, and stood there to die. And need I go to Greece and Rome? Is not obedience—is not simple loyalty to simple duty—the basis of all that is greatest in England's honour too? Is not this the glory of Balaclava?

> "Forward, the Light Brigade!
> Take the guns, Nolan said:
> Into the valley of Death
> Rode the six hundred.
> Theirs not to make reply,
> Theirs not to reason why,
> Theirs but to do and die:
> Into the valley of Death
> Rode the six hundred."

That was twenty years ago; and was there not another such instance—an instance of men in scores preferring death to disobedience some ten years ago? It was at the wreck of the *Birkenhead*. The good ship had crashed at sunset against a sunken rock; the boats were too few, the sea was rushing in; sharks were thrusting their horrible black fins through the white breakers of the boiling surf; and amid the shrieks of women and children some one clamoured that all should save themselves who could. Then, clear and loud, rang out the voice of the good colonel, bidding the men to their ranks. That order meant nothing less than death, death in those raging waters,—death among those savage sharks—but it was instantly obeyed. In perfect order the boats were pushed from the shattered vessel, rowing the women and children to the shore, while, inch by inch, the ship sank down and down, but still under steadfast men, till the last great wave rolled over her, and "obedient even unto death," brave men—loyal to their chief, loyal to England, loyal to God—sank to their noble burial under the bloody surf.

III. I will mention but one virtue more out of many, which is simply indispensable to him among you who would be soberminded: it is *diligence*. It has a lower and a higher sense, but remember that, in its very lowest sense of all, it is necessary. A diligent man is not indeed always holy, but an idle man cannot be. A diligent man will not always be unassaulted by temptation, but an idle man never is. He who can sit for hours in his room, doing nothing, thinking of nothing, talking of nothing, and of things worse than nothing—he who can deliberately make pleasure, and not progress, moral and intellectual, the sole object of his school-life—in him there can be no sobermindedness. And why? Because the faintest trace of it would impress on him the two great truths, one that the work which God requires of us all to do is vast, and the other, that the time to do it in is short. The great work of the ancient physician begins with the memorable words: " Life is short; art long; opportunity fleeting; experiment slippery; judgment difficult." But perhaps you do not think that the time for work is short? Alas! you soon will know it; swiftly, imperceptibly does boyhood flow into youth, and youth into manhood; and much is he to be pitied who, after a boyhood ingloriously wasted, if not pitiably degraded, suddenly finds himself standing upon the threshold of manhood, a bankrupt in strength and virtue, because, instead of living on the just income of the present, he has been madly squandering that vigour of his youth which was meant to be the capital of his future. I would entreat you for your own sake, for England's sake—you, the hopes of this great nation, you who are to bear up the ancient honours of this godly and virtuous island—never be idle. If you are, sadly and soon shall the days of emptiness and dreariness set in, the youth of folly succeeded by the old age of cards; but if, from boyhood onward, you are wise and self-denying, you will find that the time for lofty pleasures can never pass away. Look at the mountain-ash. Early in summer it clothes itself in its delicate and odorous flowers; and, when these fall, for a time it has nothing but leaf to show: but look at it again in autumn, and then, "decorated from outmost fringe to topmost pinnacle," it is one pyramid of glowing scarlet. That brilliant fruitage of its maturity is nothing in the world but the ripened blossom of its youth. Be you like the mountain-ash. Gather when young, and you shall possess when old the riches of knowledge and of wisdom. Nor this alone, but the mere act of gathering, the mere grandeur of a pure and spiritual ideal, the mere effect of time duly appreciated and wisely used, shall save you from a thousand remorseful memories and vague regrets—shall help you to be in God's sight soberminded,—*i.e.* to acquire your bodies, to save your souls.

I have kept you too long; yet allow me one last word. I have tried to show you that seriousness, obedience, diligence are necessary to sober-mindedness; as frivolity, presumption, idleness are its utter bane. And to you, who listen with meek heart and due reverence to the messages of God,—to you who wish to learn—who have tried to learn—the dignity of seriousness, the grace of obedience, the inexorable duty of a manly diligence,—to you I say, respect yourselves: respect yourselves, for God made you, for Christ redeemed you; respect yourselves for the dignity of God's image is upon you, and the seal of your redemption has been marked upon your brows. *Dominamini.* Rule-

rule yourselves; rule the advocates of sin and folly; rule every evil thing that would assault and thwart you. In the name of Christ your Saviour be kings and priests. Thou shalt tread upon the lion and the adder, the young lion and the dragon shalt thou trample under feet. Go forth in this confidence; go forth from strength to strength. You will meet with difficulties; stand up to them with dauntless front. You will meet the sorceress—drive her to her knees. Stronger are they that are with, than they that are against you. Against you are all the shams, the emptinesses, the frivolities,—all the passing fashions; all the lying atheisms; all the prurient vanities;—with you is all that is sweet and strong, all supreme and noble men, all divine and eternal principles; and above all, there is your Father God. With the aid of His Holy Spirit in the present, with the gift of His free forgiveness for all the past, be faithful to Him, be faithful to yourselves, be faithful to your fellow-men; and then, let the earth be smitten into ruin, and the heaven be shrivelled into smoke, but you—like all the saints and children of the kingdom—you shall be partakers of God's eternity, and even in this world shall not have lived in vain.

October 18, 1874. (*Preached also at Eton.*)

SERMON XXVII.

NOT FAR FROM THE KINGDOM OF HEAVEN.

MARK xii. 84.

"Thou art not far from the kingdom of Heaven."

A CERTAIN Scribe, struck with the wisdom with which our Blessed Lord had silenced the captious questions of Pharisees and Sadducees, stood up and asked Him "Which was the first and greatest commandment?" It is one of those miserable questions which are sure to come in vogue when the letter is exalted above the spirit, and theology held in more account than life. The rabbis, with the fatal ingenuity of a perverse literalism, had counted up the 365 prohibitions and 248 precepts of the Mosaic Law; and, understanding nothing of the royal unity of law as directly involved in the unity of God—nothing of the fact that outward service is valueless without the love of the heart—nothing of the fact that a man may only offend in one point, and yet be guilty of all—they were constantly discussing the relative importance of fringes and phylacteries, the relative heinousness of forswearing by the temple and forswearing by its gold. Not so our Lord. He, as ever, going straight to the heart of the matter, laid down one eternal principle. Pointing, perhaps, to the Scribe's phylactery, in which, on a strip of folded parchment, was written the text to which He referred, He said, "Hear, oh Israel; the Lord our God is one Lord;" and He added that we must love God with all the heart that lives and worships, with all the soul which enjoys and feels, with all the understanding which thinks and questions, with all the strength which achieves and wills. And this alone comprises all; but, being fallen and guilty, man requires something more, both as an illustration and a test. Love to man, then, is the natural sequence, the necessary condition of love to God. The second table is but a method of our fulfilment of the first; there is no less, no greater; nothing subordinate, nothing unnecessary. Was not this what Moses himself had symbolized when he had bade them wear tassels on the hem of the garment—two, as the tables of the law were two—each consisting of various threads, as the details of the general commandments were many, but both bound together by one prominent cord of brilliant blue, as if to show that their unity—nay, their very existence—depended on the one indivisible law of heavenly love? Of this even the better Pharisees were aware. The Scribe at once recognised the truth—at once referred it to that grand passage of the prophet Micah, which had shown that to do justly, and to love mercy, and to walk humbly with our God, was better than holocausts and hecatombs of all the cattle upon a thousand hills.

1. Our Lord was pleased with the candour, the wisdom, the enthusiasm, of his reply. It was His special tenderness, it was His immense love, that He would never break the bruised reed or quench the smoking flax. In His infinite holiness, in His heavenly innocence, He did not loathe the leper's touch or the harlot's tears. Though these Scribes and Pharisees

would have embittered to the very dregs any life less noble than His, He could praise even His worst foes, and gently and kindly said to the Scribe, " Thou art not far from the kingdom of heaven." To such a nature as that of the Scribe—a nature not ungenerous, if very faulty, not unenlightened, though much misled—how precious, how healing, would these words have been. Oh! let us not be all so afraid of words of hearty encouragement and honest praise. They reinspire the fading effort; they reinvigorate the trembling arm; they fall like the dew of heaven upon the fainting soul. The sunbeam touches the mountain, and at its touch the heavy load of winter which the hurricane could not dislodge melts and slips insensibly away, and where but yesterday was snow, to-day is green grass and gentian flower. It is even so with words of sympathy, which are so rare, alas! while they can cheer or bless, but which only, when they are useless, fall thick as a dust over the buried dust. But Christ was not thus jealous of making anyone a trifle happier. He knew how to give natural encouragement and generous praise. " Blessed art thou, Simon Barjona;" " Behold an Israelite indeed;" " I have not found so great faith, no, not in Israel;" " She hath done what she could;" " Thou art not far from the kingdom of heaven:"— such are a few of Christ's words of approval. It is something to abstain from slander, and censoriousness, and the hard luxury of injustice; something to be like that good man who passed everything which he had to say of others through the three sieves: Is it just? Is it necessary? Is it kind? But it is more to be like Christ, to be generous and cordial, to have "the glow of sympathy" with "the bloom of modesty;" not to be too vain to appreciate; not to be too envious to help and cheer.

2. "Thou art not far from the kingdom of heaven." What was this kingdom of heaven? Our Lord, at different times, used it in different senses: sometimes of the new dispensation which was dawning on a weary and wicked world; sometimes of individual righteousness and joy in believing; sometimes of the glory in heaven to come. But with Him who is an eternal Now, these three senses are one. To be of the kingdom of heaven is nothing less than Christianity, salvation, eternal life. And this Scribe was not far from the kingdom of heaven; he was listening to its precepts; he was talking to its King; it was but to believe, to repent, to pray, and all—the secret of the past, the blessedness of the present, the glories of the future—all, all were his.

And is it not ours? is it not yours and mine? Oh, as far as mere privileges are concerned, it is infinitely more ours than it was this Scribe's. The cross upon our foreheads can only be obliterated, the title-deeds of our birthright only lost, by our own apostasy. The late king of Prussia was one day playing with some little children, and asked them to what realm of nature various things belonged. He showed them a precious stone, and they said to the mineral kingdom; a rose, and they said to the vegetable; a leopard's skin, and they said to the animal. "And to what kingdom do I belong?" he asked, pointing to himself. "To the kingdom of heaven," said one sweet little voice in prompt reply. Yes; oh that we had the grace always, at all moments, to remember it! You, and I, and every baptised Christian in this Christian land, are by birth, by baptism, by inheritance, by privileges, members of the kingdom of heaven.

3. I see you seated in this fair house of God, silent,

attentive, reverent. It is the blessed Sabbath day, and for many of you a Sabbath of special significance. You have been hearing the solemn organ-music; you have been joining in psalm, and canticle, and hymn. Free, and quick, and sharper than any two-edged sword, the Word of God is in your hands. All of you have lived in Christian homes. Most of you have had a father's high example and a mother's yearning prayers. I know that you pray. I know that God does not suffer your consciences to sleep. I know that in moments of guilt, in moments of peril, in moments of remorse, amid the busy labours of the day, amid the silent watches of the night, I know that that Voice says to you, "My son, if sinners entice thee, consent thou not;" or, "Be not weary in well doing;" or, "Be sure your sin will find you out;" or, "What is this that thou hast done?" And in all this, outwardly and visibly, and here and now, it is true of the very guiltiest among you, that "Thou art not far from the kingdom of heaven."

4. Not far: yet you may not be therein. These are but Christian privileges; they go for nothing, or, rather, they go only for this: the certainty of a dread responsibility, the possibility of a deeper condemnation. Do not think that if you be wicked, and hard, and proud, and sensual, and impenitent, that it will help you to have said, "Lord, Lord," or to have borne the Christian's name. "Trust ye not in lying words, saying, the temple of the Lord, the temple of the Lord, the temple of the Lord are these." It did not avail King Uzziah to stand in the holy place, or to swing the golden censer, when lo! on his forehead was the leprous spot. It did not avail Balaam, the splendid sorcerer, to have uttered many a glorious truth, when he committed that last, worst, most accursed, most detestable of sins, by doing

the devil's work and corrupting others; and so, after wishing that he might die the death of the righteous, and his last end be like his, he perished, as he deserved, by the pitiless, griding, contemptuous swords of those whom he had striven to seduce, in the red battle among the routed enemies of God. Not to be far from the kingdom of God is still to be outside, and that outside is cold, and waste, and dark; and without are dogs; and pride, and lust, and shame, and the *mala mentis gaudia* are there. Judas was an apostle; Judas was not far from the kingdom of heaven; yet Judas committed the foulest sin that history records to us; and how did Judas die?

II. But, my brethren, there is a yet nearer and better sense in which it may be said of many of you, "Thou art not far from the kingdom of heaven." For far the most of you, not all—I will not say all, but far the most of you—not in outward privileges only, but also in conduct and principles, in heart and life, possess many of its gifts. In knowledge and awakenment, in docility and sweetness, in graceful obedience and cordial gratitude, in manly diligence and unswerving truthfulness, I believe that there are many of you to whom, as to the candid Scribe, the living Saviour might have uttered the same gentle and approving words. We do not despise these virtues: nay, we love, we honour, we rejoice in them; and yet, remember always, they bespeak no change in heart; they are not enough; they may coexist with a state of sin, and therefore are not a state of grace. In spite of them the heart may not be God's. The tree is not tested by its green leaves or by its vernal blossoms, but by its fruit; and if, for all its green leaves, its root be as rottenness and its blossoms go up as dust, who then shall stay the uplifted axe? If it bear fruit—

if not, cut it down; why cumbereth it the ground? You do not swear; you do not break the Sabbath day; you do not steal; you do not lie; you are not guilty of drunkenness; you have never led others into sin; you have not spoken wicked blasphemy; you do not sport with your own deceiving, and foam out your own shame. You do well. But do not even the Gentiles so? It is not Christ only who condemns such sins; it is not from the pulpit only that they are reprobated; the world, too, brands them; it does not admit to the cheat, the liar, the drunkard, the blasphemer, her title of gentleman. Nay, the world goes even farther. Its tone is far more severe than that of some you; it condemns wasteful gluttony; it condemns aimless idleness; it condemns inordinate amusement; it condemns the sacrifice of duty to pleasure; it condemns the consuming much and producing little; it condemns the "sitting down at the feast of life and going away without paying the reckoning." And all this is so far good; yet all this does not yet make a man of the kingdom of heaven. These are not the one thing needful; they are not repentance; not the new birth; and "Verily, verily, I say unto you, except a man be born again, he cannot enter the kingdom of heaven."

III. "Thou art not far from the kingdom of heaven." The doors of paradise are open near you; you may breathe snatches of its odours; you may catch echoes of its melodies; you may feel, at times, the sweetness of its angel presences, the hovering of its angel wings. Oh, *si non procul es, intra!* Oh, it needs but the violence of a faithful purpose, one spring over the threshold, and you are safe. But stop! there is an amulet, a charm on that threshold. There shall in no wise enter anything that defileth: for one word is written on that threshold, over which none can lightly tread. What is that one word? It is repentance. That kingdom of heaven is eternal, is infinite; it has many mansions; but the gate is single, the path narrow, the roof low. Think you that you can enter full of evil and wicked thoughts? think you that you can enter swollen with wind and the rank mist of your own sensual conceit? He who would enter must bow the insolent head and purify the corrupted heart. He must break, if need be, his old life in two, and fling away the worser half. He must cut a deep line between his present and his past. In one word he must be converted; he must be born again.

IV. It is not often that any crisis of life comes to us consciously and suddenly. As the tree falls so it lies; but as the tree has been gradually and gradually leaning, so it falls. And thus it is that the lost soul seldom knows what was its last opportunity, what the last little act that consummated its ruin—for what poor mess of pottage it sold its heaven. It is done on a common day; it is done in an ordinary hour; no sigh of pity runs through the shuddering foliage; no wing of angel flashes from the silent blue. Yet surely, inevitably, "he that avoideth not small faults, by little and little falleth into greater." A watch may be but a second wrong; a mere touch would regulate it; the opportunity is neglected; the second goes on increasing; it becomes an hour, many hours; and alas! how soon does the watch become wrong wholly, not only useless, but misleading. You who have been confirmed, and who have forgotten, and have not kept the vow of your confirmation, you know how fatally it is so. And you know, too, that on no occasion probably in all life is a human soul brought face to face with the test of a known conscious choice between good and evil, between blessing and cursing, between life and death, between God and Satan, between the world and heaven, between the lusts of the flesh and the aspirations of the soul,—on no occasion probably are the interests of the spiritual life staked, as it were, so absolutely on a single die—as it was to you on the day of your confirmation, as it will be to-morrow to nearly one hundred of you more. There are in life unknown, unconscious crises; tomorrow will be to many of you a known, a conscious crisis; on the spirit in which you meet it, in which you have been preparing to meet it, in which you mean to carry out its obligations, in which you purpose to approach its new and sacred privileges, how much of the peace or misery, of the shame or nobleness, of your future life depends! Almost might we apply to it the solemn appeal and fancy of the poet:

> "There is a light cloud near the moon:
> 'Tis passing now, 'twill pass full soon;
> If, by the time its vapoury sail
> Hath ceased her shaded orb to vail,
> Thine heart within thee be not changed,
> Then God and man are both avenged,
> Dark will thy doom be—darker still
> Thine immortality of ill."[1]

Oh! of that great occasion of your life it is true, if it be true of any moment of life, *Ex hoc momento pendet æternitas.* And you, whose choice was made for you long ago—you whose service is pledged—whose military oath is recorded; can it, shall it, be that any of you will be among the enemies of good,—you among those who increase, and not diminish the sum of the world's wickedness—you of them who, out of their own base, wretched weakness, pause not to imperil their own souls and the souls of others—you among those who offend Christ's little ones—you under the scope of those words of

[1] Byron, *Siege of Corinth.*

immeasurable ruin from the lips of immeasurable Love ? Oh, your place is not there. Leave even now that banded apostasy ; for you know not whether ever again it will be possible for you to do so. Death is always uncertain. Who knows but even now, for some of us, for you or me, the fatal bowstring may have twanged, the fatal arrow have leapt from the string ? If it have, no sevenfold shield can stay its flight. Yet, though we know not for how long, we still have time—be it but one day, one hour, one week—to repent and to turn to God. And if the arrow smite us—be it soon or be it late—it shall have no sting, no victory then. It shall but glance down from heaven the welcome, the blessed signal, that, pure, happy, redeemed, forgiven, we may pass into the Presence of our God—not far from the kingdom of heaven now, we shall be in it—in it for ever and for ever—then.

March 14, 1875.

SERMON XXVIII.

RUNNERS FOR A PRIZE.

1 Cor. ix. 24.

"Know ye not that they which run in a race, run all, but one receiveth the prize? So run that ye may obtain."

Phil. iii. 13.

"This one thing I do, forgetting those things which are behind, and reaching forth unto those things which are before, I press toward the mark for the prize of the high calling of God in Christ Jesus."

Heb. xii. 1, 2.

"Wherefore seeing we also are compassed about with so great a cloud of witnesses, let us lay aside every weight, and the sin which doth so easily beset us, and let us run with patience the race that is set before us, looking unto Jesus, the author and finisher of our faith."

These three texts are in themselves a sermon. They show how deeply the imagery and incidents of the Isthmian games — which were simply the athletic sports of Greece—had impressed the quick imagination of that great apostle, with whom, for convenience' sake, I may here also class the unknown author of the Epistle to the Hebrews. Writing, for instance, to Corinth, the gay and dissolute capital of Achaia, and appealing to the spectacle with which they were all so familiar, and of which they were all so proud, he tells them that, as they had seen their chosen youth striving

in the racecourse, so they were to run, that they might
obtain. In the lively imaginations of his Greek converts,
the words would summon up a vivid picture—the level
stadium under its flooding sunshine—the intent gaze of
the thronging multitudes—the strained muscles, the
passionate eagerness, the strong determination of the
runners — the judges distributing to the successful
athletes those green garlands of Isthmian pine—
the glad, bright faces, the hearty congratulations, the
loud applause of the victor's friends. On such familiar
reminiscences he founds high moral lessons — he
translates to a loftier region the scenes of daily life,
and bathes common incidents in the pure light which
falls on them from high teachings of the moral law.
In this he does but follow the example of his Master,
Christ, and the intense and searching simplicity of His
habitual illustrations. He, as I have said elsewhere,
"spoke of green fields, and springing flowers, and
budding trees; of the red or lowering sky; of sunrise and sunset; of wind and rain; of light and
storm; of clouds and lightning; of stream and river;
of stars and lamps; of salt and bread; of nets and
fish; of quivering bulrushes and burning weeds; of
rent garments and bursting wine-skins; of precious
pearls and lost pieces of money." To follow such pre-
cedents needs no apology, nor need I hesitate to say
that it is your just-concluded races and your athletic
sports—as real to you as the Isthmian games were
to the people of Corinth—which have suggested my
thoughts to-day. Those races and sports may, to the
thoughtful mind, shadow forth much that lies beyond
themselves. You will be able to think of many suggestive incidents on which I shall not touch. You
have seen some, for instance, put down their names

who, when the time came—either from accident, or because they had meanwhile changed their minds, or because they had not trained—did not appear at the starting-point at all. Is there nothing like this in the Christian life? You have seen some start well, run for a time even in the front, then falter, flag, fall into the rear, drop out of the course altogether. Is there nothing like this in the Christian life? Again: you have seen a disheartened runner, cheered by a word of encouragement, pluck up strength, pass his rival, spring to the front, and win the prize. Is there nothing like this in the Christian race? Yes; there is something like all these things. In this racecourse of a holy life where God has placed us, some put down their names indeed to run, but never even start. Others begin to run and fall out; others stop short from weakness and irresolution; others deliberately turn aside. The race sweeps on, but they are not in it. The prizes are given, but there is no prize for them.

But in the few plain words which I shall speak this morning I will not dwell on these or other illustrations, because it will be enough to consider briefly those main contrasts and main resemblances which, in the texts which I have read to you, were seized with such unerring accuracy by St. Paul himself:—

I. Now the first contrast which struck St. Paul was this. In the Isthmian races many ran, but one alone could win; for that one there was the flush of success—the thrill, the happiness, the exultation of triumph; for the others—though they may have deserved as well, though their failure may have been solely due to accident, though they may have used their best efforts—there was failure, mortification, defeat—they had to go home with their downcast looks, their frustrated endeavours, their disappointed hearts. It is so, alas! in most of earth's too numerous competitions; the success of one means the failure of many; and men, it has been said, grow by degrees each to deem of himself " as only one among the myriad of horses set to drag on the chariot of Time—to deem that his only pleasure is to snatch what provender he can as he rushes along the way—that his only glory is to surpass his yoke-fellows in speed—and that, anon, when his strength fails, the chariot will pass over him, and millions of hoofs will trample him to dust." But, thank God! so it is not in our heavenly race. How miserable would it be if it were! What a happy thought it is that none who enter that race are defeated; that no rivalries can enter into it; no jealousies spoil; no failure embitter. Like the sweet air, like the summer sunshine, the glories and rewards of it may be enjoyed to the very full by all who truly seek them: if one succeeds, the faces of all are brightened; and so far from envy at what this man is famed for, or for what another is preferred—the individual happiness is so thoroughly the general happiness—that, like the common light reflected from within a globe of crystal, the radiances of each pure spirit are but multiplied and made intense by myriads of reflections. Run only in the Christian race, and the prize is yours. You need not be like the brave adventurer who wrote with diamond on the window-pane—

"Fain would I climb, but that I fear to fall,"

nor need the warning written beneath it by the Maiden Queen,—

"If thy heart fail thee, do not climb at all."

No; let not your heart be troubled. In your Father's house are many mansions; in your Father's hand are many crowns; and though myriads fail, yet the goal, thank God! shall be reached by a great multitude whom no man can number, of all peoples and nations and languages; and I heard the number of them, even ten thousand times ten thousand, and thousands of thousands.

And that prize, those crowns,—*there* is a second contrast. All that the racers got directly, their sole prize ostensibly, was a withering garland of green pine. They struggled for a shadow; the shout of popular applause, empty and evanescent as the quivering air which gave it breath, fame which palled before the week was over, hollow glories and disappointing successes, which would neither sate the soul's hunger nor quench its thirst. Those green leaves, from a tree which grew on every hill, and withered before the sun had set—what a type were they of all earth's prizes! The world has never even deceived itself about them, and in thousands of proverbs and allegories has branded the bitterness of its own chosen pleasures, and the inanity of its own cherished hopes. The cloud of Ixion, the stone of Sisyphus, the wasted voice of Echo, the self-withering infatuation of Narcissus, Pygmalion pining for love of a statue, Midas starving in the midst of gold, the wings of Icarus, melting even while he soared, and harrowing his soul with the coming terror of the inevitable fall,—such are earth's treasures; and even were they as real as they are illusory, how short a time—for what a brief and fleeting spell of youth—they last! "Ai! ai!" sings the sweet Greek poet, "when the soft plants perish in the garden, the bright green parsley and the curly blooming anethus, they live again and spring for another year; but we, the great, and strong, wise men, we, when once we die, forgotten in the hollow grave,

εὕδομες εὖ μάλα μακρὸν ἀτέρμονα νήγρετον ὕπνον

we sleep the long, long, illimitable sleep that never wakes." And all sacred teaching, and all Christian song echo the same thing; the things which men seek, the Scriptures tell us, are but as the grass of the fading flower—as the stream which fails in summer—as clusters of the poisonous vine—as apples of Sodom, that fill the mouth with gravel and bitterness—as stones of the wilderness, which cannot be turned to bread: and—as the light lyrist was forced to sing,—

"And false the light on Glory's plume
  As fading hues of even ;
And Valour's wreath, and Beauty's bloom
  Are garlands given to the tomb :
    There's nothing true but heaven."

Nothing but that,—but that is the prize for which we run; the peace of God, the deliverance from sin, the eternal glory and the crown, not of withering pine but of immortal amaranth, the crown incorruptible, undefiled, that fadeth not away.

II. But if there are these two *contrasts* between the single as compared to the universal success, and the poor compared to the infinite reward, there are also some instructive *resemblances* between the racer's running and the Christian's life.

1. Here, for instance, was one : that both races inevitably required present effort and past self-denial. "He who striveth for the mastery," says St. Paul to the Corinthians, "is temperate in all things." You know perfectly well that it is useless for an ordinary boy to run in a race who has not, at least in some measure,

trained himself to run; useless for him to run sluggishly and lazily, without trying to do his best. It is not the loose, effeminate, lymphatic boy, who eats, and drinks, and is self-indulgent and lethargic, and who is loth to give himself any trouble, it is not this kind of boy who can carry off prizes in such—or indeed in any—competitions. He must at least be active and vigorous, and put his heart and will into what he does. Oh remember all of you the moral of this: if you would run the Christian race—the holy race for which God has placed you each in this stadium of the world—you too must be temperate in all things, not gluttonous, not soft, not half-hearted; you must, as St. Paul says, crucify the flesh with its affections and lusts; you must mortify your members that are upon the earth; you must subdue your body as with blows, and lead it about as a slave to that nobler reason which dominates in every soul wherein vice and falseness have not, like a cancer, eaten it utterly away. To have been baptised, to have been confirmed, to have had your names put down—to have put down your own names for that race—when you don't intend to run at all, or not to run in earnest, or to run only as pleases yourself—this in the Christian life, whether you call it apostasy or hypocrisy, and though for a time your sin may not find you out, is just certain wrath and deadly ruin. And do not be deceived into thinking that it will be easy to change at any time, or to repent when you like. So as by fire— a fire which shall burn and scathe in proportion to the shamefulness of your guilt—not otherwise. It is not easy to run God's race. You have heard, indeed, of saints who have made their lives,—not foul, weak, degraded, as some lives are—not like a fretting plaguespot to all who come near them—but beautiful to God kindled, like beacon-lights upon the holy hills; do you think they reached those heights at a bound? No! they were men of like passions with ourselves; their dangers, their weaknesses, their temptations were ours; but because they fought the good fight, because they did not live at random, because they lived lives of prayer and self-denial and watchfulness, not lives of sham repentances, followed by unbroken transgressions—because, whereinsoever they had fallen into sin they turned from every sin which they had ever committed to do that which was lawful and right—thus it was that they gained the love of God, and His seal was on their foreheads; and they ran and won, and they wrought, and fought and overcame.

2. There then is one resemblance—both races required effort; here is a second, that they who run in either must get rid of every impediment, must lay aside every weight, $\kappa a\lambda\ \tau\dot{\eta}\nu\ \epsilon\dot{\upsilon}\pi\epsilon\rho\acute{\iota}\sigma\tau a\tau o\nu\ \dot{a}\mu a\rho\tau\acute{\iota}a\nu$, and the besetting sin, the sin that clings to the limbs like an enfolding robe. If you had to win a race on which your very life depended, would you try to run it laden under a crushing burden? would you try it with a log tied to your feet? would you clothe yourself for it in a long entangling cloak? Yet it is no less absurd to try to run the Christian race with all the heavy load upon you of worldly purposes and unrepented sins. This must not, cannot be. How many have asked the impenitent question of the wicked king,

"May one be pardoned and retain the offence?"

and when met by the stern *Non licet* of conscience, have been forced like him to the despairing cry,

"O wretched state! oh bosom black as death!
O limed soul that, struggling to be free,
Art more enslaved."

And there is the same thought in the *Idylls* of our great living poet; where Arthur's knight, Sir Lancelot, disgraced, and by a great guilt, goes down and sits by the river and sees the high reed wave, and says with a heart that almost bursts with sorrow—

> "I needs must break
> These bonds that so defame me. . . .
> . . . But if I would not, oh may God,
> I pray Him, send a sudden angel down
> To seize me by the hair and bear me far,
> And fling me deep in that forgotten mere
> Amid the tumbled fragments of the hills."

He well knew that until the guilt was utterly abandoned, was bitterly repented of, he could not be true to God's ideal of him, he could not die a holy man.

III. I will mention only one more resemblance which struck St. Paul, which was that the runner, like the Christian, must ever keep his eye upon the goal. In that race there must be no pause, but steady perseverance; no swerving aside, but unbroken progress; no looking back, but straining forward; no meaner object to distract or to divert, "but this one thing I do." Here, too, there is the warning of wise and dearly-bought experience in the legends of antiquity. Atalanta stops to pick up the golden apples, and she is worsted in the race. Orpheus has regained, with his Eurydice, the verge of light—he looks back, and *Ibi omnis effusus labor*—wasted is all his toil. Nor is it otherwise in Scripture. Remember what came to Israel sighing for the fleshpots of Egypt. Remember Lot's wife; she looked back to the guilty city, and the suffocating whirlwind caught her in its sulphurous winding-sheets, and she became a salt pillar on Sodom's plain. Our Lord Himself pointed the same warnings. "No man, having put his hand to the plough, and looking back, is fit for the kingdom of God;" and "Let the dead bury their dead. Follow thou Me!"

Such, then, are some of the contrasts, some of the resemblances, between the Christian's and the runner's race; the contrasts that, in the Christian race, all, not one, may win, and that the prize is not a few shillings, or a few withering pine-leaves, but an immortal crown; and the resemblances, that the heavenly race, like the earthly, can be won only by effort—can be won only by laying aside every weight—can be won only by steadily fixing the eye upon the goal. Oh let us all—for the life of all is a race—keep these things steadily in mind. Let us try to help each other, for we are brothers in the great family of God. Let us strive in earnest, for the reward is infinite. Let us keep our eye upon the hope set before us, without which our life, even if it be not a curse to others, must be a failure to ourselves. In the race of school life, with its not ungenerous emulations, on which for many of you no little of your future must depend; in the race of life itself, in which nothing can save you from shame and sorrow but energy, prudence, temperance, self-denial, self-purification, singleness of aim; in the race of your Christian calling, on which depends not only the happiness, the nobleness, the purity of your lives, but even the safety of your immortal souls;—be strong, be earnest, be sincere. The stadium may be long or short, it may as it were be a mile, or half-a-mile, or 200 yards—but the exceeding immortality—'the dateless and irrevoluble circles of eternity'—is for all who can say, "I have finished my race; I have kept the faith; henceforth there is laid up for me a crown of glory, which the Lord the Righteous Judge, shall give me on that day."

April 4, 1875.

SERMON XXIX.

THE CONTINUITY OF GODLINESS.

Psalm lxiii. 1.

"O God, Thou art my God, early will I seek Thee."

I ENDEAVOURED last Sunday to sketch for you something of the history of the human conscience in its various phases of agitation and of peace. I wish this morning to urge upon you the grandeur and the happiness which result from an *early* devotion to the law of conscience; I desire to show how sad is the loss of *continuity* in a pure and holy life;—may my words, under the blessing of the Holy Spirit of God, enable you to realise the truth that not to have sinned is infinitely better than even, having sinned, to have been forgiven,—that a Paradise never wholly lost is transcendently sweeter than even a Paradise regained!

Each of us at birth is placed in a garden of Eden; for each of us there grows in that garden a Tree of Life, and a Tree of the Knowledge of good and evil; it is possible for each of us even to the last to walk that garden with peaceful feet unterrified by the flaming sword. We cannot indeed do this—since we are very frail— by being absolutely sinless, as are the angels in heaven, but we can do it by living, through God's grace, free from wilful, free from presumptuous, free from habitual, free from deadly sins. Yes, there have been some,—some like us,—some, not greater favourites of God than we, since God has no favourites,[1]—whose life, like a day which is golden to the last, has been spent, if not in the Paradise of faultless holiness, yet at least in the Paradise of an approving conscience,—in the Paradise of Peace with God. Some, the very happiest, the very divinest they,—but, alas! not many. You know how often this evanescence of man's early hopefulness is touched upon in Holy Scripture. It is compared to seeds that do not bear;—to trees whose leaf withereth;—to blossoms that go up as dust;—to the morning cloud that melteth;—to the early dew that is exhaled.[2] And Literature too dwells frequently on this loss of Eden,—this falling of man from his first innocence. "There is," says one, "in every child of man an ideal primitive being which nature has designed with her most maternal hand, but which man too often strangles or corrupts."[3] "From what have I not fallen," writes another, "if the child which I remember was indeed myself."[4] "Childhood," says yet another, "is an everlasting promise which no man keeps." The most eloquent of English divines compares the beginning of such lives to a young trooper riding into battle blithe and gay, in all the bravery of soul and dress, and its end to the same soldier riding back,—weary, and stained, and wounded,—a defeated and shattered man.[5] "How," says Shakespeare,

> "How like a younker, or a prodigal,
> The scarfèd bark puts from her native bay,
> Hugged and embraced by the strumpet wind
> How like a prodigal doth she return
> With overweathered ribs and ragged sails,
> Lean, rent, and beggared by the strumpet wind."[6]

[1] οὐκ ἔστι προσωπολήπτης ὁ θεός, Acts x. 34.
[2] Matt. xiii. 22. Jude 12. Is. v. 24. Hos. vi. 4.
[3] Sainte-Beuve.   [4] Charles Lamb.
[5] Bishop Jer. Taylor.   [6] *Merchant of Venice*, ii. 6.

We come, says Wordsworth, with the splendour of heaven about our infancy, but it grows less and less bright as we pass from childhood to boyhood, and from boyhood to youth, until

> "At last the man beholds it die away,
> And fade into the light of common day."[1]

Now of course these utterances and illustrations of Scripture and of literature would be worse than useless if they were not drawn from, and founded on, the common facts of life. But, alas! the facts to which they allude are only too common. There is but too rarely in life that noble continuity,—that continuity of goodness, —which at least in Christian lands we might expect. For what do we see? Some there are—let us hope the very fewest—who seem to be radically contemptible: their infancy wayward, their boyhood corrupt, their manhood infamous; as soon as they are born, they go astray and speak lies.[2] But infinitely more common than these are men whose lives are not wholly bad, but discontinuous. Like the Joash and Manasseh of Scripture, like the Nero or Henry VIII. of history, they begin well; they show early signs of modesty and humility, and generosity and self-restraint; but, as life advances, star by star, every early virtue seems to expire from their souls, and to leave them in the midnight of wasted lives and guilty hearts. Or else, on the contrary, they begin badly; they waste their boyhood, they stain their manhood, nor are they perhaps converted till they

---

[1] *Ode on the Intimations of Immortality from the Recollections of early Childhood.*

[2] Comp. Shakspeare, *K. Rich. III.*, act iv. sc. 4:

> "Tetchy and wayward was thy infancy;
> Thy schooldays desperate, frightful, wild, and furious;
> Thy prime of manhood daring, bold, and venturou
> Thine age confirmed, proud, subtle, sly, and bloody

have terribly imperilled the possibilities of earthly
happiness,—like St Augustine, like Ignatius Loyola, like
John Bunyan,—saved indeed, but so as by fire. But
beside these three classes, some, thank God! there are,
whose lives of unbroken holiness have been like a
summer dawn, which broadens unclouded into the boundless day.[1] Such a life—growing in wisdom and stature
and favour with God and man—was lived, for our example, in the shop of the village carpenter at Nazareth
by the Son of God on earth ; and such, " as the flower
of roses in the spring of the year, as lilies by the rivers
of water," have been the lives of some of the sweetest
of his earthly children. Such,—trained to faithfulness
from infancy,[2]—was Timotheus, the young and gentle
companion of St. Paul. Such was the holy St. Anthony,
who, at an age not much older than the eldest of you,
retired from a world hopelessly corrupt to serve God
in the desert solitudes. Such was the wise St. Benedict,
who, when not much older than even the youngest of
you, subdued every evil impulse of his nature by prayer
and fasting in his mountain cell. Such was St. Louis of
France, who, not in the cell or in the desert, but in
courts of kings and the camp of crusaders, lived worthy
of that sainted mother who said that she would rather
see him dead at her feet than know that he had
committed a mortal sin.[3] Such were St. Thomas of
Aquinum, and St. Bernard of Clairvaux, and St. Edmund
of Canterbury, and our own Edward VI. of England,
and many and many another whose names, known or
unknown on earth, are written for ever in the Lamb's
book of life. There was no violent break in the
life of these men ;—no wasted opportunities to be

[1] Prov. iv. 18.   [2] 2 Tim. i. 5.
[3] Blanche of Castile (Tillemont, *Vie de St.-Louis*).

toiled after; no years which the locust had eaten to be restored;—no lost virtues to be recovered;—no habitual vices to be unlearnt. And this is the life at which you, who are still young, should aim; this is the only safe, the only happy life; the only life fit for children of the light; the only life worthy of our high vocation; the only life which fulfils the Saviour's precept, "Be ye perfect, as your Father in heaven is perfect."[1]

And this surely is the very object of your training at a school which, before and above all other things, must be a Christian school. It is, so far as we can, to teach you from the first to do God's will, not your own, until God's will *is* your own;—to do, not what you like, but what you ought, till ought and like are identical; —to act not as you wish, but as you will, until what you will to do, because it is right, is also what you wish to do, because it is sweet;—to do your duty when it is hard until, in small things as well as great, by habit, and by instinct, and by second nature, it becomes to you as easy as it is always blessed. Yes! this is what, if we be not faithless to our high vocation, *we* should teach;—this is what, if you be not faithless to the lessons of your boyhood, *you* should learn, until the best description of your life, spent as God would have it spent, shall be this,—"They will go from strength to strength, and unto the God of gods appeareth every one of them in Sion."[2]

Now I know well that this is not the rule, or the maxim, or the idea of the world. The world is full of base and foolish proverbs upon this subject: and more and more I notice with indignation amid our recent literature books which, with I know not what sickly and

[1] Matt. v. 48.   [2] Ps. lxxxiv. 7.

sensual eloquence, are trying secretly and surreptitiously to preach some devil's gospel that sin is not sin, nor corruption corruption, nor shame shame. I see with indignation in some recent books what I can only call an Hellenic taint—some poisonous exhalation from the buried infamies of the past—the subtle treachery of an ill-concealed corruption. You, elder boys, be not deceived. Would you linger by the stagnant pool because its surface is filmed with the iridescence of decay? would you make your home in the barren and burning desert, because its lying mirage has a charm? Is a cheek beautiful because it wears the flush of drunkenness or the hectic of consumption? If you would be Christians—and if not it were better for you at once to die—if you would be anything but corrupt and bad, spurn, I pray you, with execration this would-be wisdom which is earthly, sensual, devilish;[1] —this insinuation, which would have made a good pagan blush, about the permissibility of wickedness, and the sinlessness of sin. There is but one rule for you, but one rule of safety and of happiness, and it is this: "Enter not into the path of the wicked, and go not in the way of evil men."[2] No sophistry can teach you to gather grapes of thorns or figs of thistles; no philosophy has the secret of touching pitch and not being defiled, or fire and not being burned. Suffer yourself to be deluded on this point by the mocking irony of the powers of evil, and you shall be untaught indeed, but it can only be by bitter experience. As the Cornish proverb says, "He who will not be ruled by the rudder, must be ruled by the rock."

---

[1] σοφία . . . ἐπίγειος ψυχικὴ δαιμονιώδης. James iv. 15.
[2] Prov. iv. 14.

So then I repeat to you that, as

> "The white stone, unfractured, ranks as most precious,
> The blue lotos, unblemished, has the sweetest perfume,"[1]

so the soul which has never wilfully tampered with sin is God's most beautiful creation. The subject is so large that my treatment of it has been necessarily fragmentary and incomplete, and I fear even that you may not have understood me, but let me, for a moment or two longer, illustrate to you this truth on ground not often trodden in sermons. There are two great men, the very greatest among all our writers, a contrast of whose lives will perhaps make you remember the lesson which this morning I have tried to teach. Those two are Shakespeare and Milton. And here let no idolatry of Shakespeare's oceanic genius blind us to a lesson which his own nobleness of heart would have been the first to urge. It is not that we little natures are seeking to dwarf the greatness of a lofty soul, which, with all its errors, was perhaps transcendently better as well as transcendently greater than our own; but it is that the very greatest, in proportion to their greatness, would most wish us to learn the lesson of their lives. Now there were in the life and conduct of Shakespeare very noble elements of calm and self-respect, and elevation and moral insight, on which, if time permitted, it would be a happiness to dwell, and when we read that faithful and humble passage of his last will—*I commend my soul into the hands of God my Creator, hoping, and assuredly believing, through the merits of Jesus Christ my Saviour, to be made partaker of life everlasting*—

---

[1] *The Sorrows of Han*, a Chinese Tragedy (*Quart. Review*, lxxxi. p. 85).

we are reminded of his own words about the great statesman-Cardinal, that

> "Then, and not till then, he felt himself,
> And found the blessedness of being little;
> And, to add greater honors to his age
> Than man could give him—he died fearing God."[1]

And yet there is enough, and, alas! more than enough, in Shakespeare's writings, to show that he had not passed through life unscathed; to show that his soul had not escaped the tinge of corruption; to show that when he exclaims so earnestly—

> "Give me that man
> That is not passion's slave, and I will wear him
> In my heart's core, ay, in my heart of heart,"[2]—

he was not thinking of himself. His sonnets, alas! are not the only poems which make us tremble lest "out of the grave of Shakespeare's genius should start the ghost of Shakespeare's guilt." He could see the divineness of human purity; he knew well the beauty of moral self-restraint; he could be kindled to the white heat of moral indignation; he could say, even of the favourite creation of his own fancy:—

> "I know thee not, old man;—fall to thy prayers;
> How ill white hairs become a fool and jester!
> I have long dreamed of such a kind of man,
> So surfeit-swelled, so old, and so profane;
> But being awake I do despise my dream.
> * * * * *
> Reply not to me with a fool-born jest,
> Presume not that I am the thing I was;
> For Heaven doth know, so shall the world perceive,
> That I have turned away my former self."[3]

But it would be very idle and very false to say that he was always thus true to his own self, always thus

---

[1] *K. Henry VIII.*, act. iv. sc. 2.   [2] *Hamlet*, act iii. sc. 2.
[3] *King Henry IV.*, Part II., act v. sc. 5.

faithful to that which is pure and honourable, and lovely, and of good report? And if I judge him rightly in his greatness, I think that, when he *had* risen into the light of God's truth and love, when he had learnt in his heart, no less than with his intellect, how sacred and divine is the blush of modesty on a young human cheek,—when God's pity had come like a dewy twilight "to close the oppressive splendour of his day,"—then, feeling in the depths of a heart that even in its failures had never ceased to see its God, how infinitely grander and more permanent was the moral law than is the most dazzling glory of man, he would have been glad to resign the fame of having written *Hamlet* and *King Lear* for the Paradise of having never known the guilt of the unfaithful ; and that he, like the very greatest of his English predecessors, Chaucer, the bright herald of English song, would have wept bitter tears for every evil word that he had penned, and would have wished his very name obliterated rather than that thought or memory of him should make one soul care less for virtue, or shrink less from sin.[1]

And therefore it is—though I have but a moment to dwell on it—therefore it is that in its unity, in its lofty dignity, in its vestal purity, in its sunlike path of unswerving and undaunted consistency, the life of Milton, with all its blindness, and its poverty, and its unsuccess, and its persecutions, seems to me,

[1] No one who knows Chaucer will hesitate to admit with Wordsworth that "if Chaucer is sometimes a coarse moralist, he is still a great one." Many passages of the noblest and holiest purport might be quoted from his poems. Yet he expresses contrition for such of his writings as "sonnen unto sin, and prays Christ of His mercy to forgive him for the guilt he had incurred thereby." "He is said to have cried out repeatedly on his death-bed, 'Woe is me that I cannot recall and annul these things ! but, alas ! they are continued from man to man, and I cannot do what I desire.'"—Southey.

in its continuity of goodness, a finer poem, and one of God's own inspiring, than ever the intellect of Shakespeare conceived. No "*Wild oats theory*," no familiarity with wickedness, no indifferent tampering with evil, no varnishing of bad passions with the thin and poisonous veneer of sham philosophy, could have produced such a man as this. He has himself told us in grave and strong language the ideal and theory of his life. That ideal—and would to God that some of you were brave and firm and highminded enough to adopt it too—was this:—It was, even as a boy, to make labour and intent study his portion in this life;[1] it was to draw his inspiration from "devout prayer to that Eternal Spirit who can enrich with all utterance and knowledge, and sends out His seraphim with the hallowed fire of His altar to touch and purify the lips of whom He pleases;"[2] it was to encourage in his own soul such an honest haughtiness of innocence and self-respect as to render it impossible to him to sink and plunge into the low descents of unlawful degradations; it was even without the oath of knighthood to be born with the free and gentle spirit of the Christian knight;[3] it was to cherish that fine reservedness of natural disposition and moral discipline, which, from his very boyhood, should bring home to his inmost soul the truth, that, "the body is for the Lord, and the Lord for the body." And I say that if, as Milton's latest biographer has imagined the scene,[4] this pure and noble youth, with these high theories of life, had stepped into one of those tavern-meetings of wild wits

---

[1] Milton, *Reason of Church Government* (Works, ed. Mitford, iii. 141). Again in his *Apology* he speaks of "the wearisome labours and studious watchings in which I have spent and lived out almost whole youth." [2] Works. iii. 148. [3] *Apology, &c.* (Works, iii. 271).
[4] Masson's *Life of Milton*, ii. 404.

and careless livers among whom the less happy Shakespeare passed his days—had he hushed those loose jests, and that unseemly talking, with the grave rebuke that "he who would not be frustrate of his hope to write well hereafter in laudable things, ought himselfe to bee a true Poem, that is, a composition and patterne of the best and honorablest things,"[1]—I say that if the young Milton, in the gravity of a faithful and high-thinking innocence, had appeared among them and spoken thus, some might have laughed, and some resented, and some have blushed, but I read the greatest of human intellects very wrongly if, as he gazed on that bold youth, there would not have been in the eyes of Shakespeare a light of silent tears, and in the soul of Shakespeare a pang of sadness, a prayer of penitence, as his heart went sorrowing through all that faultful part.

Yes, because "there is an inevitable congruity between the tree and its fruit:" yes, because "he who would lay up for his mature years a store of that great virtue of magnanimity, which should look the whole world in the face unabashed, and dare to do the noblest things he has ever thought, that man must begin by preserving for himself from his earliest youth, and in the most secret sessions of his memory, a spotless title to self-respect."[2] It is then to "this hill-top of sanctity and goodness, above which there is no other ascent but to the love of God,"[3] that I would lead your footsteps, that I would turn your eyes. It may be that you will sin; and if so, assuredly you will suffer; and then you may repent, or you may not repent; and then will come what comes hereafter. But there is *one* lesson

---

[1] *Apology, &c.* (Works, iii. 270). [2] Masson's *Milton, ubi supra.*
[3] Milton, Works, iii. 167.

which, if you learn it, shall be as much more to you than all other lessons, as Eternity is more than Time—it is to "*keep innocency, and take heed to that which is right, for that shall bring a man peace at the last;*" it is to say now, and as boys at school, as the one steady purpose and inspiration of a life spent in the continuity of holiness—*O God, Thou art my God: early will I seek Thee;* it is to take Christ as your Captain even now, in your earliest years, and following the divine and perfect example, to be from the first ἐν τοῖς τοῦ Πατρὸς, in your Father's House, and about your Father's business—to *grow* in wisdom and stature, and favour with God and man.

October 12, 1873.

SERMON XXX.

HOW TO RESIST THE DEVIL.

1 Pet. v. 8.

"Be sober, be vigilant; because your adversary the devil, as a roaring lion, walketh about, seeking whom he may devour: whom resist stedfast in the faith."

So speaks the Epistle of to-day. "Resist the devil and he will flee from you." Such is the warning and the promise of this evening's Second Lesson. "Get thee behind Me, Satan." Such, as the eternal defiance for all His children, was the answer to the tempter of our Saviour Christ.

I am not going to speak for a moment of what is called the personality of the tempter. Whether there be indeed an evil spirit, who, walking this world unseen, finds the delight of a detestable malignity in corrupting the soul of man, and sometimes by fleshly impulses, sometimes by worldly ambitions, sometimes by sins which seem apart from both, teaches man to destroy himself and to defy his God; or whether, on the other hand, these impulses, these seductions, these subtle and violent depravities, are the inevitable consequences of man's double nature and man's unfettered will; on either of these suppositions, the facts of our life remain the same, equally incapable of theoretical explanation, equally momentous in practical significance. It is of this practical significance that I alone would speak, and I do so in the intense desire that God may bring home my words to your hearts, and by leading you to be more sober and watchful, may thereby make you more holy, and so more happy in your life here, more sure hereafter to inherit that blessedness which eye hath not seen nor ear heard, but which God will give to all them that seek Him in sincerity and truth.

II. I am speaking to tempted souls ; every preacher in every church in England is speaking this day to tempted souls. The forms of the temptation may be very different; the difficulty with which you have to wrestle in life may be wholly different from that of the boy who sits next to you. Though the seven deadly sins have close affinities with one another, they do not equally tempt the same heart. And yet, by one or other of these —by pride and anger, by profanity or disobedience, by sloth or covetousness, by dishonesty or lust—by one or other in the perilous list of temptations—to one or other, in the dark catalogue of sins—we all are tempted. But it is one thing to be tempted, another thing to fall. A temptation is not a sin. "*Sentire tentationem*," to be strongly tempted, is common to every one of us; "*consentire tentationi*," to be guilty of wickedness, need be the misery of none. The devil may suggest, but until suggestion has become acceptance we are still innocent. A flash of rage instantly checked; a pang of envy at once crushed down into the heart; an evil image and an impure thought, hardly present to the consciousness, till, like the viper on the apostle's hand, it is shaken off into the flame of our own moral indignation; anything that degrades us instantly flung away from us with every nerve and fibre of the strong and faithful soul—these are not sins. You may sometimes see a little black cloud on some summer's day, a few hundred feet above the earth, instantly dissipated by glorious sunbeams, or dashed into beneficent rain; well, such a cloud leaves no stain on the blue illimitable sky. When there is a swaying of the heart, when there is a yielding in the will, when there is a cherishing of the guilty purpose—then and then only does temptation become sin. To all of us, to the very best and noblest—the devil will suggest. Scarcely a day, perhaps, in which he will not come in some guise or other; it may be with plausible insinuations and lying promises, all glitter and fascination, as, rustling through the fallen leaves of the forbidden tree, he crept upon the careless hour of Eve; it may be in sudden assaults of overwhelming passion, a lion with flaming eye and thundering roar, as he came bounding and crashing upon David's soul; it may be disguised like an angel of light, with subtle perversion of vices, which look half akin to virtues, as he stole in the wilderness upon the weary and fasting Christ: but oh, remember this, whether he come in stealth or in fury—with honeyed whisper or with fierce threat—with the murderer's dagger or with the liar's mask—in one way or other " Satan desires to have you that he may sift you as wheat." Every one of you will be placed under that winnowing foot of the devil; every one of you subjected to searching, piercing, exploring power, by which sin will find you out, and compel you, perhaps in shame and ignominy, to show what you are. Well, when the devil thus comes to you, remember this: not to resist is agony and ruin; to resist is possible, and may be easy; the means of resistance are sobriety and watchfulness; the end of resistance is certain victory—resist the devil and he will flee from you.

III. How and when to resist—it is on this subject

that I want to give you one or two plain hints. And the very first and most important of all which should press upon you is, resist the devil inwardly; resist him in your own heart; for far, far more easily is the outward enemy resisted if the inward man be not laid waste. You know how Scripture dwells on this. " My son, give me thy heart." "Keep thine heart with all diligence, for out of it are the issues of life." " Out of the heart proceed evil thoughts,"—and then all the rest. " Who can say I have made my heart pure, I am cleansed from my sin?" Alas! one alone—our Saviour Jesus— could say it absolutely; by the grace of His Holy Spirit His saints and children have at all times been able, in their measure, to say it too. And there are two reasons why it is of infinite importance. The one is that the guilty heart is in itself a source of anguish. In the great romance Vathek, if I remember rightly, enters the Hall of Eblis, and there sees the spirits of evil seated in splendour at a banquet, on thrones of gold, yet over the brow of each there pass spasms of agony; and when he would know the cause, one of them pushes aside from his own breast the purple robe, and lays his finger beside his heart; and there, about the heart, there plays in gnawing torture a perpetual flame. The sinner's heart is like that; if he be only a secret apostate, not an open evil-doer, the flame is there. Not infrequently the restraints of society, the dread of detection, the terribleness of consequences, the absence of possibility— even it may be some shred of compunction and natural horror, saves a man from the actual commission of a sin; he may die almost in the odour of sanctity, and yet all the while may have been in secret sacrificing to devils, and selling his immortal soul for a nothing—a fancy—or it might have been a consuming desire, which has continued unfulfilled, so that his wish of wickedness has been like that stolen robe which Achan would have worn, but never did, and which was consumed with him to ashes under that heap of hurled stones and burning fire which marked the thief's burial-place in Achor's vale. The interpretation which Christ gave of the sixth and of the seventh commandments show too fatally that the thought of wickedness is sin; but how often is it that the thought of wickedness only continues to be a thought of wickedness? How often does the black fountain of the inwardly bad heart not break forth in the black torrent of the outwardly bad life? How often does he who wilfully thinks of evil, not wish for evil, not purpose evil, not commit evil? Scarcely, alas! ever. It is easiest of all to resist Satan at this stage of evil thought. But if you do not, if you give him $\pi o\hat{v}$ $\sigma\tau\hat{\omega}$, if you yield to him this leverage, he will with it upheave the temple of your soul from its very foundations. He will not necessarily do it with violence. He will but drop the bad seed in the little cranny of the wall, or the little neglected crevice on the temple floor, and just as you may see the pestilent elder-trees have done in more than one old wall of this college, silently and day by day it will enlarge its dwelling-place, until it will break the starred mosaic, or split the solid masonry with its mere natural growth. How easy it would have been to crush that seed, or at the worst to pluck up that little seedling by the roots! But the bare thought grows first into the strong imagination, then into the evil motion, last into the perilous consent; and so, little by little, it gains in strength, and little by little it is met by feebler resistance, or at last by none at all.

IV. My first suggestion, then, to you is, resist inwardly; and my second is like it, for it is, resist step by step. The heathen poet here chimes in with the preacher.

"*Obsta principiis : sero medicina paratur.*"

Resist the beginnings of evil; a mere remedy is all too late. If you have not resisted at the stage of thought, then summon every power of your soul to resist at the stage of the act. Fight inch by inch; fight step by step;—if not at the thought, then at the act; if not at the act, then at the habit; if not even at the habit, then, at least, at the frightful surrender—the utter massacre of the last defenders of all that is holy or pure within you. But bear in mind that each stage of the losing battle is more perilous, more difficult than the last. It is easier to frighten the enemy than to rout him by a charge; easier to rout than to await his onset; easier to defeat him then than to recover one lost inch of ground; easier to recover an inch than to rally finally the demoralised and broken troops. There is more hope for a boy who may have had bad thoughts than for one who has let them pass into bad words; and more hope for bad words than for bad deeds; and more hope again for him who hath sinned once than for him who has sinned twice, and for the sinner of a week than for the sinner of a month. Oh, if any of you have lost the drawbridge, in God's name drive back the enemy from the wall; if he has reached the wall, fight for the portcullis; if he has carried the portcullis, rally every shattered power and wounded energy, and die rather than admit him at the gate. And don't have any truce or any parleys; don't stop even to bury your dead. Your enemy hates you, and he is as false as he is deadly. He will say, " Only this once. You are tired of fighting; give me the fortress only now, I promise you that I will evacuate it whenever you like ; if not, at any rate you can at any time drive me out.

> "Be mine and Sin's for one short hour ; others
> Be all thy life the happiest man of men."

Oh, do not believe him! He is a liar from the beginning. A boy may be tempted to lie, to steal, to wrong his neighbour, to indulge some bad passion, and thinks that "*once*" cannot matter. Oh, pause ! That one sin—is it not the trickling rill, which must become the bounding torrent, the broad river, the waste, troubled, discoloured sea ? You drop a stone out of your hand : is it not the very law of gravitation that, if it falls twelve feet the first second, it will fall forty-eight feet the next second, and 108 feet the third second, and 300 feet the fifth second ; and that, if it fall for ten seconds— do you know how many feet of air in that last second it will have rushed through ? In that last second it will have rushed through 1200 feet, till earth stops it. Even with that prodigiously increasing momentum, even with that rushing acceleration of velocity, is the increase and multiplication of unchecked sin ;—and too often it falls on and on, until it is dashed to shivers on the rock of death.

V. But, as a last warning, it seems sometimes that the spirits of evil, as though to induce a fatal security, as though to lull a wholesome alarm,—attack the soul, not coarsely and openly, but gently, caressingly, gradually, insidiously. There are times when the devil comes upon us, not with the insinuated apostasy, but with the quoted Scripture ; not with the gross offer, but the subtle treason; not as a raging enemy, but as the soft, smiling, flattering, caressing friend. Souls there are which have been overwhelmed, not by the beating of waves and storms, but the noiseless stealing as of the muddy tide upon the coasts of Lancashire, "always shallow, yet always just high enough to drown." Oh beware the devil when he steals upon you in the normal tone of a surrounding society, or still worse in the pleasant guise of a would-be friend. There may be a companion whom you are inclined to like; whose society is pleasant to you; to whom you feel greatly drawn, or by whose notice you, being younger or smaller, are flattered;—well if, after a very short time, you get to see that, however plausible, he is not a good boy,— not a boy who will do you any good,—that his influence over you,—that which subtly, by look, and word, and deed, flows in upon your soul from his—is weakening all that is best and purest in you, and hardening all that is worst—then, most of all, be sober, be vigilant,— then most of all resist a gradual, an insidious, attack. Which is best, that you should cast off your bad friendship, or that you should lose your immortal soul? It cannot be that there are none with whom you can enjoy that blessed and beautiful thing, a free, pure, noble, natural school friendship,—a thing as blessed and beautiful as a low and sneaking friendship is leprous and accursed. But even if it were not so, better utter loneliness than evil communications;—better to be a friendless boy than to dwell in Mesech, and have your habitation among the tents of Kedar. But, as I have often warned you, since it is the case that the worst of all tempters are often human tempters, how fearful is the guilt alike of the instability which passively acts as a temptation to the strong, or of the wickedness which dares to take the tempter's office and to sacrifice the weak! And whether for strong or weak, what guilt to turn into a source of mutual degeneracy that happy companionship between friend and friend which God's mercy meant for a mutual safeguard and an inestimable boon!

VI. There then are three hints meant alike for the youngest of you, and for the eldest. Resist *in the heart;* resist *step by step;* resist *insidious* attacks, no less than sudden attacks. And, in one word more, resist soberly, watchfully: — soberly, because even that which is lawful is not always expedient; watchfully, because the assault may come violently at any moment, may be coming imperceptibly at every moment. However it comes, you will, some day, find yourself in tangible manner, face to face with the awful final choice between good and evil; and when a soul's destiny hangs trembling and wavering, then even the mere dust in the balance may decide the deathful dipping of the scale. So that all which you have heard is very practical; oh, when you leave this chapel, will you take pity on yourselves, will you *make* it practical. And as, at once, the fiery darts begin to fall on you—perhaps this very day to fall on you,—will you hold up against them the shield of faith, will you wield against him who hurls them the Spirit's sword? If so, you are safe. The other day an English clergyman visited the two fine ships which have just sailed on their voyage of Arctic discovery into the land of snow and darkness; and he found the brave captain full of confidence; and raising his eyes in the cabin, he saw there, as almost its only ornament, an illuminated text; and the text was, Have faith in God! "Ah, there," he said, pointing to the text, "there is the true pole!" We like to think of those gallant men carrying with them into the cold and midnight that faith, that hope; it is a faith which will lighten their darkness more than the stars that glitter over the floes of ice; it is a hope which will make the heavens glow with a more vivid splendour, than the Aurora which flushes the fields of snow. Take with you that faith, that hope: you too may sail hereafter, in your little boat of life, into the cold, into the hunger, into the darkness, into the exploration of unknown hopes. Gigantic powers will fight against you there, more terrible than the midnight, more paralysing than the northern cold. Νήψατε, γρηγορήσατε. Be sober, be vigilant; have faith in God and in His Son our Lord Jesus Christ, and He will give you the victory; resist the devil, and he will flee from you.

June 12, 1875.

SERMON XXXI.

HOLIDAY ADVICE.

MARK vi. 31.

"And He said unto them, Come ye yourselves apart into a desert place, and rest awhile."

AFTER another term,—another of these epochs of school life which pass so rapidly, which seem so short, and yet of which each one is so fraught with infinite issues of possibility for the health of souls and the happiness of lives—the holidays are now close at hand. We are going to enjoy a period of rest (or, which is the same thing, since mere rest can never satisfy a reasonable being for more than a very short time)—of changed scenes, and of changed endeavours, which many of us need, and from which I hope we all shall profit. Those who have deserved it most thoroughly will enjoy it most entirely. To talk of rest when there has been no work is a mockery—it is then a pleasure we have no right to,—a reward we have not earned; and it will then be as little refreshful as is the sleep of night to one who has yawned and slept through half the day. But I believe sincerely that all, or very nearly all, of you have earned the rest fairly; and when this is the case, how delightful the holidays are! I think that of the rare unmingled pleasures which life has to offer, few are to be compared, in sweetness and intensity, to the summer holidays of a good boy in a happy home. The mere joy of going home; the ever-brightening consciousness of the glad reception that awaits us there; the sense of mute regard and unchanged friendship in each familiar object as it flashes into sight—the bridge, the river, the village, the church, the smiling faces of those who have known us from childhood, the dear old house nestling in its ancestral trees, the nursery where we slept, the garden where we played as little children when there were none who did not love us, the father's welcome, the mother's kiss—the eager visit to each well-remembered nook, the well-earned prize to be shown with so much pleasure, the plans for many long, long happy days—even those tender touches of sadness in the sunshine, the well-remembered portrait of some dear dead face, the churchyard where the green sod and the cross of flowers mark a little brother's or a little sister's grave—every silent, every voiceful appeal to that which each of us has in him of purest and sweetest—well, as he contemplated these, might the poet sing:—

> "Ah, dear delights, that o'er my soul,
>   On Memory's wing-like shadows fly;
> Ah, flowers that Joy from Eden stole,
>   While Innocence stood laughing by."

II. Now God forbid that in one word which I shall say I should darken by the faintest shadow of a shade—were it even but as the shadow of a bird's wing as it flits across the summer noon—this, which for every good, high-minded, true-hearted boy may be one of the brightest and purest of life's joys. Clouds for every one of you, as life goes on, will gather fast enough over the sunlight, and ever longer and longer will the inevitable shadows of the evening fall; but he who has known rightly how to use the innocent sunshine while it lasted, knows, at his darkest hour, that the great sun is still shining, though it be scarfed by earthly vapours or hidden behind the shadow of the world. I love happiness. I believe in happiness. I am sure that God meant us for happiness. I think that we are all the better for happiness. I long that every one of you should be as happy as God gives it to any of His children to be. And though mere pleasure is a far lower thing, I do not even look with a dubious eye on pleasure. I know that many turn it into a Marah fountain, scorching and poisonous; but I know too that innocence can sweeten it. No good man can be a foe to happiness; no good man need be a foe to innocent pleasure. God meant us to have something of both; and the better we are, the more generous, the more pure, the more unselfish, the more we shall have of both. For there is but one form of happiness which can long satisfy the soul which God has made. It is when happiness is not sought at all for its own sake, but comes as the natural law of a noble existence; it is when duty and delight are synonymous and coincident; it is when peace is the reward of faithfulness, not the aim of self-indulgence; it is when gladness is found in the service of others, not in the satisfaction of self; it is when the psalm of life is, "Lo, I come to do Thy will, O my God. I am content to do it; yea, Thy law is within my heart."

> "Who follows pleasure, pleasure slays,
> God's wrath upon himself he wreaks:
> But all delights attend his days
> Who takes with thanks, but never seeks."

And this is what our Lord Himself intended when He said, "Seek ye first the kingdom of God and His righteousness, and all other things shall be added unto you." I would try to make your rest more enjoyable, by being spent but as a prelude of that rest which remaineth for the people of God. I would wish your homes to be yet dearer, as being but dim reflections of the home in heaven. " Blessed are they that are thus homesick, for they shall come at last to their Father's house." You are entering on a rest—I would make the rest more enjoyable.

III. I would ask you then during these holidays, and indeed always, to bear in mind that *all life is an education.* I use the word not of books, not of science, not of languages, but in its very widest sense, of that wisdom which is far loftier than knowledge, because it is health of mind, and self-content, and well-directed industry, and perfect kindliness. The true education of life—and, for all we know, it may go on even beyond the grave—is never attained until the awful, eternal difference between right and wrong is fully, finally, personally, practically, irrevocably learned. Alas! the experience of every day teaches us that the lesson, which looks so simple, is in reality terribly difficult; at all times, I fear, and especially in youth, we get easily confused in our judgments about wrong-doing; easily blunted in the edge of our moral sense; easily apt to estimate the seriousness of sin, only by the gravity of its consequences, not by the fatality of its nature. "I saw in Rome," says a modern writer, "an old coin, a silver denarius, all coated and crusted with green and purple rust. I called it rust, but I was told that it was copper; the alloy thrown out from the silver until there was none left within, the silver was all pure. It takes ages to do it, but it does get done. Souls are like that. Something moves in them slowly, till the debasement is all thrown out. Some day perhaps the very tarnish shall be taken off." Well, there is this alloy, this tarnish in all of us, and the education of life is to purge it all away; if we do not do this ourselves, God in mercy helps us to do it by sorrows, by disappointments, by failures, by judgments,

> "By fires far fiercer than are blown to prove
> And purge the silver ore adulterate."

But to this wider education, all the narrower may tend. Moral growth, almost of necessity, involves intellectual growth. For though it needs no intellect to see the difference between right and wrong—though herein many a dull boy may be as good as gold, and many a clever boy may be weak, and loose, and bad, yet if only the heart be in the right place, the training of the mind has a double moral importance, not only as saving the soul from the many wretched temptations which idleness brings in its train, but also as deepening and strengthening the sense of right. A well-trained mind, a well-stored memory, a well-developed intellect will help to disentangle the soul from the fatal and subtle sophistries of sin. And if you would be happy you must not think that your education may cease for these seven weeks. They are far too long for anyone to waste, nor will they pass without leaving their mark upon you for good or for evil. Many a boy spoils his holidays—makes them a burden to himself and a weariness to his friends—by having nothing to do. A boy with nothing to do is at once miserable and disagreeable. But a sensible boy will never be without something to do; and the hours of hearty play and vigorous exercise will come all the more freshly and delightfully if they be varied by good reading or honest work. And the holidays are especially a valuable time for removing that sad ignorance of your own literature—that blank unacquaintance with the thoughts that breathe and words that burn—with all that glowing poetry and heart-ennobling eloquence in which your own language abounds.

> " We must be free or die that speak the tongue
> That Shakespeare spoke ; tho faith and morals hold
> That Milton held."

To know souls like theirs—to understand them and enjoy them—is in itself an education, and a very liberal one. These strong and noble guardians, these beautiful and inspiring thoughts, will save the empty house of the mind from a thousand villainous and contemptible intruders—they will make you loftier, wiser, better,—at once more useful and more happy. If you are to do any high service in the world—and to do high service every one of you should aim—then, even in the holidays, add to your faith virtue, and to virtue knowledge. They are a trinity of gifts spiritual, of which the eternal unity is a heavenly wisdom. "You must not only listen, but read; you must not only read, but think: knowledge without common sense is folly; without method it is waste; without kindness it is fanaticism ; without religion it is death."

IV. And remember that life is an education mainly that it may be also *a service*. You cannot realise too early and too wholly that we are not our own—that no man liveth to himself; that love is the divinest, the sweetest, the most comprehensive of all the virtues; that if love to God be the motive, love to man is the main end and aim of all earthly existence. It is one of those simple principles which should be the guide of all life, and sins against it are very fatal. This is why charity covereth a multitude of sins. This is why the most sternly terrible words which Christ ever spoke were words against those wretches who are not only sinners themselves, but the direct wilful cause of sin in others. And you must not fancy that you can lay aside this view of life at home. Oh! remember that as to father and to brother the most generous and manly services, so to mother and to sister the most chivalrous self-renouncement, the most delicate courtesies, are due. I do not suppose that any of you are boys of the low type who mainly think of home as a place for indulging in eating, and drinking, and laziness; but I do know that some boys are very apt to think that at home they need take no trouble to be unselfish or agreeable. And how in such cases do discontent, fretfulness, little disobediences to parents, quarrels and bickerings between brothers and sisters, poison even the sweet charities of the home. Where these are, home almost ceases to be. But the sweetest and happiest homes—homes to which men in weary life look back with yearnings too deep for tears— homes whose recollections lingers round our manhood like light, and the sunshine, and the sweet air, into which no base things can intrude—are homes where brethren dwell together in unity; where because all love God, all love their brothers also; where because all are very dear to all, each is dearer to each than to himself.

V. And, lastly, as life is an education, and as life is a service, so too life is *a struggle*. The wheels of time will not stand still for you because you are at home; nor will the powers of evil sleep. The great problems, the great trials, the great temptations of life will go on for you there as here. You will be away, indeed, from school, but you will not be away from yourselves. As the labour of Christ was a ceaseless effort for others, so remember that His very rest was a ceaseless prayer. What we have ever to bear in mind is this: that there is but one final and fatal evening to life, to beauty, to goodness, to happiness. It is sin. All our dangers, all our sorrows—every pang of remorse, every ache of shame, every access of despair—comes from sin. It is sin that crowds the wards of the prison-house; it is sin that throngs the cells of the asylum and goads the suicide to the river-bank; it is sin which, when it stops far short of these desperate extremities, yet makes the heart gather blackness, and stains the path of life with tears. And how does sin thus gain a footing in human hearts? Only in one of two ways—stealthy, insidious intrusion, or sudden, violent assault. Both attacks need equal watchfulness. When a Josiah degenerates, when a David murders, when a Peter blasphemes— what does it mean? Alas! it means the same as when those who know what is right do what is wrong; it means that their principles are not yet established; it means that there is no depth of earth in the stony place where the good seed of teaching has fallen; it means, in a word, that they have not yet learnt that life is an education and a struggle; it means that they have slept when they should have watched; have been careless when they should have prayed. Even at home, even in the holidays, yea, even till the end of life, Watch and pray, lest ye enter into temptation.

VI. It only remains, on the one hand, to hope that all who return may, after a rest well earned and wisely spent, return here in health, in happiness, in good spirits, with high resolves, with loving, earnest hearts, to a diligent and prosperous term; and, on the other hand, to bid a very hearty and kind farewell to those who leave us. From every one of them we part in perfect kindness; from most with sincere regret. And for those who have done their duty here and been blessed—those over whose happy years at school the blessing of God has fallen like a line of light—those who have learnt by glad experience the dignity of duty, the holiness of innocence, the happiness of work—we know that by God's grace we shall hear of them again with pride and pleasure. And if there be any who have not yet fully, bravely, wholly, learnt to refuse the evil and to choose the good, to them we say that there, at the Holy Table of the Lord—there, where side by side we shall kneel, all of us sinners, yet all of us redeemed—there, more than at any other spot on earth, is to be found for all who faithfully and humbly seek it, the pledge of past forgiveness, of present consolation, of future hope. For all of us alike, with the end of this term, will be shut and ended another volume, wherein is written by Time, the great transcriber, the history of ourselves. In two more days the last page will have been turned, the solemn *finis* written.

> "Whose hands shall dare to open and explore
> Those volumes, closed and clasped for overmore!
> Not mine. With reverential feet I pass,
> I hear a voice that cries 'Alas! Alas!'
> Whatever hath been written shall remain,
> Nor be erased, nor written o'er again;
> The unwritten only still belongs to thee,
> Take heed, and ponder well, what that shall be."

July 25, 1876.

SERMON XXXII.

BLAMELESS AND HARMLESS.

Phil. ii. 15.

"Blameless and harmless, the sons of God, without rebuke."

I. These beautiful words are suggested to me by the conclusion of to-day's Epistle: they are an amplification of that word "blameless," which is there the most prominent conception. They seem no unfit subject for our morning thoughts. I do not desire to treat of them elaborately, or theologically. It is better that the passing thoughts, by which, week after week, we would lead you heavenwards, should be spontaneous and simple; and very often I should rejoice if the text could be the only sermon; if there were any means of engraving the text alone upon your hearts and consciences—more than content if so all else that is said, and he who says it, were alike forgotten.

II. And I think you all will feel that these words—"blameless and harmless, the sons of God without rebuke"—are very exquisite words—words worthy to linger in our memory as with the music of a lyric song. They describe the most consummate of attainments—the loftiest of ideals. They are the brightest commentary on the exhortation, "Be ye perfect, even as your Father in heaven is perfect;" they are the finest description of what Jesus was, and of what the followers of Jesus ought to be.

III. The word "blameless" means free from every form of wilful wrong or intentional misdoing against our fellow-men; the word "harmless" means sincere, simple, without admixture of sin and vileness in the sight of God. To be the first is far, far the easier. It would not be so if the word "blameless" meant "unblamed;" for no man, however blameless, can escape being blamed. The experience of ages has shown that the shield of innocence, which a good man carries with him through the world, cannot be so white that none will throw dust at it. Some of the holiest and noblest men that ever lived have been—and sometimes all through their lives—very targets for the arrows of abuse. So long as Envy has restless eyes, and Calumny a fertile imagination, and Malice a myriad of voices which bellow in the shade—so long will there be enemies, persecutors, and slanderers of the very saints of God.

The stainless purity of Joseph saved him not from infamous accusations; nor the noble meekness of Moses from bitter criticisms; nor the splendid services of Samuel from open ingratitude. Of the stern self-denial of John the Baptist they could say only, He hath a devil; of the boundless sympathy of the Saviour of mankind, they dared to mutter, "Behold a glutton and a wine-bibber, a friend of publicans and sinners." If ever we feel discouraged at the thought that there are natures which guilelessness fails to disarm, or unselfishness to win, let the Cross reveal to us the high lesson that we may still be utterly blameless, though it may be that we live no day unblamed. And if they have called the Master of the house Beelzebub, they have done the same to them of His household, and some of them have even

> "Stood pilloried on Infamy's high stage,
> And borne the pelting scorn of half an age."

IV. Yet blamelessness is often recognised. In those school-reports which, term by term, pass in hundreds through my hands, and which we send home to your parents as our estimate of your conduct and character, I always observe with deep pleasure that the very large majority are favourable and good reports. Not a few of them are the warm expression of hearty praise. It is quite exceptional if any boy is singled out for censure as idle or unruly, as untrustworthy or corrupt. And now and then in these reports one comes across the word "blameless;" and it is a deep pleasure to be able to endorse it; for of all characters it is the very highest that can be given, and the one which must most delight a parent's heart. If any of you have ever received that report—if any of you ever earn it hereafter—as I hope many of you will strive to do—be well assured that, since it is never lightly given, it shows you to have won the love and the confidence of those who are set over you. It means no mere negative character—no mere absence of overt misdoings. It would never be given to a conceited, or saturnine, or ill-conditioned boy, or to one who is content with the superficial standard and the vulgar average. It would imply diligence, and purity, and faithfulness, and good influence over others; and that modest humility, that courteous sweetness, that happy geniality, that natural appreciation of all kindness, which are only found in the fairest dispositions, and which are to the nature of a boy like the very dew of God upon the opening flowers of life. And yet, though rare indeed are such gifts and graces, how far more easy is it to be thus blameless to men, than to be harmless—ἀκέραιος—unmixed with any taint of evil, before God. For this is innocence—this is holiness. It is to be an Israelite indeed, in whom is no guile—it is to know the beatitude of the pure in heart, who see God's face, and His name is in their foreheads—it is to have that "state of mind for which all alike sigh, and the want of which makes life a failure for most : it is to enjoy that heaven, which is everywhere if we could but enter it, and yet almost nowhere, because so few of us can." It is not, alas! from want of knowledge that we do not enter this heaven. I do not doubt that the youngest of you knows well what is meant by being harmless in the sight of God; and that, if you were asked to write down your notion of what a boy should be if he were striving to walk as a true disciple of Christ, you could do it perfectly well. I once tried the experiment. I set to a form of boys, not older than most of you, the task of sketching for me their notion of a right noble and perfect youthful character. The answers were remarkable. In details they all differed; in substance they were all the same. Few boys omitted any essential point in the fair unity of virtues; all gave outlines of character which, were they realised, would cause this earth to blossom once more like the garden of the Lord. What could one say on reading these ideals? What but "They have well spoken all that they have spoken : oh! that there were such a heart in them!" What but "If ye know these things, happy are ye if ye do them." For indeed, and alas! I do not suppose that even the youngest boy ever becomes a bad boy for want of knowing better. The Ten Commandments are plain enough; the directions of duty unmistakably authoritative; the voice of conscience is indisputably clear. But men sin because they do not see the fatal degradation of the ruined future in the seductive whisper of the tempting present; they sin because, in the first instance, the intense voice of passion drowns the low whisper of conscience; they continue in sin because the dull, heavy chains of habit fetter the enfeebled resistance of reason. They choose death rather than life, because they have not faith; they love the darkness rather than the light, because their deeds are evil.

V. But the question is, Is this quite an universal experience? Have none but Jesus ever been in this life blameless and harmless—the sons of God without rebuke? Yes, some have been; and what some have been, all may be—gentle, faithful, beautiful to God—"transparent as crystal; active as fire; pure and tender as grace; strong, generous, enduring, as the hearts of martyrs." It has been so, for instance, in the conquest of the commonest vices, and the attainment of the rarest of virtues. The love of money is the root of all evil; yet avarice has been absolutely non-existent in some lofty souls. As one case in thousands, take that of our own Edmund of Canterbury, whom nothing could persuade to keep under lock and key the little which he did not spend in charity, and who, leaving it loose in his window-sill, would often strew it over with ashes, saying, "Ashes to ashes; dust to dust." Sensuality, again, is the most frightful curse and scourge of a guilty world, yet perfect chastity has been reached even by the young. Just as the mere presence of the youthful Cato overawed the profligate Romans in their Saturnalia, so in the young Bernardino of Siena, though beautiful and graceful in person, there was even in his boyhood such angel modesty, such noble dignity, that, if he merely entered a room, all that was foolish and foul in the conversation of his companions was hushed at once into shamed silence. Or, to take one more common sin, it is scarcely one in a million who does not sometimes yield to irritability. Yet we are told of one who died not many years ago—the famous Curé d'Ars—that, though at every moment you might see him surrounded, pressed, harassed by indiscreet multitudes, wearied by idle questions, besieged by impossible demands, assailed by cruel calumnies, rewarded by base ingratitude, yet he was never seen unequal to himself, always gracious, lovable, sympathising, smiling; no word of passion passed his lips, no cloud of vexation overshadowed his countenance. Now if these and other virtues—faith, meekness, temperance, brotherly kindness, charity—have shone so perfectly in the lives of the saints of God, knowing, as we do, that there is a solidarity in the virtues as in the vices, and that one virtue usually lies close beside another, like the pearls that touch each other in the same necklace—while one vice is usually found in closest proximity to another, like burning links of the same iron chain—we might naturally expect that where one virtue thus existed in its perfectness, the others also would be found. And so it has ever been. Yes; we read of many of these high saints, blameless and harmless, the sons of God without rebuke. Such in the old world were Socrates, the wise teacher, and Marcus Aurelius, the stainless Emperor. Such was the great founder, St. Benedict of Nursia; such was the great scholar, St. Thomas of Aquino; such was the brave crusader, St. Louis of France; such the saintly painter, Angelico of Fiesole; such was Melanchthon, the gentle reformer; such was

Whitefield, the fervent preacher; such was Howard, the prison philanthropist; such was Henry Martyn, the self-denying missionary; such were hundreds more, whose names and memories are to all good men as beacon-lights upon the holy hills; and thousands more, whose names, unknown on earth, are written in heaven, and who have left the world sweeter and brighter than before. Nor have we only read of them: we have known them, we have loved them, we have seen their faces, and not in dreams; we have watched, and grown better as we watched, the width of their sympathy, the manliness of their modest worth. We have seen them even among the young, and when we turned, wearied and saddened, from the churlishness and the childishness of natures swollen with the rank wind of pride, or repellent with the morbid corruption of selfishness, our souls have been refreshed by their unselfish sorrow, their unaffected delicacy, their spontaneous charity, their ingenuous relf-reproach. Cedars were these in God's fair garden—constellations in the firmament of Christian nobleness. Clean hands had they, and pure hearts; and they spake the truth, and did the thing that was right, and never slandered, and did not think much of themselves, but were lowly in their own eyes; and therefore they did not fall. These are they who came in their white robes out of much tribulation; and the Shepherd of their souls feedeth them in green pastures, and hath led them forth for ever beside the still waters of comfort. And when we contemplate such lives—when from this low smoke and stir, and contact with so much that is mean and vile—we raise our eyes to the sunlit heights whereon they sit in their solemn choirs and sweet societies, is there any but the very deadest heart, which feels no more beauty in the picture, "Blameless and harmless, the sons of God without rebuke"?—no more force in the encouragement, "Oh! serve the Lord in the beauty of holiness"?

But perhaps one and another may say, But how can *we* be this? We are not this. We are so far from blameless, that our faults are gross and glaring to ourselves, and still more so to others. We have been neither humble, nor loving, nor grateful, nor obedient, nor pure; our words are often shameful; our acts often dishonourable; our thoughts—oh! what a desperate wickedness is often there! Why then do you preach this lovely ideal of innocence to us who are not innocent—to us, the harvest of whose life has not been golden grain, but coarse, and sour, and rank—like the grass that groweth on the house-tops, wherewith the mower filleth not his hand, nor he that gathereth the sheaves his bosom? Ah! wait, my brethren, before you say all this. This ideal is open to you. For if innocence can never again be yours, repentance can. If not yours can be the blessedness of them to whom the Lord imputeth no sin, and in whose spirit there is no guile, yet yours *can* be the blessedness of him whose unrighteousness is forgiven, whose sin is covered. "The prayers of Penitence," says the grand old allegory of Homer, "are the daughters of God." They are lame, for they cannot keep up with the rushing feet and desperate bound of Guilt and Retribution; they are wrinkled, for they live amid silence, and sorrow, and chastisement; they have downcast eyes, for it is among the guilty that their work is thrown. But when Guilt has been accomplished and Retribution come—when Mercy has played her part and Vengeance has leapt upon the stage—then, with uplifted hands and streaming eyes, and with voices of anguish that pierce the heavens, they calm the awakened wrath, and do much to heal the havoc and the ruin of man's iniquity. Oh ! if indeed you hate sin, and desire to be delivered from its slavery and from its stain—if indeed you are not an insolent rebel and a hardened offender—the means of grace are open; there is yet a white robe for you in the holy land—your foot may still traverse the streets of gold—your lips drink of the clear river which flows out of the throne of God and of the Lamb. For the love of God still pleads with you; His Holy Spirit still strives to wean you from your living death. Be humble, be sincere, be in earnest; and then, if you resolve, if you watch, if you pray, if you strive, if you believe—you may be divinely restored, progressively sanctified; and though now your sins are hateful to God, and odious to man, and degrading to yourselves—though you feel, however you brazen and brave it out, yet, at every better and truer moment, that sin is misery and that sin is weakness—yet even you—for His sake who died that you may live—by His power, whose word released the demoniac, and whose touch purified the leper—even you, like God's fairest and holiest saints, may by repentance become now, and may be more and more hereafter, " blameless and harmless, the sons of God without rebuke."

Sept. 26, 1875.

SERMON XXXIII.

HANDWRITINGS ON THE WALL.

DAN. v. 25.

"And this is the writing that was written, Menê, Menê, Tekêl, Upharsin."

THE Book of Daniel, which now enters into the cycle of Sunday First Lessons, presents a series of pictures so solemn, so stately, so striking, that I think even the dullest imagination must be somewhat stirred by them. In chapter after chapter, like Titanic frescoes in some Eastern temple, you have scenes, set side by side with marvellous contrast, of youthful temperance and regal luxury; of tyrannous insolence and intrepid faithfulness; of colossal sacrilege and sweeping retribution. In the first chapter, four young Jewish boys, glowing with modesty and hardihood, refusing the wine and the dainties of the palace, grow up fairer and sweeter on pulse and water than the pampered minions among whom they live. In the second, one of these Jewish boys interprets the dark dream-secrets which baffle the Chaldæan sages. In the next, the other three of those four boys stand steadfast, even to the fire, against the worship of the golden image in Dura's plain; and in the fourth, the great Nebuchadnezzar, at the moment of intoxicating exultation, is smitten suddenly with shameful madness; but is restored to grandeur when the lesson of humility is learnt. In the fifth, which we shall read as the Evening Lesson, the deadly warning flashes on the walls of the banquet-house; and after it,—as lightning follows thunder,—the stroke of ruin falls. Are not these plain lessons which he who runs may read? Lessons that health is granted to self-denial, and that beauty is the sacrament of goodness:—that God sends a glistering angel, if need be, to keep virtue safe;—that there is laughter in heaven at human pride; that there is joy in heaven at human penitence; that there is vengeance in heaven for human crimes. And how full are these chapters of memorable utterance valuable to all boys who aspire to live a noble life? May they not be specially valuable to you, the sons of an heroic island, and of a school which must be above all a school which was meant to be the stern yet tender nurse of manly simplicity and self-denying work? "Our God whom we serve is able to deliver us out of the burning fiery furnace; but if not, be it known unto thee, O king, that we will not serve thy gods, nor worship the golden image which thou hast set up"—there rings the glorious trumpet-note of undaunted obstinacy and defiant faithfulness. "Hew the tree down, and destroy it; yet leave the stump in the tender grass of the field;"—there is the stern Nemesis of self-satisfaction, and the last chance for utter penitence;—Mene, Mene, Tekel, Upharsin—"Numbered, numbered, weighed, and they shall divide;"—there is the doom that follows neglected warning.

II. You know the story. "Belshazzar the king made a great feast to a thousand of his lords, and drank wine before the thousand." So, as with a crashing overture of orchestral music, the tale begins. Imagine the following splendour for yourselves;—that vast Babylonian palace, with its kiosks and fountains, its hanging gardens, and long arcades; every wall glowing with its weird images of Pagan symbolism; every portal guarded by colossal forms of winged cherubim, half-animal, half-human, staring through the dusk, with calm eyes, on the little lives of men; and everywhere, sweeping through court after court and chamber after chamber, the long and gorgeous processions of Chaldæan conquerors, portrayed with vermilion, exceeding in dyed attire; and gathered there the princes, the wives, the concubines,—all that the satraps could display of magnificence, and all that the harems hid of loveliness, as though in scorn of the enemy without, vainly thundering at those brazen gates. And, at last, as though sacrilege were needed to fire the mad festivity, they pledged their gods of brass and stone in those great cups of consecrated gold which Solomon had made for the Temple of the Eternal. And then the awful disturbance of the feast: that ghastly apparition; that something which looked like the spectral semblance of the fingers of some gigantic hand, moving slowly along the wall where the central lamp flung its most vivid light; and those seeming letters, which, as it moved, passed from under its dark shadow into a baleful glare; and while it moved, and when it went, the king, with fixed eyes, and ashy looks, and knees that smote together, staring in the very paralysis of fear, not, as before, on the crimson annals of Chaldæan conquest, but on some awful decree of an offended God recorded in hieroglyphs of undecipherable fire. The wild cry which summoned his magicians; the entrance of the queen-mother, to tell her son of the Jewish boy—an old man now—whom his father had taken captive, and

in whom was the spirit of the holy gods; and how
Daniel came, and read those fearful letters into the
four words :—

> "Menê, Menê, Tekêl, Upharsin—
> Numbered, numbered, weighed, and they shall divide;"—[1]

all this you know. Short was the space for repentance.
In that night was Belshazzar, king of the Chaldæans,
slain. "That night," as an English poet has written
it—

> "That night they slew him on his father's throne,
> The deed unnoticed, and the hand unknown:
> Crownless and sceptreless Belshazzar lay,
> A robe of purple round a form of clay."

III. You must not think that this was the only
warning which Belshazzar had received. If it came
too late, that was because it was the warning of retribution, not the warning of mercy; it was only because
all previous warnings had been neglected and despised.
His father's dreams of the shattered colossus and the
felled tree; the brute madness which had afflicted him;
the besieging of his own city; the fact that the shouts
of an enemy might have mingled with the very songs
of his banquet;—these were all warnings to this crowned
fool, but they had all been fruitless. Do not similar
warnings come to every sinner, long before the warning
of his doom? If any of you are living a life of sin,
have they not come to you? Have there been for you
no dreams in the darkness? no voices in the silence?
no hauntings of fear? no burdens of remorse? no
memories of innocence? no aches of shame? no qualms
of sickness? no echoing, as of ghostly footfalls, in the
far-off corridors of life? And later on, if these have
all been neglected, are you conscious now of no deriding,
deadly enemy doing siege to the golden Babylon of life?

[1] *Dividentes* (sc. *erunt*).

—no attempts of your own to drown in dead sloth, or hardened perversity, the hoarse murmurs of that approaching foe? And if in spite of all these the soul still sin and sin,—hardened to the pain of sin,—ceasing to feel its shame, lulled in its dead security—then has no history, has no biography, told you what you, young as you are, can hardly yet have yourselves experienced, that there comes at last sometimes—and sometimes, alas! too late—a handwriting upon the wall, which is only the handwriting of doom?

IV. But though my text is taken from this hand writing upon the wall, which was the doom of Belshazzar, it is with the earlier, less terrible warnings, that I have to do;—the warnings full of gentleness and mercy, which tell us of destruction while it still is distant, which bid us seek refuge while there is time to fly. Those warnings are always written on the palace wall of life; raise your eyes, and you will see them running, like a legible inscription, round the cornice of your banquet-house of youth. But is it not literally an every day experience that an inscription always before the eyes is little heeded? I imagine that the ancient Athenians paid little heed to the moral sentences which were carved upon the Hermæ in every street. I imagine that the Turks of Constantinople have taken but little notice of that ὁ Χριστὸς νικᾷ which remains, legible and unobliterated, like a prophecy which shall still be fulfilled, upon their central mosque. To come nearer home,—there are four noble, inspiring lines carved over the fireplace of a large room in this college; but do they enter specially into the life of those who daily see them? and, in another room, there is engraved upon a clock a very solemn Greek word;[1] but of all

[1] ἐξαγοράζου.

who know what that word means, do all try their very utmost to construe it in the noble version of an earnest, vigorous, self-denying life ? And just in the same way do we not, all of us alike, often thus neglect and forget the notices of God ? Yes; and that is why in dealing with us He is obliged, now and then, to *make* us see them—to force their meaning into us,—to interpret them again, when the dimmed wall has been painted over with other symbols, and familiarity has made them meaningless to eyes that will not see. And these reminders from God of truths which we have forgotten come sometimes very terribly; not whispered, but shouted,—not shouted only, but cut deep—not only cut deep before the eyes, but branded in letters of fire upon the soul. When palsying sickness is the debt due from weakened manhood to sinful youth;—when the loss of the last chance brings home to us the sense of the squandered opportunity; when the cold light of heaven, bursting through the drawn curtains of the hypocrite, shows him to himself and to others, not as he wished to be thought, but as he is; above all, when sin has been punished by God's suffering us to fall into deeper and deadlier sin, and crime flings its glare of illumination on the self-deception which said of sin, "There is no harm in it"—then it is that God puts forth the fingers of a man's hand, and His inscription, once unheeded, flashes into letters of fire. And—since be sure your sins will find you out—so must it be, sooner or later, to every sinner to whom repentance calls in vain. So that what I have been trying to urge on you to-day is to read those milder warnings, to listen to those stiller, smaller voices, which come to us, not at some terrible crisis, but at quiet moments, and ere we sleep at night, and on our knees, and when we read our Bibles, and in this chapel, and before Holy Communions, and in every blessed means of grace. For indeed those words, written once in the palace of Belshazzar, are for us written for ever in the house of life; and each one of you, in your own hearts, may still read the Mene, Mene, Tekel, Peres, as they were left by the awful moving of the spectral hand.

V. I will only try for the brief remainder of our time to brighten for you into legibility one of the many meanings of that first twice-repeated word. Mene, Mene—numbered, numbered. The last numbering—when all that we have, and all that we are, is numbered and finished—that will come to us all. But what ought we to number now? I would say especially, number your opportunities. Each *moment* is an opportunity, and if, as the old sundial says, *Ex hoc momento pendit æternitas*, what an opportunity, what a mass of opportunities must each day be! And each *prayer* is an opportunity. Have you never longed to open your whole heart to some friend who could help you in the difficulties and trials of your boyhood and inexperience —father, or mother, or elder brother, or teacher,—who might, once for all, influence, perhaps for good, your whole life, give you advice, give you help, give you comfort, save you it may be from years of folly and wretchedness? Ay, but after all, the very best of men cannot help you, and save you, and enlighten you as your God and Father can, as your Friend and Saviour can;—and what an opportunity then every prayer you utter as you clasp His feet! And each *Sunday* is an opportunity,— an opportunity by religious thoughts, religious services, religious studies, to raise your souls above the routine and frivolity of daily life, and to warn you not only against all sin, and impurity, and temptation, but also against all lazy, and unguarded, and dangerous hours. And these years of your *school-life* are an opportunity —number them. Consider how great is the weight they have to bear, and how much depends on your forming here a manly and sober view of duty, and making here a manly and stern choice between what is good and what is vile. And, numbering thus, " Seek to make your weeks roll round like the wheels of a chariot which is to carry you along the road of God's commands and purposes, and to bring you constantly nearer to the gates of Heaven." Do this, and then be sure that the Spirit of God will descend upon you week by week and day by day ; and the satisfaction of your Saviour, week by week, and day by day, will wash away your sins ; and each day will tell another, and each night certify another of your daily approach to God.

VI. But the word Mene is repeated, and I want you to see, lastly, that if you do not thus soberly and thankfully number your opportunities, and your days, and your prayers, and your sabbaths, a sadder, more disastrous numbering awaits you. How if, some day, in awful bitterness, you have to number, not your blessings, but your *sins ?* How if, like David, you have to say, " My sins have taken such hold upon me that I am not able to look up ; they are more in number than the hairs of my head, therefore my heart faileth me " ? Ah, in that day the gentle Mene of warning will burst into the flaming Mene of terror. For there is nothing more dreadful than a numbering of sins. The dead leaf falls, the chill wind sweeps it away : how slight a thing it seems : but go into the forest, and there see those dead leaves rolling in ghastly heaps, putrescent, numberless, into the dank and herbless soil ; they are not a slight thing then! Even so it is with the dead leaves which strew the floor of life—dead leaves of sins from which the life is gone—of sins which you have done with, but which have not done with you. Let me help you to judge of the sadness of such numberings. Two hundred years ago there lived a great poet, of humble rank, but of noblest character, who from boyhood had taken intense toil as his lot in life, who turned with fastidious haughtiness from every form of corruption, and cherished from his earliest years the dignity of a holy self-respect. Yet great as he was, and good as he was, and much as he had done, this great poet, John Milton, wrote on his twenty-third birthday :—

> "My hasting days fly on in full career,
> And my late spring no bud or blossom showeth.
>   *   *   *   *   *
> And inward ripeness doth much less appear
> Than some more timely-happy spirits endueth.
> Yet be it more or less, or soon or slow,
> It shall be still, in strictest measure even,
> In that same lot, however near or high,
> Towards which time leads me, and the will of Heaven."

In this vow and retrospect, if there be any sadness, it is only the sadness of the faithful, who when he has done all that is commanded him, yet, from the very loftiness of an ideal which towers so high above his attainments, says still, " I am an unprofitable servant." And now contrast these with the sad, remorseful verses written in his Bible by another poet, Hartley Coleridge, on his twenty-fifth birthday :—

> "When I received this volume small
> My years were barely seventeen,
> When it was hoped I should be all
> Which once, alas! I might have been.

> "And now my years are twenty-five,
> And every mother hopes her lamb,
> And every happy child alive,
> May never be what now I am."

And then after lines of deep pathos and remorseful memory, he humbly adds :—

> "Of what men are, and why they are
> So weak, so woefully beguiled,
> Much have I learnt; but better far,
> I know my soul is reconciled."

Once more, contrast this sorrow of bitter repentance with the hopeless, the cynical despair of these lines by a third poet—Lord Byron—on his thirty-third birthday :—

> "Through life's dull road, so dim and dirty,
> I have dragg'd to three-and-thirty.
> What have these years left to me?
> Nothing, except thirty-three."

Who was it that wrote thus? He was a man of noble rank, of vigorous health, of great beauty, of splendid genius; how had he used these great gifts? Not for man's good—not for God's glory—not, oh not, as you will see, for his own happiness. Those gifts were squandered, that beauty defaced, that strength abused, that genius laid like incense on unhallowed altars. It began when he was a Harrow boy. He had been a bad boy, and he grew up into a godless man. And when the days of numbering came how unspeakably sad, how utterly heartrending they were. What a difference between the white ashes and the gray heart of Byron at thirty-three, or the deep remorse and humble penitence of Hartley Coleridge of twenty-five, and the calm nobleness and conscious strength of Milton at twenty-three! And in all Byron's later poems, however finely uttered, there is the same bitterness, the same despair; the same wail that the bloom of the heart has fled as fast as the blush upon the cheek; that he has been driven over the shoals of guilt; that the magnet is lost, the sail shivered; that

> "Oh could I feel as I have felt, or be as I have been,
> Or weep, as I could once have wept, in many a vanished scene!
> As springs in deserts found seem sweet, all brackish tho' they be.
> So, 'midst the withered waste of life, those tears would flow to me."

And on his very last birthday, but three months before his death, he writes, though still young:—

> "My days are in the yellow leaf,
> The flower, the fruits of love are gone,
> The worm, the canker, and the grief
> Are mine alone."

You see it is all Mene, Mene—numbered, numbered. Ay, and it is Tekel too; weighed in the balances of God, weighed in the balances of the sanctuary, weighed even in the balances of his own judgment, he is found wanting. And oh, do not think that this is only the sorrow and the shipwreck of splendid genius! The wretchedest, craziest, most worthless shallop may be wrecked as hopelessly as the stateliest ship; and the meanest, dullest, stupidest, least-gifted schoolboy—as he may save his soul, and make it, through Christ's redemption, worthy to live with God, so may also lose his soul, with misery as intense and remorse as shameful—though he cannot utter them—as a poet or a king. Mene, Mene, Tekel, is for everyone of us: ay, and far away a voice peals forth in the distance, "Upharsin," "And they shall divide." Ay! be not deceived; good is not evil, and a state of sin is not a state of grace, and the angels shall divide the just from the wicked as the reapers divide wheat from tares. Oh then, if you would save many and many a future year, and the long hereafter, from the scathing misery of vain remorse,—if you would not have the sole remembrance of your boyhood to be a bitter sigh—read that warning word on the walls of the inner temple—number ere God numbers—pray to Him, ere it be too late, "So teach us to number our days that we may apply our hearts unto wisdom."

October 17, 1875.

SERMON XXXIV.

THE COURAGE OF THE SAINTS POSSIBLE IN BOYHOOD.

PSALM xvi. 3.

"All my delight is upon the saints, that are in the earth: and upon such as excel in virtue."

ONE morning, among the high Alps, I happened to be on a glacier which lay deep beneath a circle of stupendous hills, when the first beam of sunrise smote the highest summit of Monte Rosa. As I gazed from the yet unbroken darkness of the valley, so vivid was the lustre of that ray of gold upon the snow, that it looked like a flame of intensest crimson; and even while I gazed, the whole "pomp and prodigality of heaven" began to be unfolded before me. Until they burned like watchfires of advancing angels, mountain-crest after mountain-crest caught the risen splendour, and it flowed down their mighty crags in rivers of ever-broadening gold, until not only was the East full of glory and flame, but the West too echoed back the dawn in bright reflection, and the peaks which had caught the earliest blaze were lost in blue sky and boundless light,—and it was day. I never think of the Saints of God without their recalling to my memory those sunlit hills. *We* may be wandering in the dangerous darkness; but *they* are the proof that the Sun has risen,—they are the prophecy of the lingering day. And hence, to-morrow —which is All Saints' Day—is a day which I can never pass unnoticed,—a day which imperiously dictates the subject of the Sermon. But though that subject be embarrassing from its very vastness, yet, if I do nothing else, I shall regard it as a good end gained, by God's blessing, if I teach you to think much of All Saints' Day, and never to let it pass without trying to realize its noble lessons. It will be something to have quickened your "delight in the saints that are in the earth, and in them that excel in virtue." For while the world says, "Be as others are; do what others do; think as others think; let custom lie upon you heavy as death; leave not my beaten path, or you will be prosecuted;" Christ, on the other hand, says, " Follow not the multitude to do evil; aim at that only which is greatest; strive for that only which is best; be perfect as your Father in Heaven is perfect." And oh, it is good for us thus to lift up our eyes unto the hills! It is good for us in the midst of lives so inconsistent, so dwarfed, so conventional as ours, to bear in mind how much greater and better others have been;—how dauntlessly good, how magnificently victorious over vice and sin. Their high examples teach us how we may rise above our nothingness;—how little we are when we live the selfish life of the world; how great we may be, if we live as the Sons of God.

I. Once get this view of things,—the view that we read of the good, and wise, and holy, only that we may strive to become like them,—and then all History, all Biography, will become to you radiant with bright examples. No virtue will lack its illustration; no age its glory. Among the many many reasons why it is most desirable that you should not only read more, but read better and higher books than those cheap and trashy fictions—the mere refuse of tenth-rate literature, not worthy of the name of literature at all, which I see so often in the hands of some of you—is that you may get to see what great and good men have been. If I were asked what reading was best adapted to fill the soul of an English boy with high imaginations, and to keep his heart pure, and to give him lofty aims, and to store his mind with lovely and inspiring imagery, I should say, first of all, the best poems of our best poets; and next to this, the histories and lives of our loftier brethren in the great family of God.

II. But if we know how to read aright,—then in all ages, and from all nations, passes before us the glorious procession of the Saints of Christ. Go back to the earliest dawn of history, and think of Abraham, the elect Chaldee, and his simple unselfish life in the nomad tent; of Isaac, and those meditations in the fields at eventide, which kept his heart at peace; of Jacob, and how he wrestled in mighty prayer; of Joseph, the young, the self-controlled, the pure, and that grave protest which he left as his eternal legacy to the tempted youth of every age, "How can I do this great wickedness and sin against God?" Think then of the man Moses, so meek, and so heroic; of Gideon's modest intrepidity; of David's passionate repentance; of Hezekiah's utter and childlike faith. Then read the grand old Hebrew prophets;—Elijah, the rough ascetic, and Daniel, the polished courtier, and Isaiah, the eloquent statesman, and Jeremiah, the timid priest, and Amos, the bold gatherer of sycamore-leaves,—all uttering before apostate peoples and angry kings their dauntless protest for truth and God. And when the Maccabean patriots have closed the chequered story of Jewish fortune, we see John in his mantle of camel's hair, and we see the heavens opened and the dove descend on the head of Him who was the King of all Saints, and the Desire of all nations. Then we sit beside Paul the aged, chained to the rude legionary in his Roman prison. And as the drama of history advances, we stand in the gardens of Nero and see the martyrs die in their shirts of flame; we fly with the hermits to the desert solitudes; the sweet serious countenances of the Benedictines look down on us from their holy cells; we listen in the lecture-rooms of the saintly scholars, and see the beautiful face of St. Edmund of Canterbury, the pallor of which became "of a fair shining red" when he spoke of Christ or of holy things. We watch the heroic struggles of the first witnesses against a corrupted Church, and give our admiring pity to the dying agonies of a Fra Dolcino, a Savonarola, and a Huss. Anon, the thunder-tones of Luther wake an echo in our souls. Our hearts glow as, with a Vincent de Paul, we found the Sisterhoods of Mercy, and with a Howard gauge the depths of guilt and misery in the prisons of Europe. And to this long line of the world's noblest, I add the wisest and the purest of the heathen. As we dwell on the communion of saints, I recall Socrates,

> "That white soul, clothed in a satyr's form,
> That shone beneath the laurels day by day,
> And, fired with burning faith in God and right,
> Doubted men's doubts away." [1]

I think of Epictetus, poor and a slave, and lame, and the darling of the immortals.[2] I think of that bright

---

[1] *Songs of Two Worlds.* 2nd series.
[2] "Δοῦλος Ἐπίκτητος γενόμην κατὰ σῶμ ἀνάπηρος καὶ πενίην Ἶρος καὶ φίλος ἀθανάτοις."
    See Brucker, *Hist. Crit. Philos. II.* ii. 568.

consummate flower of Pagan chivalry, the sad, great warrior, philosopher and moralist, the Emperor Marcus Aurelius Antoninus. High heroes of unselfishness, pure ideals of excellence, the world's true soldiers, the world's true nobles, the world's best gentlemen! To think of them, to live with them, is to be stimulated, and encouraged, and refreshed. In life we meet the churl and the scoundrel, and we see that in human souls the ape and the tiger are not yet dead; but—are we angered, are we weary, are we discouraged?—then the high faith of these saints, their golden hope, their courage, their sweetness, their temperance, their magnanimity, restore to us our shaken faith in human nature; they show us what men *may* be by showing what they *have* been; they make us say to our souls, "The waves may seethe with mud, but be thou as the promontory on which they break." "Whatever any one does or says, thou must be good; just as if the gold, or the emerald, or the purple were always saying thus, 'Whatever any one does or says, I must be emerald and keep my colour.'"[1]

III. All Saints' Day bears to us, then, this witness, that we too are called to be saints; that this is the will of God, even our sanctification. Now perhaps some might think that there is a certain irony, a certain unreality, in telling the ordinary dull, commonplace schoolboy, whose moral sense seems often dormant, whose words are often bad, whose standard is often low, whose life is generally of the average, that God bids him strive after saintliness. He is living too often a life in which good and evil are not wrestling shoulder to shoulder in all the passionate energy of deadly struggle, but in which they are "lying down flat

[1] M. Aurel. Anton. vii. 15.

on the ground" in fatal truce; the common vulgar life, in which the boy is neither good nor bad, but just haphazard: neither cold nor hot, but just lukewarm; the life of the sandy desert, in which every pebble is a rock; the life of the flat plain, in which "every molehill is a mountain and every thistle a forest tree." It sounds like irony to tell this average every-day lad,— not very ideal in his habits, not very intelligent in his pursuits, not very noble in his instincts, not very delicate in his sensibilities,—that he is to be a saint. Ah! believe me there should be no irony in it; none, if you believe in the "communion of saints": none, if you be the soldier and servant of Him who is the King of Saints; none, if you wish, in the furthest future, to share in such honour and beatitude as have all His saints. And All Saints' Day is meant to teach you this; it is meant to make you believe in the divine within you, and read on your souls the heraldic blazonry of their high origin from God.

IV. But since it would be vague if I were merely to bid you follow God's saints and try and excel in all virtues, I will, for the remainder of our time, single out but one saintly virtue, such that if you have it, all the rest will follow it.

That virtue is moral courage.

You all love courage; you all despise cowardice. Of course you do; every Englishman does. At Waterloo, one of our allied Belgian regiments took fright, turned cowards, and ran away: our British fellows were so indignant at this poltroonery that they turned half round and fired a parting volley into the rear of these flying friends. But this kind of courage—the courage which faces physical danger—though the world surrounds it with such halo of glory, is just a matter of course. The saints of God have ever had it, and never thought much of it. The "flush and flashy spirits," who would try to taunt saints with cowardice, do so only in ignorant falsehood. "We could tell them," says one "of those who fought with savage beasts, yea, of maidens who stept to face them as coolly as a modern bully into the ring. We could tell them of those who drank molten lead as cheerfully as they do the juice of the grape, and played with the red fire and the bickering flames as gaily as they with the golden curls. And what do they talk of war? Have they forgot Cromwell's iron band, who made their chivalry to skip? or the Scots Cameronians, who seven times, with their Christian chief, received the thanks of Marlborough, that first of English captains? or Gustavus Adolphus, whose camp sang psalms in every tent? or Nelson's Methodists, who were the most trusted of that hero's crew?"[1] But I say that this courage—this gallantry and battle brunt in the temper of men—this tenacity of the tiger, "who leaps with bare breast and unarmed claws upon surrounding deaths"—is a matter of course. Some of the very best of men have shared it with some of the vorst; and a Catiline and a Borgia, no less than a Bayard or a Sidney, have died with their hands upon the sword-hilt and their feet towards the foe. But how far loftier—how truly saintly—is the moral courage of the brave and good; the courage which braves opinion in the cause of right; the courage which confronts tyranny to protect the weak; the courage which faces destruction to put down a wicked custom; the courage which escapes the average—which breaks loose from the conventional! Duke George was a powerful prince and Luther a poor monk: it was moral courage when Luther

[1] Edward Irving. I have altered one or two expressions.

said, "If I had duty to do in Leipzig, I would ride into Leipzig though it rained Duke Georges nine days running."[1] Take one of the most conspicuous instances which history affords. The veteran Stilicho had conquered Alaric and his Goths. The Romans invite the hero and his ward—a stupid, cowardly boy, the Emperor Honorius—to gladiatorial games in honour of the victory. The Empire has been Christian for a hundred years, yet these infamous and brutalizing shows still continue. They are defended with all sorts of devil's sophistry. Deadened by custom, people argue "that the gladiators themselves like them; that they gain their livelihood by them; that they train the multitude to bravery; that, at any rate, the enjoyment of the respectable many is worth more than the anguish of a squalid few." The games begin; the tall, strong men enter the arena; the tragic cry echoes through the amphitheatre, "*Ave, Cæsar, morituri te salutamus;*" the swords are drawn, and at an instant's signal will be bathed in blood. At that very instant down leaps into the arena a rude, ignorant monk,[2] who, however rude and ignorant, can tear to pieces by the strength of righteousness all these devil's cobwebs of guilty custom and guilty acquiescence. "The gladiators shall not fight," he exclaims: "are you going to thank God by shedding innocent blood?" A yell of execration rises from those 80,000 spectators. "Who is this impudent wretch who dares to set himself up as knowing better than we do; who dares to accuse eighty thousand people —Christians too—of doing wrong? Down with him! Pelt him! Cut him down!" Stones are hurled at him;

[1] "What a reservoir of dukes to ride into!"—Carlyle, *Hero Worship*.
[2] His name was Telemachus or Almachus. Theodoret, *His* v. 62. Alban Butler, *Lives of the Saints*. Jan. 1.

the gladiators, angry at his interference, run him through with their swords; he falls dead, and his body is kicked aside, and the games go on, and the people—Christians and all—shout applause. Ay! they go on, and the people shout, but for the last time. Their eyes are opened; their sophistry is at an end; the blood of a martyr is on their souls. Shame stops for ever the massacre of gladiators; the hearts of Christians were no longer " brazed by damnèd custom," and because one poor ignorant hermit has moral courage, "one more habitual crime was wiped away from the annals of the world."

V. This was a poor monk's doing, and think not that the race of such heroes is dead. I could give you dozens of such instances of moral courage, infinitely beneficent, if time permitted. I will give you one of quite modern days, of which some of the actors are living now—the moral courage of the missionary, giving up all, suffering, dying, to put down another bad custom —the custom of kidnapping—by Christians too—in the Southern Seas. Transfer your thoughts from the Coliseum of Rome to the coral islands of the Pacific. There stand a large multitude of swarthy savages, stark-naked, and brutally ignorant, armed with bows and clubs and poisoned arrows; and among them stand, unarmed, two English bishops: one of them with his quick ear, and ready gift of language, is learning, with incredible rapidity, how to preach to these poor degraded savages the good tidings of the gospel of peace; the quick eagle eye of the other is noting every change of countenance which,—should it become dubious and threatening,—must instantly warn them to reach their boat. And sometimes it does threaten, and then these two English gentlemen and bishops, of gentle birth, of gentle education, have to plunge into the white breakers that foam over the reef, and amid waters haunted by sharks, and devilfish, and stinging jellies, to swim to their boat, while about them whizzes and splashes into the water a flight of arrows, each one of which, if it only graze, means horrible death—death by lockjaw arising from the wound.—And one of those bishops is living; and there four years ago, the other, in the midst of that high service, died by the clubs of savages, whom he daily risked his life to save; and they laid him in an open boat to float away over the bright blue water, with his hands crossed, and a palm upon his breast.

VI. Is not looking at such a life something like looking at a hill-top fired by the first beams of the rising sun? Such palms and such crowns are hardly for us who would "go to heaven in an easy chair." By the side of such lives and such self-denials, do not our lives look very vulgar and very selfish? Yes, but remember two things: one, that such lives are at the best but a pale reflex and faint echo of His life, the life of the Son of God, by whose precepts they were guided, by whose Spirit they were inspired; the other that that life of Christ on earth was meant as the example, not only to God's saints, but to all men, and to all schoolboys too. Oh, do not slide into the fatal treason and delusion of supposing that you can give your boyhood to sin, and ignorance, and idleness, and offer only the dregs of your life to God. As the boy is, so mostly the man is; and when I see some wretched dullard, leaving behind him wherever he goes a trail of vice and meanness as a boy, it will not surprise me much to see the same trail behind the footsteps of the man. But let me look at the opposite picture. There was at Eton, not many years ago, a boy hale and strong and fresh coloured, and athletic—a boy frank as the day, and diligent, and docile—not particularly clever, but always high in his form; captain of the boats; in the cricket eleven; very popular, yet very good. Now it was a bad tradition, a bad custom there, that, at certain gatherings, songs were sometimes sung which were coarse songs, and which were not fit for a gentleman, much less for a Christian (and every right-minded boy should be both) to sing; and this boy of whom I speak—ready to risk popularity, ready to face sneers, ready to seem presumptuous even among his elders—declared that, in his presence, at that gathering, such songs should not be sung; and when such a song was sung he got up then and there, and left the room, and thereby stopped the bad custom. That boy of whom I now tell you grew up to be that man of whom I have just told you. That boy was Coley Patteson in 1845; that man was Dr. Coleridge Patteson, the martyr Bishop of Melanesia, in 1871. Even a boy, then, you see can do at school the duty of a saint; because even a boy can do what is right, and shame the devil; because even a boy can boldly rebuke vice, and patiently suffer for the truth's sake. Will you—will any one of you—do the same? Will you have courage to do what you know to be right, and to put down at all cost what you know to be wrong. Will you try to rise above bad customs? Will you make it a duty to "escape the average"? Most boys do not. The average boy, the ordinary boy, if a school have a vicious tone, catches that vicious tone, and leaves it worse himself, and worse for others. If a house is unchristian, he adopts the tone of his house. If a form is dishonest, he will become like the rest of his form. If one or two bad boys can set a bad tone, do you think that one or two good boys cannot set, and cannot restore, a good tone? Yes! for sin is cowardice, and sin is weakness, and sin is misery; and we were born to be brave, and strong, and happy, and the instincts of most boys will be on the right side if they have but fair play. Do all you can to act up to those instincts yourself, and to foster them in others. Do not follow the multitude to do evil. Be as the wheat, even if the tares around you are so many that hereafter they will have to be gathered in bundles for the burning. LET THIS be your lesson from All Saints' Day. Thus, may each and all of you begin here, and begin now, your high training as Saints of God.

October 31, 1875.

SERMON XXXV.

THE TRIPLE SANCTIFICATION.

1 Thess. v. 23.

"And the very God of peace sanctify you wholly; and I pray God your whole spirit and soul and body be preserved blameless unto the coming of our Lord Jesus Christ."

Body—soul—spirit: it is the combination of these three which makes up our mortal nature; it is the due relations between these three which constitute our sole possible happiness; it is the right training of these three that is the object of that lifelong education which should begin with our earliest years, and end only with the grave.

I. Let us begin with the body. When we consider what we are, why we are here, whence we came, and whither we are going, what facts strike us at once about our mortal bodies? The first obvious fact is that subtle chemistry, that exquisite mechanism, that perfect adaptation, which brings home to us our creation by some divine power—which proves to us that "It is He that hath made us, and not we ourselves." The next is, that as we did not create, so neither can we preserve ourselves. So delicate are the harmonies of our earthly frames, so exquisite is the agony which might be caused us by derangements, almost infinitesimal, in their structure; so " strange " is it

> " That a harp of a thousand string
> Should keep in tune so long,"

that we at once see ourselves to be but " as brittle glass in His hand; not only could He crush us with a motion of His hand, but were He even to withdraw His hand we should fall and break of our own selves." The third thing is, that these bodies are subjected to laws that cannot be broken; cannot, that is, be broken without certain and often terrible suffering; laws which we must therefore conclude to be the express will of Him who made us. The last fact is, that these bodies are lent to us for a time, and for a time only. They grow, they strengthen, they decay, they die. It is the lesson of the falling leaf. First it glitters in the glad, light green; then it passes into summer's burnished splendour and autumn's gorgeous colouring; then it hangs sere and ragged in the chilly wind; last, it flutters down, to be trodden into the common soil. So is it—so will it be, with all of us. It would be strange and painful to count how many have sat in this chapel, even in the last few years, who have already passed away—some of them in early youth—and who, by the inevitable law of death, lie cold under the cold sod now. And we do not know how soon the same end awaits us; but we do know, all of us, that, at the longest, only

> " A few more years shall roll,
> A few more seasons come,"

before we too shall be numbered among the dead. And we do know, for God has revealed to us, that we shall arise again, to be judged according to our works; we shall rise again to receive the things done in the body—those same things, not other things—whether they be good, or whether they be evil.

And from all these facts we see clearly the meaning of Scripture when it tells us, that our members are members of Christ, and our bodies temples of the Holy Ghost. Our bodies are not ourselves, but they are an essential part of ourselves, and if we do not train them into obedience to God's laws, they react fatally upon ourselves, until we become their slaves, and not their masters; and as is said so terribly by Zophar of a wicked man, in the book of Job, "His bones are full of the sin of his youth, which shall lie down with him in the dust." What, then, are the duties which spring from these considerations? How are we to train, how to save, how to sanctify our mortal bodies? Immense mistakes have been made on this subject in all ages; it was a mistake when the ancient philosophers regarded the body as a prison-house of which to be ashamed; a mistake when the mediæval monks regarded it as an enemy to be crushed; a mistake, more brutal and fatal by far than these, when whole nations gave themselves up to bodily indulgences, and said, with the infamous inscription on the statue of Sardanapalus, "Eat, drink, enjoy thyself, the rest is nothing." Against all these errors the testimony of our faith is clear. To each Christian it says, Thy body is not a prison-house, but a temple of the Holy Ghost, who dwelleth in thee; thy body is not an enemy, but a redeemed and sacred instrument of righteousness; thy body is not to be made the prey and victim of its appetites and baser impulses, nor art thou, as a mere beast of the field, made to be thus taken and destroyed, but thou art a child of God and an heir of heaven. He, then, has sanctified the body who has so trained himself in youth "that his body is the ready servant of his will, and does with ease and pleasure all the work that, as a mechanism, it is capable of; . . . . who, no stunted ascetic, is full of life and fire, but whose passions are trained to come to heel by a vigorous will, the servant of a tender conscience; who has learnt to love all beauty, whether of nature or art; to hate all vileness, and to respect others as himself." And what are the means to this? Three words, the words of our catechism, admirably sum them up. Those three words are temperance, soberness, chastity; those three words sum up all our duties to the body, and exclude all sins against it; those three words are the secrets of its beauty, its cheerfulness, its health. In this, as in all things else, obedience is infinite blessing; self-pleasing is utter ruin; perfect duty is perfect happiness. And the opposites of these—gluttony, drunkenness, impurity— oh, who shall count their victims? Among the living, how does the moan of their anguish arise to God, and the air tremble with the sighing of these "Gehazis whose leprosy is not upon the forehead." And from the pale nations of the dead, how, with the agony upon their ravaged faces, start they up in myriads—from Sychar, the city of drunkenness, from Kibroth-Hattaavah, the graves of lust! Oh, if ever your boyhood has but one pure aspiration, one solemn moment, one serious thought, recognise the high duty of carefully guarding your mortal bodies in sanctification and honour; recognise that none can sin against their mortal bodies without, sooner or later, being smitten by the iron weapon, and stricken through by the bow of steel; and if ever—whether by careless hours, or false friendships, or guilty imaginations, or subtle degeneracies—you be tempted to lay waste their sanctities, lift your eyes, and let these awful consequences of sin be to you as the fiery swords of cherubim waved to bar your entrance from the knowledge of evil, and mark where they crouch in the shadow, the terrible executioners of violated laws. Wicked sophistries of corrupt companions, wicked whisperings of evil passion, may try to deceive you; but be not deceived, for because of these things cometh the wrath of God upon the children of disobedience. Watch and pray, lest ye enter into temptation.

II. But the body is not the only thing which we have to train; many men are too noble, too fastidious, to sacrifice all life to its vilest passions. If man were composed only of body or spirit, this would be enough; but it is not enough: between the body and the spirit there is what is here called the soul, by which is meant, not what we commonly mean by the soul—not the divine and immortal part of us—but the mind, and the emotions, and the natural life. And, if we are to be presented blameless at the coming of Christ, this also must be sanctified. For a man may be temperate, sober, chaste, and yet no child of God; or, on the other hand, he may be idle, irreverent, covetous, disobedient, ungrateful, conceited, childish, dishonourable, false; or supposing he be none of these, he may yet be a lover of the world, a lover of his own self, selfishly absorbed in the career of ambition, in the culture of intellect, in the pursuit of wealth. And such are never safe; they are never to be trusted. Morality without religion has never in this world's history been an adequate defence. Need you any other proof of it than ancient Greece? She satisfied the intellect. She was full of grace, beauty, brightness, and knowledge; yet how utter, how shameful, how irremediably despicable was her brief and unpitied fall. How distressing is the life even of her philosophers;

how did they become vain in their imaginations, and their foolish heart was darkened; how, professing themselves to be wise, did they become fools; how more and more, falling from that starry heaven of their intellect, did they sow to the flesh, and of the flesh reap corruption. But even if the natural life does not sink thus, yet even then it is miserable and insufficient; for it is God's decree that nothing short of Himself should fill or satisfy the soul. If this soul be unsanctified, if its desires and affections be not fixed on God, then all life is a failure; and all who have lived and died with everything which the world could give them, yet without God, might cry to the Christian as the soul of Gawain shrilled into the ear of the holy king,

> "Farewell: there is an isle of rest for thee;
> But I am blown along a wandering wind,
> And hollow, hollow, hollow all delight."

No soul, then, is sanctified which has not learnt that the object, and the one object, of life is not what we *have*—for a man's life consisteth not in the abundance of things which he possesseth; and not what we *are*—for our wretched little gifts and attainments are absolutely nothing unto God, except in so far as they be used for the good of others; but what we *do* and what we speak—affections set on things above—the soul which is athirst for God, and the one hope that, however unworthy we be, and however imperfect, we may still be suffered to make our brethren better and not worse, and to spread God's kingdom among men.

III. And so we come to the best, the highest, the divinest part of man—man's spirit, which is none other than the Spirit of God within him. In one sense it needs not to be sanctified, being itself sacred; but it needs to be sanctified in the sense of being preserved from the contagion and the conquest of the body and the mind. For the spirit may be quenched, though it cannot be sophisticated; and it may be overpowered, though it cannot be depraved. Our sins never arise because we are too ignorant to know our duty, but because we are too weak to do it. When a boy disgraces himself by any form of sin, it is never because he does not know better, but because, being weak as water, he cannot excel, and because his spirit has no power over the impulse of the body or the temptation of the mind. Only do not think that weakness is a plea, or infirmity an excuse; nay, since you *might* be strong and not weak, such weakness is a sin, and such infirmity a shame; and if *we* cannot teach you this, life will teach it you by very rude and very agonising shocks. Nature, at any rate, accepts no idle promises, and listens to no weak excuses; and he who "will not be taught by the rudder must be taught by the rock." So that if you would shun this utter shipwreck, you must, by prayer, and penitence, and thoughtfulness, and humility, see that your spirit controls the warring lusts of the body and purifies the wandering affections of the soul. If not, yours will be one more of those wretched dual lives we see; the lives that face both ways; the lives rent by a fatal schism of disunion; the lives which are like bells jangled out of tune; the lives perfectly clear in their convictions, utterly contemptible in their actions. And oh, let me earnestly warn you against the fatal delusion that such a dual, such a divided, such a disharmonious life as this, is enough for God; that there is either virtue or religion in this miserable moral see-saw: that it is sufficient for us to do homage with our lips to what is good, while all the while our unregenerate hearts are full of worldly imagination, and our unsanctified bodies are made the instruments of unrighteousness. Oh, believe me, the spirit cannot serve God while the soul and the body persist in serving sin. Do you need any illustration of the state I mean? There was once an English minister, who, having designed for his king an act of wickedness, went home and wrote in his private diary a pious prayer: do you think that that was a prayer which God loved, and which God would hear? There was once an English conspirator, who talked open infidelity to all around him, and who, even on the scaffold, uttered the piteous words, "Oh God, if there be a God, save my soul, if I have a soul," who yet, the moment that he was left alone, was heard to fling himself on his knees with passionate entreaties to the very God whom he had just denied: do you think those prayers would be heard? Ah, God is merciful, but I am quite sure that this is a very dangerous, a very awful, a supremely wretched state. Yet, is it a state wholly alien to all our experiences? Have you never known a boy go straight out of this chapel to walk in the way of sinners and sit in the seat of the scornful? Have you never known a boy rise from his very knees to defile his lips with wicked talking, and his actions with wilful sin? Have you never known a boy "wet the face of a sin with a tear, and breathe upon it with a sigh," and fancy that he has prayed against it at the Holy Communion; and then go and plunge into it recklessly again, and go through the same farce once more? Why is this? It is because he deceives himself; it is because he is not living up to his light; not obeying the best part of his nature; not allowing his spirit—which means his reason and his conscience—to be the supreme guide of his life. It means too often that, both bodily and mentally, he has fallen into bad habits; and that "habit can, in direct opposition to every conviction of the mind, and even but little aided by the elements of temptation, induce a repetition of unworthy actions." And if you feel, any one of you, that this is your state, then realise at once your danger and your duty: your duty, because your present life is a violation of all that God in His mercy intended for you; your danger, because if this be continued, it can only end in moral death. Oh, "great is the effort, great, and not so easy as it seems, to be good and not bad." If you would be sanctified, learn to be discontent with your dishonour, ashamed of your weakness, penitent for your sins. Arise in tears, and go to your Father; arise in shame and remorse, and cast yourself at your Saviour's feet. Struggle on, and deal very sternly with yourselves. Walk very humbly with your God. Struggle on, if it be only inch by inch, till the rout is resistance, and the resistance victory. I could not tell you to do this if you had to struggle unaided: but it is not so. Stronger is He that is with you than he that is against you. God is with you; His will is your sanctification. For you Christ died. May He—I pray it with my whole heart—may He sanctify you wholly, body, soul, and spirit. Yonder Holy Table, yonder loving Communion, yonder memorial of His body broken and His blood shed for you, is the pledge of His desire to save you. Faithful is He that calleth you, who also will do it.

November 7, 1875.

SERMON XXXVI.

TRUTHFULNESS AND HONESTY.

Ps. li. 6.

" But lo, Thou requirest truth in the inward parts.

I. You all remember how, in the first book of the Bible, there is a tree of the knowledge of good and evil, and the first tendency to sin is to linger in its neighbourhood, and the first impulse to sin is to look at it as a tree to be desired, and the first act of sin is to pluck its fruit. On that tree of death we will not look to-day. In the last book of the Bible there is another tree—a tree planted by the river of the water of life, in the midst of the Paradise of God,—a tree whose leaves are for the healing of the nations. And the path to this tree is open; the fiery sword of the cherubim does not wave around it, nor asp creep under its shadow, nor awful mandates warn us from it. Nay, but we are invited, we are bidden, to draw near to it by heavenly voices, and to pluck from it

" A perpetual feast of nectared sweets,
  Where no crude surfeit reigns."

II. It bears twelve manner of fruit, and to-day I want you to pluck one of them—the fruit of truthfulness. All the fruits of the Spirit which this tree bears grow very close to each other; nay, they touch each other on the same stem, and where one grows the others are rarely wanting. This is the sole resemblance between the tree of life and the upas of evil. Indulge but one sin, and that sin by a fatal law engenders others; cherish but one virtue, and its diffusive healthiness will sweeten and purify the whole spirit. In the career of that criminal who now lies in prison awaiting the death due to his revolting crime we have a fearful illustration how one vice—in his case inordinate vanity—brought a promising and high-spirited boy first to sensuality, then to cruelty, then to horrible murder, and so to a shameful fate and an execrated name.[1] So it is that when but one vice has betrayed the wicket-gate, a hundred devils rush in and take possession of the fort. But the other—the sweeter, the more blessed truth— is that, even so, one virtue fairly, honestly, rigidly followed may be a safeguard and a defence—may be a fortress of impregnable refuge against every assault of the enemy—may be an inch of rock amid the waste of angry waters. This I hope will become partly clear when I have spoken of one virtue to-day—the virtue of truthfulness.

III. Let us begin at the very lowest step. I have known some natures to which a lie was a thing simply impossible. They could not lie if they would; they would not if they could. In the very clearness of their eyes, in the very openness of their faces, you may see a transparent truthfulness—an utter impossibility of anything serpentine and base. Hopeful, manly, noble natures these! Even if they go astray, they have one strong anchor to save them from drifting to perdition : one indissoluble chain to tie them to the shore. I thank God that truthfulness has ever been held a right

[1] Wainwright.

English virtue, and that every Englishman worthy the name of Englishman would echo the lines of the poet—

> "Thou hast betrayed thy nature, and thy name,
> Not rendering true answer, as beseems
> Thy fealty, nor like a noble knight:
> . . . . .
> This is a shameful thing for men to lie."

Ask the brightest virtue of our English Alfred, and Asser will tell you that it was truthfulness; ask the chief characteristic of the good Lord Falkland, and Clarendon will record that he abhorred the semblance of falsity; ask the most prominent strength of the great Duke of Wellington, and Gleig will answer, "He always told the truth." But though we may be proud of truth-telling as a national virtue, yet all good men have loved it. Take the Jews. "As for lies," says David, "I hate and abhor them." Take the Romans. When a man had pledged his word to Hannibal that he would return, and, going back to the camp for a moment on some trivial pretext, returned no more, the Romans, because though he had kept the promise to the ear he had broken it to the sense, branded him with the just ignominy of their contempt. Take the Greeks. Of their noblest—of Aristides and Epaminondas—we are expressly told that they would never, even in boyish sport, say what was other than the fact. The house of Glaucus, the son of Epicydes, is torn up, root and branch, because he had even meditated a lie; and at the very dawn of poetry the old Greek bard exclaims—

> ἐχθρὸς γάρ μοι κεῖνος ὅμως Ἀΐδαο πυλῄσιν . . .
> "Who dares think one thing and another tell,
> My soul detests him as the gates of hell."

Nor has it been otherwise in modern history. When the Emperor Sigismund, at the Council of Constance, is charged with having broken his word to Huss, there, before prelates and princes, it is visible to every one in that vast hall how the blush mantles on his guilty cheek; and all goes ill with Harold after he has broken his oath to the Norman; and it is all down-hill and ruin with Francis the First when he has violated the treaty of Madrid. And shall English boys, the sons of the gallant gentlemen who have made England what she is—shall English boys degenerate into the shame and cowardice of falsehood? God forbid! And when—as sometimes, alas! happens—an English boy can look you in the face, with all the air of openness, with all the affectation perhaps of injured innocence, with all the semblance perhaps of just indignation,—and will, to rebut a charge, or to parry a suspicion,—knowing, as he does know, that his word will be taken—will look you in the face and tell you a lie (a thing which he cannot do, unless everything wholesome in his nature has been sapped by that effeminate cowardice, which is the leprosy of the weakest and the feeblest of natures)— I say when an English boy can do this, there is nothing which so all but drives one to despise him, all but compels one to despair of him. I hardly know what can become of such a boy; I can but dimly read the prophecy of one more to join the miserable multitude of the world's living dead; of those who live for evil and not for good; of those through whose selfishness and through whose corruption the world is a world of misery and shame. From being such as this I utterly acquit the vast majority of you. If it were ever conceivable that England could train many of such a breed, then

> "Bear me from the harbour's mouth,
> Wild wind. I seek another sky.
> And I will see before I die
> The palms and temples of the south."

IV. Yes; but consider, is there not "a manslaughter upon truth," as well as a murder? Are there not more who, though they could not thus lie deliberately and designedly and in cold blood, are not so strong in virtue, so armed in the "hauberk's twisted mail" of sturdy integrity, as never to be surprised into a falsehood. As timid creatures fly from danger into the nearest refuge, so too often if a boy has committed some, perhaps even a quite venial fault, a sudden question (which I, for my part, think it my duty never to ask) may startle him into a denial which is a lie. Put him on his guard, and the boy who has any honesty in him at all will be safe at least from this worst aggravation of the offence; but do you not see how far braver, stronger, more hopeful, is a nature that could not even in the first instance, under any surprise, thus run its head into the strangling noose of falsehood, but at once, but naturally, but inevitably, but instinctively, but at whatever cost, tells the truth and shames the devil? Now what I would urge on you to-day is—now in this sacred place, here in the sight of God—to register a resolve in heaven that as for you, come what will, you will never stain your soul, you will never burden your life, you will never wound your conscience, with a lie. Oh, block up, I entreat you, in your souls not only every avenue, but every lane, and byepath, and little winding way to falsehood. And do not be content with the vow that no lie shall ever defile your lips, but nothing which has the most distant odour or complexion of a lie; no half lie or quarter lie; no sneaking subterfuge; no bragging exaggeration; no prevaricating ambiguity; no stammering suggestion; no half confession; no lie which, because it is half the truth, is ever the greatest of lies. And oh! if any one of you has ever given a promise to your father, or mother, or brother, or master for your good, consider that promise as a pledge, made for your own protection, in the very hearing of your God; and let your word be as your bond, and your bond be as your oath, and that oath sworn on the inviolable altar of your hearts. Let that promise be as a strong chain to bind you to integrity: let it be as a vast barrier to screen you from temptation. And, as a part of this subject, let me, as my distinct duty, however painful, warn you with all affection, but with all honest plainness and in no doubtful words, against that dishonesty, that unfairness, that (let us here at all events call things by their right plain English names)—that cheating in work which, deceive yourselves about it as you will, saps all honest industry, defrauds your fellows of their just dues, and proves a boy to be unworthy of the confidence which is, and which I hope always will be, placed in him till he has justly forfeited it. With this it is perfectly shocking to think that even the dullest and most ignorant of you should feel a spark of sympathy, because it is nothing more or less than a mean thing, a blot and a stain upon anyone's character,—into which a boy may perhaps fall once from weakness and thoughtlessness, and not from radical falsity, but into which if any boy who has a conscience does fall, he will at least be most heartily ashamed of it, and feel for it a sincere and bitter repentance. That such practices, if unchecked, must simply ruin for life anyone of you hereafter—that they would earn you the contempt even of a man of the world of ordinary honour,—this is bad enough; but it is even worse to have in the character a poisonous fibre which may make a whole life shifty and worthless. I have known boys—thrown in large schools at eight years old—placed in forms where not one boy was free from this miserable meanness,—and yet never led for one moment to make either of those wretched excuses which are so often made—either that the examination was so important, which makes the fraud only greater, or that it was so unimportant, which only makes the temptation less—but able to say that not from that early childhood have they ever shown up one word which was not most strictly their own, or got one mark which they had not most honestly deserved. I am sure that many of you could say the same, and I am sure also that I could name those that could. But oh! that every one of you could say it; or, if it has not been so hitherto, that you would vow that henceforth you will scorn dishonesty as a base and slavish thing. I do most confidently hope that the coming examination will not be stained by one single instance of this un-English and mean offence. If there be decadence, as men say there is, in the proud old honesty of England—if there be forgery and swindling in our commercial enterprises— if there be adulteration and trickery in our trade—if among foreign nations the word of an Englishman is no longer as his bond—if, as the blood of martyrs has shown, the villanies of people who call themselves our countrymen have come to be distrusted by the very savages of the Pacific,—then let every one who has the honour of England at heart see that faith, and honour, and fairness, and simplicity, and honesty, and any other noble name we like to call it—in one word, see that truthfulness be as the very girdle of the loins of English boys.

V. I have left myself no time to show you how falsity in word or action gives a crookedness to the whole character; but you may be sure of this, that it does lead, and that quite inevitably, to self-delusion and hypocrisy—to a cheating of ourselves and a cheating of God.

> " To thine own self be true,
> And it shall follow as the night the day,
> Thou canst not then be false to any man."

Now to be true to yourself is to know that you were made for virtue, made for integrity, made to keep your body in sanctification and honour, made a child of God and an heir of heaven; and that to be either indolent or wicked, to either waste your own blessings, like the beasts which perish, or to add to the sin and sorrow of others, like the evil spirits of the pit, is to personate another, not yourself, and to give the lie to your nature and to your God. And the reason why the truthful man is the less likely to do this is because he is the less likely to lie to himself. Some natures are so false that they " partly take themselves for true: " such dupes of their own worthlessness, that they do not realise that their course of life is morally detestable. Why is this? partly because they make lying excuses to themselves; partly because all the vile work of their lives is done in the back places and dark closets of their own natures, where, since no ray of God's eternity can pierce, they hide themselves in their most interior secrecy. But the honest man when he errs most deeply will still be honest about it—he at least will tell no lies about his sin either to himself or to his God. Oh! it is an awful thing to stand as a guilty soul before the eye of God; but he will stand there with more of hope and less of shame, who cannot " smile, and smile, and be a villain " —who has often set himself before himself, and forced himself to say "that shameful thing art thou." For he whose "conscience—that can see without light—sits in the Areopagus of his heart, surveying his thoughts, and condemning their obliquities," he, even when he stumbles, has not lost his hold of a guiding hand; he has that which David desired so passionately, and which saved David even in his worst extremities—he has truth—truth in the inward parts.

December 12, 1875.

SERMON XXXVII.

SCHOOL GAMES.

ZECH. v ii. 5.

"And the streets of the city shall be full of boys and girls playing in the streets thereof."

THE prophet is speaking here of restored Jerusalem, and as he summons up the image of its future happiness, his kindly eye dwells for a moment, in prophetic vision, on the games of the young in its bright rejoicing streets. He contemplates them with unmingled pleasure; without one touch of obtrusive sadness, or of ungenial cynicism. It is not altogether a healthy sign in our English poet, when, on revisiting the fields where once his

"Careless childhood played,
A stranger yet to pain,"

he can only say with a sigh, of the lads whom he sees on the banks of the Thames, that they are like victims playing regardless of their doom, and then draws a melancholy picture of the misfortunes of the future which lie in ambush for them,—passion, and falsehood, and remorse, and poverty, and the painful family of death. A truer and healthier feeling breathes through the lines of the sweet poet of the *Christian Year*, who, though he begins by the somewhat saddening thought,

> "The heart of childhood is all mirth,
> We frolic to and fro,
> As free and blithe, as if on earth
> Were no such thing as wo,"

yet proceeds to speak of a life enriched by such hope, and joy, and peace in believing, such brotherhood of a loving Saviour's sympathy, such tenderness of a Heavenly Father's love, as will enable the boy to sing his morning song all through the weary day of the world's strife,—as will make his age like the rich glow round the autumnal sun, and will enable him to look beyond the grave for a bliss which heart hath not conceived.

II. I think you all know that it is in this latter spirit,—with this warm and cordial sympathy,—with this faithful and untroubled hope,—that we here look upon your games. It is this that, to me at any rate, makes it a beautiful and exhilarating sight—now alas! more than ever—to see our cricket-field so lively with its hundreds of cricketers in the sunshine of a summer afternoon. Too often, amid the burdens of manhood, we are apt to be like the peevish children in the market-place to whom the gladness of boyhood appeals in vain; but it is not lightly, least of all is it with any desire whatever to answer you according to your idols, if I call it a national blessing that there are two vigorous games to absorb the superfluous energy and occupy the abundant holidays of English schools. The great Duke hardly went too far who, when he saw the boys at football under the ancient elms of Eton, said, "It was here that Waterloo was won!" These games undoubtedly do educate, or may be made to educate, much that is manly in the best and truest sense. There is a manliness which is identical with virtue; and there is—as usual—a certain spurious semblance of manliness—the devil's counterfeit of it—which I call mannishness. By manly I mean all that is eager, hearty, fearless, modest, pure; by mannish I mean that which apes the poorest externals of the lowest types of men—the premature swagger of folly, and the odious precocity of vice. And it would indeed be deplorable if the devil, and the devil's agents, thrust their debasing influences into our English games, as they always do try to thrust themselves into all good things. If, through the idleness and emptiness of the vicious and the dull, all the detestable machinery of low betting, lounging, drinking, and worldliness in its worst sense, ever gets mixed up with the athletic sports of our schools and universities, all that is most valuable in those sports will be gone. May that day be far distant, and may we so do our duty that it may never come at all!

III. I am going then to speak to you a few words about games, nor do I think it in the least degree needful to apologise for such a topic, as though it were as much beneath the dignity of the pulpit as it is alien from its conventionalities. The true, the only dignity of the pulpit which I can recognise comes from the desire to do good by speaking words which are real, and which even the youngest hearers may understand. And in drawing my subject from the circumstances of your common life, I do but humbly follow the highest examples. The prophets, the apostles did the same. Is it David the shepherd? He sings of "the ewes great with young ones," and his dreams of happiness are the green pastures and the still waters. Is it Ezekiel the priest? He dwells on the incense of the temple and the smoke of the sacrifice. Is it John the hermit? His words ring with the imagery of the desert—the rock, the serpent, the barren tree. And why need I speak of these? Did not Jesus Himself take His subjects and His illustrations from the commonest incidents of common life? Did He not speak of the whitening harvests and springing flowers, and the reed shaking by the river, and torn clothes and lost pennies, and eggs, and pearls, and fish, and weddings, and funerals, and grumbling labourers, and reapers amid the wheat and tares? Did He not rejoice in life's joys no less than He grieved over its sorrows, and did not the kindly and the kingly eyes, which were so often dim with tears amid earth's mourners, shine with a brighter glow as they watched the games of happy little ones in the green fields beside the silver sea?

IV. You spend many hours this term at cricket. You call this term "the cricketing term." The thought of this game is very prominent in your estimate of school life, and it is hardly possible to live among you without knowing how much you talk of it. And all this is thoroughly natural. If there are some people who deplore, some who are indignant at, some who cannot understand it, that is because this prominence of athletics is not free from dangers. Those dangers— to which I shall only allude but slightly—are partly general, partly individual; and though I think that by God's blessing we are largely able to avoid them, yet we must not deny that they exist. A boy, for instance, is often in danger of wholly overestimating the value of his own athletic success. Many of the best men—like Bishop Coleridge Pattison—have been good cricketers, and so have been, and are, many of the best boys I have ever known; but yet the physical gifts which may make a successful cricketer are not, you must remember, incompatible with—and not once or twice only have I seen them combined with—much that is utterly hateful and utterly contemptible; so that if it be absurd and wrong to be vain of any gift, it is more than ever absurd and wrong to be vain of those which are among the lowest. Then too there is a second danger lest games, —not so much in the actual time spent over them, as in the endless and not very fruitful gossiping about them afterwards,—should degenerate into serious waste of time, which a boy, whose future must depend on his own exertions, may regret and rue for life. There is, again, a real danger of foolish partisanships,—ungenerous dislikes,—miserable jealousies,—evil surmises,—perverse disputings. Once more, there is a constant danger of extravagant and foolish misjudgments, which utterly lose sight of the relative values and importance of things, so that a boy who, from any circumstance, is not, to use your common phrase, "good at games," is quite ludicrously underrated, perhaps even despised, defrauded of his legitimate influence. Now while you play with all heartiness, do not forget that games, however useful and delightful, are not of first-rate, not even of third, fourth, or fifth—scarcely even of tenth-rate importance in comparison with higher things. If any one were asked to name the most famous living Marlburian, a man whose works are read wherever the English language is read, he would name one, who, when he was a boy here twenty years ago, certainly never touched a bat; and there may be at this very moment, on those benches, some boy, whom you don't think much of now because he is "no good at games," of whom thousands of future Marlburians may be proud as having reflected lustre on their school, when the very names and existence have been forgotten of whole generations of boys who kicked numberless bases and won enormous scores. Well, against these dangers—of vanity, of wasted time, unchivalrous rivalries, attaching of exaggerated importance, undue and silly contempt for those who care only for other things—we must all be on our guard. I am sure that most of you are on your guard against them; and then, if I am not much mistaken, all that remains is good.

V. How much good is there, for instance, in the mere enjoyment, pure and simple, which our field on a summer afternoon represents. When we further bear in mind what an immunity this enjoyment secures to us from unhealthy lounging, aimless idleness, and vicious mischief,—when we remember how many excellent qualities it may help to bring into play—it seems to stand on still higher grounds; but even if there were nothing more in it than harmless, hearty, happy occupation, it would be a thing at which all may rejoice who look at life with the eye of faith and love. Only let one ray of God's sunlight—the sunlight of a pure and faithful heart—fall on this natural gladness, and how bright may it become! If the profane old man of the great comedy, on his death-bed, "babbled of green fields," how much more sweetly to you in after life,—perhaps as you faint on the arid plains of India, perhaps as you toil in the dingy back streets of great cities, amid haunts of poverty and crime—may come the memory of sunny cricket grounds where once you played. Like a draught of clear water in the desert—like that sparkling cup which his warriors brought to David from the well which he had loved in boyhood—you will drink of the innocent delights of these school-days, and will take heart of courage, and remember how you learnt in your youth that God is a loving and a tender Father, who, if He asked your service, asked it only for your good; and if He said, "My son, give Me thy heart," desired it, not because you can do anything for Him, but solely out of His love for you, and that He might save that boyish heart ere the evil days had come, from the vice which seduces, from the shame which crushes, from the agony which tortures, from the temptation which betrays.

VI. But, as I said, there is something more in our games than this mere happiness—good as that is. For, even from your games, you may learn some of those true qualities which will help you to do your duty bravely and happily in life. No one can be a good cricketer who does not practise—who does not take trouble—who is not glad to amend faulty ways of playing—who does not attend to rules. And in a yet better and higher sense, no one can make a first-rate cricketer if he is not ready, and steady, and quick, and bold; if he is not trained to bear a reverse with a perfectly good-humoured smile; if he is not free from the self-consciousness which is usually called being nervous; if he has not the pluck, and the patience, and the good humour, and the self-control to play out tenaciously to the very last a losing game, ready to accept defeat, but trying to the end to turn it into victory. Well, believe me, you want the very same good qualities in the great cricket-field of life. There too—in high moral and spiritual matters which affect eternity itself—it does not do to be for a single moment off your guard;—there too neglect and carelessness produce disgraceful catastrophes;—there too either over self-confidence on the one hand, or deficient nerve on the other, will end in certain defeat;—there too it is cowardice to be demoralised by the first sign of apparent failure ;—there too the highest courage is often shown by sticking to the very last to a failing cause ; —there too you must be ready at all times to give way to others, and not expect to have all the batting or all the bowling to yourself;—there too you may be unsuccessful without any fault of yours, and if it be God's will that thus for you the chance should be over, and the wickets fall, almost before you have well taken your stand, you must step from your place, not with despair, not with anger, least of all with the angry gesture and passionate curse of disappointed vanity, but bravely, and quietly, and with a manly and cheerful heart.

VII. Yes, life is a game ; a complicated game ; a difficult game; a game which requires wisdom, diligence, patience; a game of which you must learn the conditions ; a game which will try your powers ; a game in which there is not one good quality of head or heart that will not greatly help you; a game of which the forfeits are terrible, of which the issues are infinite. " It has been played for untold ages, and every one of us is one of the players in it." The rules of it have been made independently of us, but they are absolute, and we must obey them. Those rules are the laws of nature, the laws of health, the laws of intellect, above all, the moral laws of God. If we violate them from mistake, or from ignorance, some allowance may be made for us ; none, if we defy them wilfully. Obey them,—and by prayer and the grace which your Saviour will give, you *can* obey them,—and you must and will find peace unto your souls. Disobey them, and you make of life a misery, and of death a ruin. But there is one respect in which the game of life differs from our earthly games. In these there is always an element of chance ; in the game of life there is none. He who keeps the high and simple rules of it must win. He may seem indeed to lose. He may seem to die broken-hearted, in indigence, obloquy, failure. Fools may think his life madness, and his end to be without honour; but he has won, and more than won, for he is counted among the children of God, and his lot is among the saints. So that in this respect it is not with life as with your games at cricket. There a player may have done his very best, but if he has made no score, you do not cheer him, and, his chance being over, he walks in silence up the steps. Not so when any faithful player—even the humblest—leaves the game of life. He may leave it, not only amid the world's silence, but even amid its execrations; he may leave it to join

> "The crowd untold
> Of men, by the cause they served unknown,
> Who moulder in myriad graves of old—
> Never a story and never a stone;"

but as his last breath ebbs away, be it even in a sigh of sorrow, be it even with a groan of agony, how joyfully does the guardian angel utter the record, "He has done his best!" And then, upwards, and ever upwards, peals even to the glimmering summit, the glad answer, "He has done his best!" and so at last, while

> "They stand, those walls of Zion,
> All jubilant with song,
> And bright with many an angel,
> And all the martyr throng,"

he who has lost his life for Christ's sake, finds it. The poor failure of earth becomes the high success of heaven. He hears a voice he knows, a voice which thrills into his inmost soul, and oh! he cannot mistake it. It is the voice of his Saviour, heard far amid the crowding Immortalities of Heaven, and it says "Servant of God, well done!"

May 14, 1876

SERMON XXXVII.

FROM SORROW TO REPENTANCE.—THE PRODIGAL'S RETURN.

LUKE xv. 18.

"I will arise and go to my father."

I. FROM innocence to sin,—from sin to sorrow,—is there any one soul in this congregation which is not so far at least,—it may be to very different extents, but still to some extent—acquainted with this path of the prodigal? Which of us must not confess that he has gone astray like a sheep that is lost? which of us cannot testify that no jot or tittle of God's word has in his case fallen to the ground, but that every step away from God is a step in the road to death? But this third stage in the soul's journey—the path from sorrow to penitence—have we all trodden that? "I have sinned with Peter, not wept with Peter," was the dying wail of the cruel bishop. Are there none of us who must confess we have wandered like the prodigal, but we have not with him repented,—we have not, like him, returned? Yet many of us, I trust, have trodden that path of penitence. Oh, may every soul which has not trodden it begin to tread it now; may God grant that even these poor and feeble words—the last, except it may be a few words of farewell, that I shall ever utter in this position from this place, to this congregation—may be so blessed by His Holy Spirit as to help some soul here to find its Saviour,—to return from darkness to light, from the power of Satan unto God. May God grant it for His dear Son's sake!

II. We left him in the depths of his degradation,—his penal degradation,—the degradation which was the inevitable consequence of his sins,—this once gay and happy boy; we left him seated in his hunger, in his loneliness, afar from the God whom he had forsaken, abandoned of the companions by whom he had been betrayed, a lost soul, a ruined life. Sin, revealing itself to him, as sooner or later it does to all, in its native hideousness, took no further pains to make him believe in its charm or beauty. Active agencies and strong deceptions are needful only at the first; but when temptation has done its work, habit may be left to continue, and despair to finish it. Vice must come at first in full attractiveness—it must come to the boy in the guise of a friend, bold and radiant, with a smile on the face and light in the eye;—to the youth with all the mysterious enchantments of Circean beauty and Siren songs. But she comes very differently to the gloomy, to the fallen, to the suffering, to the disillusioned man. When she has once won her victim Sin may come undisguisedly as Death; being no longer a temptress to dupe, but a fury to scourge the soul, she may heap upon it the chains of its iniquities, and grate and clang upon its prison-house the locks and bars of hell.

III. But, thanks be to God, again and again are the prisoners delivered—again and again does the malice of Satan overreach itself. Because we are made in God's image, which we may deface and desecrate, but never quite lose;—because He has placed the light of

His Holy Spirit, as a lamp in our souls, which may smoulder, but never quite be quenched;—because we are His sons, and even when we have made ourselves slaves in some far country, can never quite become its citizens;—because we cannot sink so low as not to feel that we were born for God and for heaven, not for foul offices and swinish husks,—therefore not seldom is the spoiler reft of his victims. The soul which he had drugged, and well-nigh slain, shakes off its torpor; there come back to it the stirrings of its old strength; it tears off its fetters; a power not its own bursts the gates of brass and smites the bars of iron in sunder; and in spite of the thraldom of habit, in spite of the power of Satan, the duped, degraded, imprisoned soul is free.

IV. The prodigal "came to himself." He steadily faced—and oh how much is there in this!—he steadily faced his true position. He had left his home, and his father, and his mother, and the innocence of his early years; he had sought independence, and found slavery; had sought friends, and found tyrants and traitors; had sought pleasure, and found agony; had sought plenty and importance, and had found famine, detestable humiliation, and the husks of swine. Was this to be the end? Was his life worth nothing more than to be thus sacrificed? Ah no! He came to himself. The child who had played in the sunlight of his father's love,—the clear-browed lad with no taint of evil in his thoughts—the favourite son, so dear, so happy, so full of generous purpose and unselfish life—that was himself. But the loveless, thankless, graceless boy—the troubled, the corrupt, the dissolute youth—the companion of rioters and harlots—the fool who had laid waste the inner sanctities of his being, and squandered the highest heritage of his life—that was not himself. It was a guilty semblance of himself which he hated; a hideous dream of himself which he despised. "How many hired servants of my father," he thought, "have bread enough and to spare; but I—I a son, a loved son, —ἐγὼ δὲ ἀπόλλυμαι—I am perishing, am being destroyed." And as the thought of all he had been, of all he might have been, and all he was, came over him, there came too a thought of all that he yet might be. Like a soiled robe there dropped off from him the bad memories and base temptations of the last few years. A breath of vernal and holy hope came to him like a breeze of Eden beating balm upon a fevered brow. He was no longer the runaway, the self-destroyer, the boy of whom they could only think with a blush of shame;—but again he was a much-loved child in the dear old home;—again the roses of the garden bloomed around him;—again he mingled a pure voice in hymns and prayers;—again a mother's kiss was not sullied on his cheek, nor the hand of a father laid in blessing on an unworthy head. The calls of olden promise and olden prophecy came back to him. From the page of Holy Writ the voices whispered to him, "Return unto me, for I have redeemed thee"—"Turn ye, turn ye from your evil ways, for why will ye die?"—"Return, ye backsliding children, and I will heal your backslidings." And to these voices he listened. The fixed thought—ἐγω δὲ ἀπόλλυμαι —became the blessed resolve—ἀναστὰς πορεύσομαι. "I will arise and go to my father, and will say unto him, Father!"—and oh! surely in that word there will be a touching appeal—"Father, I have sinned."—Yes! I will open my heart to him; I will make no excuses; I will conceal nothing; I will confess all. And since I dare not hope, I hardly venture to desire, that all will be as before, I will say, "I am no more worthy"— I was worthy once, but alas! οὐκέτι—" I am no longer worthy to be called thy son,—make me as one of thy hired servants." He deserves to suffer—that he feels; he has no wish to escape from the consequences of his past misdeeds; no subtle desire to retain one guilty pleasure or false freedom of the past—He knows that

> " Hearts which verily repent
> Are burdened with impurity
> And comforted by chastisement;
> That punishment's the best to bear
> Which follows soonest on the sin,
> And guilt's a game where losers fare
> Better than those who seem to win."

Ay, here, my brethren, you have an answer to the question, What constitutes repentance? It is a change of heart which confesses and amends. It says, "I have sinned;" and makes no excuse, and accepts all consequences. Not as Pharaoh said, "I have sinned," and did the same thing again and again. Not as Balaam said, "I have sinned," yet proceeded from bad to worse. Not as Saul said, "I have sinned," yet laid the blame on others, and wished still to be honoured before the elders of the people. Not as Judas said, "I have sinned," and plunged into despair. No, not as these; but as Achan said, "I have sinned," and made full restitution; and as David said, "I have sinned; let me now fall into the hands of God, and not into the hands of men;" and as Job said, "I have sinned; what shall I do for thee, oh! thou Preserver of men?" With these penitent souls it is not the agony of consequences that they care for, but the shame of wrong-doing; it is not the remorse of despair, but the godly sorrow for unworthiness. It is like the sorrow of that poor penitent which an English poet, himself a penitent, has so touchingly expressed :—

> " She sat and wept beside His feet : the weight
> Of sin oppressed her heart, for all the blame
> And the poor malice of the worldly shame
> To her were past, extinct, and out of date;
> Only the sin remained—the leprous state.
>   * * * * *
> She sat and wept, and with her untressed hair
> Still wiped the feet she was so blessed to touch,
> And He wiped off the soiling of despair
> From her sweet soul, because she loved so much."

And so—yearning more than all for his father's love—the prodigal arose. If his thought was followed by a resolve, his resolve also was followed by an action. It was not only confession and self-humiliation, it was immediate return to God, immediate abandonment of sin, which proved his sincerity. There was no delay; no procrastination; no dallying with the past; no looking back to the doomed glittering city; no going over the old sins under the plea of penitence, and growing half guilty in the thoughts again. Ah ! my brethren, remember this; we are not sorry, not truly, not savingly sorry for sin, unless we do as much as even Ahab and Judas did, viz., abandon the fruits of it. And the prodigal did abandon it. He turned his back for ever on the scenes of his shame and sin; he arose and came to his father.

V. You must not think that it cost him nothing. Penitence is not a thing which costs no effort. Oh ! if it were, who would not repent ? It is not easy ; oh ! it is not easy to repent. Nothing but God's grace could enable us to do it. He alone can break the iron sinew in the neck of our pride. To confess that we have been fools, and degraded fools, and it may be hypocrites as well—to see how inferior we have been to the elder brother, whom, it may be, we have despised—to break off bad habits—to front the stern and dreary path through which alone we can reach the unific rectitude of a holy and self-denying life ;—it is not easy ; and it is, alas! so rare that this world, like the jealous elder brother of the prodigal —

> "This world will not believe a man repents ;
> And this wise world of ours is mainly right,
> For seldom doth a man repent, and use
> Both grace and strength to pick the vicious tares
> Of blood and nature wholly out of him,
> And make all clean, and plant himself afresh."

But, whether rare or difficult, it is thus alone that we can be saved. God's grace will never be wanting, only remember that there must be our own free will, our own hearty effort too. Perhaps you think that time will make you better. My brethren, time is nothing—it is a mere mode of thought; if time does anything, it only makes men worse, not better. Or perhaps you think that sorrow will make you better. It would be indeed a daring blasphemy thus to challenge God to strike, and say I will sin till the wrath falls on me, and then I will repent; but though suffering will dog the heels of your sin, it may but make you worse, not better, even as fire, though it melts the gold, does but make the clay more hard. No; you must repent as your own choice; you must amend of your own effort; you must listen to the voice wherewith God ever calls you; you must think of these very words of mine to-day as a voice whereby to-day, while yet it is the accepted time, He calls you to repentance. Either this, or the end must be that your life—that golden, that inestimable life which God gave you—must come to nothing, or better not have been. Oh, brethren! if your conscience tells you that you, at this moment, are living in unrepented sin, then believe me, not health, not happiness, not life itself, is to you of importance so unspeakable as repentance: it is, it must be, to you the very work of life.

VI. And so it was to this young prodigal. He had sinned; but all the good in him had not yet been wasted away; all the strength, and vigour, and, purity not yet quite degraded out of him. He arose, he went tottering and foot-sore, and with difficulty, and in rags, and with shame at heart, and with deep misgiving, and conscious that he had disgraced and destroyed himself, and that, being what he had been, and having done what he had done, he was utterly unworthy to pollute with his presence that pure home; sick at heart, he yet resolutely turned his face uphillward, prepared meekly to accept in punishment the worst that could befall. And along that difficult and often well-nigh despairing path of penitence—through its rending briars of strengthened temptation, and its constant failures of weakened will, up its steep rocks of difficulty, through its miry sloughs of despair—faint often and weary, yet upheld by steady purpose and inspiring hope, he struggled on. He struggled on; and at last, with a great leap of his heart, as he toiled to the last hill-top, far off in the distance, he saw his home. Ay, there it was; the blue smoke rose from its clasping foliage, the quiet silver stream that gladdened it, the peaceful fields which blossomed round it, the trees under which he and his brother had played of old. Ah! but there—within its shelter—was the mother there? Tired of wishing and of waiting, had she passed, yearning for him, to the grave? or was she still living, with a heart full of sore, sore sorrow for her son? And the father—was he alive—the old man, was he well, though sorrow had turned his hair to a deeper grey? Would he receive, would he pity his disgraced, lost, wandering boy?

VII. My boys, you know that your fathers and your mothers love you all with a deep and a tender love, yet you know that sons and daughters have sometimes sinned against their parents, and have not been forgiven. I once knew a boy who had gone wilfully to a far country. He came back years after, absolutely penniless. He came back to a friend; to the lot of that friend it fell to tell him of "heart-shaking news in long-accumulated arrears"—to tell him that his father was dead, and his sister, and his brother; and that his mother lived; and to give him the means of getting home. He got home; but day after day, as he wrote afterwards—day after day he had come up to, he had passed, he had walked to and fro in the twilight in front of the well-known door of his old home, and dared not knock, and dared not enter; barely at last, his whole heart sick and faint within him, he summoned up courage to knock; the door opened, and there was a cry of love; he was clasped, forgiven, in his mother's arms. But it is not always so. Not long ago a father had a sailor-lad—a handsome, high-spirited, gallant boy. He may have been in some way to blame—I do not know; but at any rate he was cruelly treated by his captain: he ran away from his ship, and he came to the country village where he lived. His father was an old man, a clergyman, a man who had known sorrow; yet he took the boy to an upper room, locked him up there, and next morning, in spite of tears and entreaties, took him straight back to the ship he hated, to the captain from whom he had fled. Never again— and you cannot wonder at it—never again did that boy set foot in his father's home.

VIII. But it was not so with this father in the parable: it is not so with our Father in heaven, for whom he stands. In the whole round of literature, divine and human, I know nothing equal to that wonderful outburst of impassioned and forgiving love. " And he arose and came to his father; and when he was yet a great way off"—ah! think of that, you who feel within you the first stirrings of repentance—" when he was yet a great way off, his father saw him, and had compassion, and ran, and fell on his neck, and kissed him," and barely left him time to sob out his " Father, I have sinned." Not as a slave did he receive his boy, but as a son; not as an evil-doer, but as a lost child; not with reproaches, but with unbounded tenderness. Farewell to the far country, and the cruelty, and the hunger, and the swine. Bring forth the robe, the white robe, and the ring, and shoes which he shall soil no longer in evil paths, and slay the fatted calf, " for this my son was dead, and is alive again; he was lost, and is found." And he began to be glad—an ever-deepening, ever-increasing happiness—not the ever-deepening, ever-increasing hunger of that far country, with its " began to be in want." I do not say—mark you—that that gladness would never be disturbed; I do not say that for him all struggles would be over; that for him there would be no obstructions from the past; that for him the future would not be more difficult, less peaceful, less tranquil in its self-mastery, than if he had never gone astray. " Blessed is he whose unrighteousness is forgiven, whose sin is covered." Oh! far, far more blessed is he who has no deep sin to cover, no flagrant unrighteousness to forgive. " Be the stern and sad truth spoken," says one, " that the breach which guilt has once made into the human soul is never in this mortal state repaired. It may be watched and guarded, but there is still the ruined wall, and near it the stealthy tread of the foe that would win over again his unforgotten triumph;" and to quote the high words to which I once saw the Parliament of England thrill with emotion, "It is against the ordinance of Providence, it is against the interests of man, that immediate reparation should be possible when long-continued evils have been at work; for one of the main restraints of misdoing would be removed if at any moment the consequences of misdoing could be repaired." Oh! no; be sure that for this young prodigal the *vinum demonum* which he had tasted had still its bitter dregs; temptation was not dead; not his could ever be the tranquil happiness of the unfallen; the *tutum diadema* of the pure in heart. He had been wounded by the fiery arrow, and be sure the scar remained, and sometimes throbbed. He had sat among the swine, nor could the past ever become for him as though it had not been. But he had been healed; but he had been delivered; but he had been cleansed; but now he was at home; and as long as he stayed in his father's home his soul was safe.

I have spoken to you, my brethren, solemn words. In these last addresses on sin, and righteousness, and judgment—on the fall, and ruin, and repentance of the prodigal—I have striven, as it were, to finish and summarise my witness to the great truths of God—the Father, the Son, and the Holy Spirit—as they deal with human souls. And I have kept you too long, and I must end. Yet I feel that there are some hearts among you in which my words may suggest some very serious and awful questions, which now is not the time, nor is this the place, to answer. This only I would say,

I have but a week more here as your Master, and then I depart, and my place will know me no more. And for six years you know that my house and my study have always been open—open to the very youngest boy, who, if he wished, might come to me at all times unannounced, and, however pressingly I might be occupied, you know that you were never sent away. And sometimes in sin and in sorrow, and before confirmation, some of you, uninvited and unencouraged, have come to me quite fearlessly and sought my counsels; and if I could think that the words of sympathy and advice, then once for all spoken, have been to some of you a blessing and a help to smooth your path in life,—if they have taught you always, in every difficulty, to go straight to God, and not to man—that thought would make me more happy by far than any other can. And if there be but one among you who has aught to ask me about these, or about other truths that you have heard, one week remains before I part from you, and I should hold it, as I have always done, a blessing and a privilege to help you for the last time with that help which experience and years may bring, and which may perhaps save you hereafter an erring path or an aching heart. And this may be for a few. But this I would say to all of you, Oh! do not despise the grace of God that calleth you to repentance. Some of you have wandered, some at this moment are wandering, from your father's home; some of you are sitting there, happy boys it may be to all appearance, but knowing that they are prodigals, and feeling the death-hunger in their secret souls. Oh! go up, each of you, into the tribunal of his own conscience, and ask if it be thus with thee; and if it be so, oh! unhappy one! steel not your heart against the arrow of conviction;

but, by prayer, by penitence, by amendment, arise and go to your Father. He will not cast you out, None that came to Him has He ever cast out. He will allay your hunger; He will quench your thirst; He will give you the bread of heaven; He will lead you to the water of life; He will for Christ's sake, for the sake of your Saviour — and does not this include all? — He will restore your soul, He will lead you in the path of righteousness for His name's sake.

July 15, 1876.

SERMON XXXIX.

LAST WORDS.

2 Cor. xiii. 11.

"Finally, brethren, farewell."

THE hour has come, my friends, by me long dreaded, and for the last time as your Master,—perhaps the last time for ever,—certainly the last time as far as this congregation, so dear to me, is concerned,—I stand in this pulpit to bid you all a hearty, a grateful, an affectionate farewell. There *must* be something sad and solemn in these partings. They remind us that there is nothing in this world which we can call our own; that all which God gives us is His, not ours; lent, not given; given sometimes, and then taken away; and sometimes by His mercy given back in other forms. They remind us too that our time is short. The sad hour which now has come to me will come in turn to all of you, though far less sadly, because you, I trust, will but be going to larger hopes. But at the best we, like our fathers, are only dwellers in tents. Here and there—by some sweet well, under some spreading tree, on some green spot—we linger for a time; but the evening comes at last, the stars come out, the encampment is broken up, and we must move away. And very soon we shall have made our last stay of all;

the sky will flush with the crimson of its last sunset; the last long shadows of the twilight will lengthen round us; the last farewell will be sighed forth from weary lips. After that our tent will be moved no longer; for then we hope that it will be pitched, for the last time, under the walls of the heavenly city, and the sun shall go down on us no more.

Bear with me kindly, my friends. What I said to you last Sunday about the repentance of the prodigal, was meant in truth to be my last sermon. This is to me no great occasion, but a time of sorrow, when I would rather lean on your sympathy. Most of you on the first Sunday of next term will again be gathered here; I shall think of these long lines of boyish faces; I shall recall many whom I have loved; many whose future career I shall watch with deepest interest; many whose names, though they knew it not, I have often borne to God's mercy-seat, as the High Priest bore engraved on the jewels of his breast the names of the twelve tribes of Israel. But I shall not be here. All, by God's blessing, will go on as safely, as happily —it may be more safely, more happily—without me. I am under no delusions. I have never for a moment exaggerated the importance of this change. No man is necessary, and no man's work. "Man goeth forth to his work and to his labour until the evening;" the evening of my work here has come; I depart, and it is well.

Always before when I have mounted the steps of this pulpit, the one sole desire of my heart has been to share with you those thoughts which are the bread of life;—to speak to you so that the very youngest little boy might understand;—to make every sermon an influence—infinitesimal it might be, yet real—against the power of temptation;—a warning—ineffectual it might be, yet solemn—against those bad, base spirits which would have troubled the peace of our souls;—a force—insignificant indeed, and yet appreciable—on the side of God. How can I recapitulate, how reinforce, in these few moments which alone are left me, all I have said to you of temptation and deliverance, of sin and forgiveness, of peace and trouble, of the life here and the life beyond the grave ? Nearly six years ago, to some of you who were then here as little boys, I preached my first sermon on "Ye stand this day all of you before the Lord your God," desiring to strike the keynote of our common duties in the faith of a life spent as under the Eye of God. How often have I spoken to you since of our Father, and of our Saviour, and of the Holy Ghost the Comforter; and of the tender affection which you owe to your parents, of your high duties towards one another and towards yourselves ? That, and all else, is over. You and I alike will have to give an account to God hereafter of an opportunity which now is past.

And I say farewell to you with a very heavy heart. Six years might seem too short a time to cost me such a pang in leaving you; but I knew and loved Marlborough before any of you, its present sons, were born; and when I was here but one year, as an assistant-master with Bishop Cotton, even then this place fixed itself indelibly in my deepest affections. To me our mere physical surroundings are unspeakably dear. The river valley, with its towers and trees; the forest, with its mossy glades, and primroses, and waving boughs; the West Woods, with their wild anemones and daffodils; the free fresh downs with the winds of heaven that breathe health over them; the natural amphitheatre of Martinsell, and the glorious expanse on which I had gazed so often from its green and breezy summit; and how far, far more these, the nearer scenes so bright with their thousand imperishable memories; the terrace, the mound, the cricket-field, the wilderness, the roofs of the old house rising over the clipped yews and between the groups of noble limes. And often, as on these gorgeous summer evenings the sunsets have rolled over us in their countless waves of crimson fire, I have sat in my own garden amid the woodland sights and sounds that now seem doubly precious—the peace, the coolness, the song of birds, the quiet lapse of the river heard in the stillness, the air full of the odour of rose and jasmine—and then heard the chapel bell breaking the stillness, and passed through the court with its groups of happy boys, and so into the beautiful reverence of this dear House of God, with its "solemn psalms and silver litanies"—I have thought that not often has God our Heavenly Father given better elements of happiness than His free grace has vouchsafed here to you and to me. Yet—for the outer elements of happiness are nothing if there be not peace within—these have been but the least of His mercies. Deeper has been His gift of prosperity to this place; deeper the blessing that He has saved you from sickness and from evils far deadlier than any sickness; deeper that He has given me so many kind and warm-hearted friends; deeper that He has allowed me to help some of you, to gain the affection of many, the kindliness of most, the loyalty of nearly all. Yes! dearer to me than aught else, are you to whom I have ministered, you whom I have tried to serve. Who could gaze on the spectacle of this chapel, and know how rich it is with the interests of the future, and how infinitely dear are you who sit in it to so many English homes—who, though but a stranger, could gaze on it unmoved? But to one who has been so nearly connected with it,—who has shared in so many of our bright gatherings and simple pleasures—who has seen you dedicate yourselves to God at confirmation, and confirm that confirmation at His Holy Table—oh! I cannot think over all this without deep emotion. For these things,—for the good hand of my God upon me,— for your unwearying aid, my beloved colleagues,—for all your honour, and faithfulness, and diligence, and docility, my boys, to whom I am now bidding farewell—I thank my God, and I thank you: and in the great city, among the sick and poor, amid the heat and burden, it may be among the disheartenments of labour and the strife of tongues, the memory of these things will come back to me like a cup of cold water in the desert, like the shadow of a great rock in a weary land.

And if you ask me, "Why then I leave it all?" I answer that we do not, my friends, absolutely choose our own lot in life. There are sometimes intimations of God's apparent will which come to us, whether we wish or no, like hands that beckon, like a voice that calls. Christ bids us live for others, not for ourselves; and when life opens before each of you, it will be your business, not to pick and choose the most comfortable of the posts that may be offered you, but to go where duty calls you, and where you believe that God's work may best be done. It was nearly in these words that Bishop Cotton spoke to the Marlborough boys assembled in this chapel on June 13, 1858, and the fathers of some of you were among those who heard them; and if I repeat them to you, their sons and successors, the Marlborough boys of this July 23rd, 1876, it is because I, like him who spoke them, have striven to act in their spirit. Oh! in leaving you I have not done what I liked, but what seemed to me to be a duty. And if ever any of you, who have known and loved me here, are called to choose hereafter between what you wish and what you ought, and hesitate on which side the scale should dip, then, when you recall the question of this morning's Epistle—" Know you not that so many of us as were baptized unto Jesus Christ, were baptized into His death?"—you may perhaps remember that one, who once taught and loved you, strove, even in leaving you, to give up much that was most dear to him, at what he believed to be the call of God,—was ready to let others gird him and carry him whither he would not.

And I advise you thus, and I have myself striven thus to act, in the belief that, in spite of all appearances, this is the only happiness. And as such it coincides with my text, Λοιπὸν ἀδελφοί, χαίρετε. Finally, brethren, at once "farewell" and "rejoice." In this sense I can use to you the words of the wounded runner, who brought to Athens the tidings of Marathon, and sank dying on the first threshold, Χαίρετε καὶ χαίρομεν. "Farewell, rejoice; I too rejoice." Only that the Christian adds with St. Paul, Rejoice, χαίρετε, "in the Lord." You know that I have always wished for, have always aimed at, have always thought much of, would always gladly have made any sacrifices for, your happiness. And how shall you be happy? Let me, as though I were naming you each by your names, strive for a moment to tell you how you may each be happy. It is the old, old lesson I have tried to set before you so often, but, my brethren, it is true. It is by diligence; it is by purity; it is by self-denial. It is by being clear of vice; clear of self-indulgence; clear of self-conceit. It is by that seriousness of mind which stands in awe and sins not; by that thoughtfulness of disposition which sets a right value on time and opportunity; by that resoluteness of purpose which shall arm you both against the sudden onslaughts and the insidious approaches of evil. It is thus, and thus only, that Christ can be revealed in your hearts by faith. It is thus, and thus only, that you can find happiness. But thus assuredly you *shall* find it, and thus my parting wish will be a parting prophecy.

Do you look forward, with all a boy's eagerness, to see what awaits you in the future? You need not doubt of it. At this moment, brightly or dimly, the star of its destiny is shining in your hearts. I see it in the ideal you are now setting before you, and in the purpose, or want of purpose, with which you are carrying it out. I read it in those reports of your conduct and character which I have just studied with so deep an interest. Golden threads there are in the saddest life, but it is not of golden threads that the woof of any life is woven. To all of you pain must come, and inexorable weariness, and many frustrate hopes. All of you must weep over the graves of those you most dearly love; all of you suffer from man's meanness or man's malice; and—near or far none knows, but somewhere in the shadow Death stands waiting for you all. But from one thing may God in His great mercy save you, and that is "the meeting of calamity with an accusing conscience,"—the bitter punishment which comes of sin. This alone is to be really dreaded; though the natural calamities of life happen alike to all, they come differently to the wise and to the foolish, to the wicked and to the pure. To the foolish and the wicked they come with crushing anguish and ruinous despair, but of the wise and the pure it is infinitely true that

> "He shall not dread misfortune's angry mien,
> Nor feebly sink beneath her tempest rude."

Be brave, be honest, be pure, and no real evil can befall you. "Who shall ascend into the hill of the Lord? or who shall rise up in His holy place? Even he that hath clean hands and a pure heart, and that hath not lift up his mind unto vanity, nor sworn to deceive his neighbour, he shall receive the blessing from the Lord, aud righteousness from the God of his salvation." You may have sorrows—yes; and failures—yes; and others may grow rich by fraud while you are poor; and successful by baseness while you must struggle—yes; but you would not change with them. For you have been true to the highest that you know. Lowest of all men are they who live only to gratify their senses; higher are they who have pleasure in art and nature and science; higher yet they who rejoice in deeds of simple kindliness and loathe all envy and calumny and hate; highest of all they who live in the faith of eternal thoughts, and are ready to pour out their very lives as a sacrifice, if so they may inspire others with the same holy and everlasting faith.[1] To live thus is Christ, and he that thus liveth hath eternal life. We may lose all else that the world wishes; but this cannot be torn from us either by malice or by violence. All else may be swept away, even for our good, by the billows and storms of God; this cannot be shaken and shall remain. So that when you have learnt to aim at this, you will soon learn also to desire nothing beyond it. To live thus is to be happy, and in this sense, from

---

[1] This thought is well developed in Miss Martineau's *Household Education*.

my heart of hearts, I wish you happiness. Yea, it is God's best blessing. It is the blessing which He reserves for the brave in battle. It is the peace which He sheds upon the pure in heart.

That, then, is my farewell lesson to you, and it may be summed up in the words of the Psalmist which I have quoted to you so often, "Keep innocency, and take heed to the thing that is right, for that shall bring a man peace at last;" and if you set this ideal before you, Christ will enable you to fulfil it. But I would add to it, again in St. Paul's words, the one request, "Finally, my brethren, pray for us." Oh! believe me, I mean it. It is no mere conventionality: I mean it very earnestly; I ask it of you—of all of you—as my last boon. I do not say pray for me always, or pray for me often, or even pray for me ever again: to do so would be unreal; but your Master asks you to pray for him now. Oh! I do ask every one of you, from the oldest master to the youngest little boy—I do ask you to offer up one prayer for me now. When I left the beloved and famous school where I laboured for fifteen years, on the evening of January 29th, 1871, preaching for the last time in Harrow School Chapel, I asked the Harrow boys to offer up for me one prayer. And I think that they loved enough the teacher who was leaving them to do it; and I have sometimes thought that, if my time here have been blessed and happy—and it has, my friends, been deeply blessed and abundantly happy—I have sometimes thought that, in part at least, I owed it to those prayers. And, going to scenes less full of hope and promise, I ask the same thing now of you, my Marlborough friends and my Marlborough boys. In less than one moment my voice will have waked its last echo—we shall then join for the last time—we who leave, and you who will return, in our parting hymn; and then,—after the blessing,—for one moment the heads of all of us will be bowed in prayer. Oh! will you as the last boon I ask you, will you, if I have been kind to many, have wished to be kind to all, have been wilfully unkind to none—will you in that one moment before we arise and leave the house of God, every one of you, pray for the Master who is leaving you, and for those most dear to him who have lived among you? Let me feel that during that one moment the hearts of six hundred of God's children are imploring Him for a blessing on us in our new home; for grace and consolation amid its trials and difficulties; for power to do good to the souls of others in the great city; that, whatsoever else befall us, He may teach us to do the thing that pleaseth Him—for He is our God;—that whithersoever else it guide us, His loving Spirit may lead us into the land of righteousness.

July 23, 1876.

THE END.

www.ingramcontent.com/pod-product-compliance
Lightning Source LLC
Chambersburg PA
CBHW022112290426
44112CB00008B/645